Y0-BPU-145

★★★★★★★★★★★★★★★★★★★★★★★★★

ELECTION 84

★★★★★★★★★★★★★★★★★★★★★★★

LANDSLIDE WITHOUT A MANDATE?

★★★★★★★ EDITED BY ★★★★★★★★★

ELLIS SANDOZ AND CECIL V. CRABB, JR.

LOUISIANA STATE UNIVERSITY

A MENTOR BOOK

NEW AMERICAN LIBRARY

NEW YORK AND SCARBOROUGH, ONTARIO

NAL BOOKS ARE AVAILABLE AT QUANTITY DISCOUNTS WHEN USED
TO PROMOTE PRODUCTS OR SERVICES. FOR INFORMATION PLEASE
WRITE TO PREMIUM MARKETING DIVISION, NEW AMERICAN LIBRARY,
1633 BROADWAY, NEW YORK, NEW YORK 10019.

Copyright © 1985 by Ellis Sandoz and Cecil V. Crabb, Jr.

All rights reserved

Library of Congress Catalog Card Number: 85-61720

MENTOR TRADEMARK REG. U.S. PAT. OFF. AND FOREIGN COUNTRIES
REGISTERED TRADEMARK—MARCA REGISTRADA
HECHO EN CHICAGO, U.S.A.

SIGNET, SIGNET CLASSIC, MENTOR, PLUME, MERIDIAN AND NAL BOOKS
are published by New American Library,
1633 Broadway, New York, New York 10019

First Printing, September, 1985

1 2 3 4 5 6 7 8 9

PRINTED IN THE UNITED STATES OF AMERICA

WHAT DO THE VOTERS WANT?
The Many Meanings of Election 84

Experts respond to the 1984 general election:

- The "Reagan Phenomenon"
- Election Results
- Policy Implications
- Economic Issues and Reaganomics
- The Reagan Victory and the Future of American Politics
- The New Federalism and State Elections

With Contributions by:

Ellis Sandoz, Louisiana State University
Fred I. Greenstein, Princeton University
Thomas E. Cronin, Colorado College
Charles O. Jones, University of Virginia
Daniel J. Elazar, Temple University
Stephen L. McDonald, University of Texas
Cecil V. Crabb, Jr., Louisiana State University
Walter Dean Burnham, Massachusetts Institute of Technology

ELLIS SANDOZ is professor of political science and former chairman of the department at Louisiana State University (Baton Rouge). He has written numerous articles in the fields of political philosophy and American thought, in addition to four books. Along with Cecil Crabb, he is the co-editor of *A TIDE OF DISCONTENT: The 1980 Elections and Their Meaning.*

CECIL V. CRABB, JR. is professor of political science at Louisiana State University (Baton Rouge) and served as chairman of the department for twelve years. He is the author of numerous books and articles on international relations and American foreign policy.

MENTOR and SIGNET Titles of Interest

(0451)

☐ **THE MAKING OF THE PRESIDENT® 1960 by Theodore H. White.** The masterful Pulitzer Prize winning account of the 1960 campaign and election of John F. Kennedy. (623487—$3.95)*

☐ **TO SET THE RECORD STRAIGHT: The Break-in, The Tapes, The Conspirators, The Pardon by John J. Sirica.** Judge Sirica's account of a five-year struggle to preserve rule of law in this country is "a commendable, highly readable work, enhanced by the author's unique judicial vantage point."—*Library Journal.* Told in a down-to-earth manner, it reveals the complexities of our constitution and how it protects the public interest. "The strongest and most revealing book about the Watergate Affair."—*The Washington Post* (091566—$3.50)

☐ **NONE OF THE ABOVE: Why Presidents Fail—And What Can Be Done About It by Robert Shogan.** In the past twenty years, not a single president has served two full terms. This study fully and frankly confronts our leadership crisis; shows how and why it occurred in terms of people, politics, and underlying problems involved, and offers provocative prescriptions for change. (622413—$3.95)*

*Price is $4.95 in Canada

Buy them at your local bookstore or use this convenient coupon for ordering.

NEW AMERICAN LIBRARY,
P.O. Box 999, Bergenfield, New Jersey 07621

Please send me the books I have checked above. I am enclosing $_____
(please add $1.00 to this order to cover postage and handling). Send check or money order—no cash or C.O.D.'s. Prices and numbers are subject to change without notice.

Name _____

Address _____

City _____ State _____ Zip Code _____
Allow 4-6 weeks for delivery.
This offer is subject to withdrawal without notice.

Contents

Preface

Whether the 1984 presidential election was *great* in the sense of "wonderful" depends on whether you are a Republican or a Democrat—and the authors of this book are quite divided on the matter as a consequence. But we can agree that it was great in the sense of most votes ever cast in an election in this country, the most electoral votes ever received by a presidential candidate, the most states ever won (a tie with 1972) for president. It was a great victory for President Ronald W. Reagan and Vice President George Bush. It was a true landslide. Conversely, it was a great defeat for the Democratic party and its candidates. Former Vice President Walter F. Mondale and Representative Geraldine A. Ferraro of New York, the first woman ever named to a major-party ticket, carried only Mondale's home state of Minnesota and the District of Columbia—the second greatest defeat in the party's modern history in terms of popular vote and the worst electoral vote drubbing.

This book is about the 1984 general elections, especially the presidency, but also congressional and state elections. Experts respond to the election and the Reagan phenomenon, report what happened, analyze the many aspects of the elections and their results, explore policy implications, weigh the significance of events for Reagan's second administration, and consider the question of political realignment of the country and a new (sixth) political period in our national history.

After a stage-setting introduction by Ellis Sandoz, the presidential campaign and election are presented by Thomas E. Cronin, and then Fred I. Greenstein discusses the Reagan presidency and style in comparison with other modern presidents back to Franklin D. Roosevelt. Charles O. Jones follows with a chapter devoted to the congressional elections in a detailed analysis of their character and implications for

Reagan's legislative program. Daniel J. Elazar then brings to bear the perspective of the New Federalism and state and local elections in evaluating the meaning of 1984. The lone economist in the book discusses economic issues and Reaganomics and finds a range of problems to worry about. It's not for nothing that economics is known as the dismal science, as Stephen L. McDonald methodically demonstrates. Cecil V. Crabb, Jr., next weighs the foreign policy aspects of the election and the implications for the second Reagan Administration of key trouble-spots and the question of nuclear arms reduction diplomacy. Walter Dean Burnham, then, sweeps together the whole range of election year phenomena to provide a profile of all that occurred and a theoretical and statistical interpretation of its importance for the country. The editors' conclusion reflects on what we know about American politics in the wake of momentous events that appear on the surface to show the divided mind of the electorate. If there is a *mandate* in the 1984 election, what is it?

Political scholarship, like politics itself, is animated by passion no less than reason and is both imprecise and adversarial. With Aristotle nearly two and a half millennia ago, we are incapable of making things more precise than they are, and much in politics (and political science) rests on perspective and fluctuating opinion. A sage somewhere remarked that if human beings only spoke when they were absolutely certain of their facts, a great silence would settle over the earth. We here offer with conscientious attention to detail and relevant data an in-depth analysis of the American elections of 1984; we are fully aware that definitive data on the elections can hardly be provided earlier than three years after the events. We disagree with each other about various aspects of the 1984 elections and, thereby, continue in a fruitful way the *debate* that marks the public arena and structures science itself in all free societies, not least of all in the United States of America. We would not have it any other way. The reader is invited to decide things for herself or himself!

Ellis Sandoz
Cecil V. Crabb, Jr.

Introduction:
The Silent Majority Finds
Its Voice

Ellis Sandoz

There is a story about a little boy who could not speak. His distressed parents took him to doctor after doctor, to famous medical centers in distant cities, and the physicians were totally baffled. There was no evident physiological reason for his silence. Finally, one morning the seven-year-old mute suddenly burst out at the breakfast table: "Mom, these damned pancakes are cold!"

Stunned yet delighted, the mother came to herself and stammered out, "Son, son, why is it you haven't spoken before in all these years?"

"I didn't have nothing to say," the boy responded.[1]

If there ever really was a silent majority in the country, it has plainly found its voice. If no one was listening the first time it spoke, the second try should get attention. The 1980 landslide for Reagan-Bush was a tidal wave that was widely interpreted as a negative election in which the American electorate rejected a failed presidency and voted massively *against* Carter-Mondale in a "tide of discontent."[2] So we thought, anyway. The 1984 landslide is even larger, coming within a few thousand votes of being a 50-state sweep, and it is a positive vote of support *for* Ronald Reagan. This is the first positive election in 12 years, a veritable tide of satisfaction with the incumbents' stewardship of the nation during the past 4 years. If, like the little boy, the voting majority of the American electorate had little to say before, it is now shouting at the top of its lungs that breakfast has improved markedly. It is even saying things about the menu for lunch and dinner.

Election Profile: Read 'em and Weep

Time wrote of "underestimating the amiable old actor." *The New York Times* offered the headline "A Master's Mark on Politics" on Inauguration Day. The television networks scrambled to keep everyone watching on election night by playing up the only interesting uncertainty left by then: Would the Republicans carry all 50 states? With voting still proceeding in 26 states, all three commercial networks had projected the winner by 8:30 P.M. E.S.T., and CNN (which did not stoop to such predicting itself) dutifully reported as news the projections of its rivals. Democrats could only read 'em and weep and watch the parade of states go by as the projections were confirmed one by one throughout the evening. Finally, the result was clear: Mondale would carry his home state of Minnesota after all, by a whisker (50.4 to 49.6 percent); and the District of Columbia was solidly in the Democratic Party column. That was it. Let us briefly profile the election that is thoroughly analyzed in chapters to follow. (See the Appendix for voting data.)

Electoral Votes for President 1984

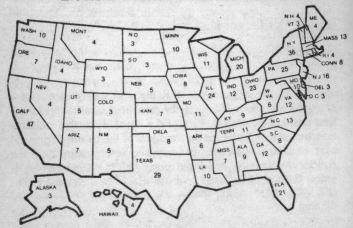

Figure 1-1

As landslides go, 1984 was a great election by any measure. Of course, George Washington won the electoral vote 69 to 0 in 1789, and James Monroe demolished John Quincy Adams 281 to 1 in 1820. But in modern times only Franklin Roosevelt's 1936 victory over Alf Landon of 523 to 8 is superior in percentage points to Reagan's victory over Mondale of 525 to 13: 98.4 percent to 97.5 percent. In absolute numbers Reagan set the record, both in electoral votes and in the popular vote in 1984 of about 54.5 million, compared with 43.9 million four years ago. The percentage split was 58.8 to 40.6, so that Reagan's popular vote landslide fell short of the 60–61 percent range of Roosevelt (60.8 in 1936), Nixon (60.9 in 1972), and LBJ (61.0 in 1964).

The demographic and regional breakdown show that Mondale-Ferraro carried the Black vote heavily (90 percent), and the Jewish and Hispanic vote by smaller margins (mid-60s percent), the Oriental vote, union households, and those making under $10,000 per year. The Republicans won nearly every other identifiable grouping of voters: every age group, every income level except the poor, most ethnic groups, male voters (64 percent), and female voters—yes, the women, too, by 55 percent. The Republicans' "gender gap" with women voters did not appreciably widen with Geraldine Ferraro on the Democratic ticket. In fact, she seems to have hurt the Democrats rather than helped, although she no doubt buoyed the spirits of many American women and gave the party some of the little excitement its ticket generated. Yet Reagan-Bush carried the New York Italian vote by an impressive 63 percent to 37 percent, including Representative Ferraro's own congressional district, despite the presence of an Italian American on the Democratic ticket. Ed Rollins, Reagan's political director, stated that Ferraro "made the South ours." Moreover, the large Black vote generated in the South by the Jesse Jackson registration drive and primaries campaign provoked white flight from the Democrats in the general election to the tune of 71 percent white vote for Reagan to 29 percent for Mondale. The other regions of the country reflected strong support for Reagan as well. The so-called yuppies (young urban professionals) who were enthusiastic for Senator Gary Hart in the Democratic primaries ended up voting for Reagan in about the same proportion as did the "born-again" Christians, 67–32 and 69–31 percent (Reagan over Mondale) respectively.[3]

On November 8 *The Washington Post* headlined: "Democrats Challenge President's Landslide as Mandate." And things did look better for the Democrats in Congress. In the Senate, the Republican majority of 55–45 in the Ninety-eighth Congress narrowed in 1984 to 53–47. With only one third of the Senate (33 seats) up for election every two years, the Republicans won 17 to hang on to a five-vote majority. In the House of Representatives, the Republicans had gained 33 seats in Reagan's 1980 win, but then lost 26 in the off-year elections of 1982. They were looking for a strong recovery in 1984 on the basis of the great popularity of Reagan (steadily at a 60 percent approval rating throughout the campaign) but had to settle for a gain of 14 seats in the Ninety-ninth Congress. This left the Democrats in control of the House, under Speaker Thomas P. "Tip" O'Neill, Jr. (D-Mass.), with a majority of 71 seats, the House divided 253 Democrats to 182 Republicans, with one disputed and, therefore, undecided race. Then, in January 1985 one of the Democratic House leaders, Representative Gillis W. Long (La.) died, creating a vacancy filled by special election in March, when his widow, Cathy Long, won his old seat. Finally, in the states, the governorships were split in favor of Democrats 35 to 15 going into the 1984 elections. Only 13 states elected governors at that time, and the result was eight Republican and five Democratic winners for a Republican net gain of one (see Chapter 5). Some significant gains for Republicans occurred in state races for legislative seats and local offices, a suggestion that the conservative mood of the country as reflected in Reagan's popularity was having some effect on state politics.

The disappointing "coattails" of the mighty Reagan landslide, from the Republican viewpoint, will be analyzed in detail later in Chapter 4. It is the basis of the *Post*'s headline and means that Congress is, even more so than usual, a force to be reckoned with because of the narrowed Republican majority in the Senate and Democratic control of the House. The problem is aggravated by the fact that Reagan cannot succeed himself again for a third term—because of constitutional limitation, even if a 74-year-old man might wish to run again three years hence—and this makes him a "lame duck," thereby supposedly lessening his leverage with congressmen and senators. Getting legislation through Congress is seldom easy, and getting an ambitious legislative program through the Ninety-ninth Congress will be a challenge for President Reagan. Moreover, it is a challenge for analysts of American politics looking for "mandates" and "realignments" of the country in what could have been a "critical" election. What is the wily American voter up to now?—or is it confusion, or, perhaps, political schizophrenia that he suffers from? On the day after the election, House Minority Leader Robert H. Michel (R-Ill.) petulantly blamed the small Republican gain in that body on the President himself: Reagan "really never, in my opinion, joined that issue of what it really means to have the numbers in the House" and was preoccupied with making a 50-state sweep to the neglect of GOP congressional candidates.[4] A cooler answer is that when times are good economically and the country at peace, the incumbent is hard to beat. Nineteen-eighty-four was the year of the incumbent, as subsequent analysis will show in detail (see especially Chapters 4 and 8, below). In the elemental logic of one Texas voter, *"If it ain't broke don't fix it!"* Probably everything else we have to say on this subject is covered by that unassailable maxim.

The impeccable logic of the Texan has its more sophisticated equivalent in Charles O. Jones's phrase: "Inertia was purposely built into our system." As we ponder the heady question of the meaning of a landslide without evident mandate, the congressional elections will seem less anomalous if we bear in mind the salient psychology of the Reagan reelection campaign itself: *support the incumbent!* When things are going well in the economy, patriotism at home and esteem abroad both on the rise, the people of the country still asking themselves Reagan's 1980 campaign question and agreeing that they are, indeed, better off now than four years ago, then everyone holding office tends to share some of the credit and to benefit at the ballot box. There is intellectual incongruity and emotional dissonance in saying under these circumstances, support the President but turn the Democratic rascals out of Congress. Reagan's coattails were prodigiously long from this angle, extending to virtually all incumbents who sought reelection to Congress.

Aside from the psychology of the election, there are also

several objective factors of importance in seeing why Republicans picked up relatively few seats in the House (and lost two in the Senate), despite the enormous popularity of their presidential ticket. Perhaps chief among these is that predominantly Democratic state legislatures had charge of redrawing congressional districts after the 1980 census. Not surprisingly, they did this in the American gerrymandering tradition so as to maximize the Democratic vote. Further, many Democrats continue to fill uncontested seats, and in any event, there were only 27 *open* seats in the House in 1984, 18 of which were won by Republicans. In the remaining 407 seats occupied by incumbent congressmen, a record 392 (or 96.1 percent) won reelection in an incumbent's dream year. Also, there is the singular factor of congressional district politics, personal rapport of the congressman or congresswoman with a unique constituency on local causes and issues, and the insularity of the campaign in the district by comparison with the national campaign. Added to these elements are the general atrophy of political party partisanship and the continuing rise of ticket-splitting, further reasons why the Reagan-Bush landslide did not extend to Congress in the form of large, overt Republican gains.

Political and Constitutional Setting of Elections

It is worth pausing to notice that the 1984 elections peacefully empowered thousands of officials in this country, high and petty, to wear the mantle of legitimate authority for a time. When one considers that there is an election somewhere in the United States nearly every week year in and year out, and that we elect an estimated 521,000 officials to various positions, we have a glimmering of one more explanation of why Americans tend not to be terribly excited by even presidential elections and why turnout is relatively low—much to the consternation of the League of Women Voters and political scientists. Free government is, for Americans, no novelty. Still, these elections are the chief consent-giving mechanism whereby a free people choose their representatives and governors who, then, wield the awesome powers of rule: the power of lawmaking, administration of justice, life and death over individuals, war and peace for the nation and world. Elections are a substitute for revolutions and lesser forms of forcible seizure of power. We accomplish this in ways grown utterly routine through centuries of historical usage, although because of our penchant for the concrete we imagine the beginning lies in the "supreme law of the land," the Constitution.

That Constitution's two-hundredth anniversary will be observed during the term for which President Reagan was recently elected. In a world in which a scant two dozen nations out of over 160 enjoy genuinely free government, liberty under law as enshrined in our Constitution and the peaceful passage of power from one set of hands to another truly are political marvels, however humdrum they seem to us. An admiring Englishman caught the wonder of it all in these lines:

> The American Constitution is the oldest written constitution in existence. It can claim, indeed, to be the first constitution in the modern world, and that it has survived so long is a tribute to the sagacity, moderation, and sense of the possible shown by its makers. When it went into effect in 1789, the French monarchy still stood; there was a Holy Roman Emperor, a Venetian Republic and a Dutch Republic, an Autocrat in St. Petersburg, a Sultan-Caliph in Constantinople, an Emperor vested with the "mandate of heaven" in Pekin and a Shogun ruling the hermit empire of Japan in the name of secluded, impotent and almost unknown Mikado. . . . *Forms and realities have changed less in the United States [during the last 200 years] than in any other political organization, even than in Tibet.*[5]

The Constitution's provisions reflect in the matter of elections the general distrust of political power and the desire for effective checks and balances in government that characterized the framers of 1787. It was a compromise between James Madison's desire that the House of Representatives be elected for three-year terms and the belief of others that "where annual terms end, tyranny begins" that resulted in two-year terms for House members. The Constitution requires four-year terms for president and six-year terms for senators (one-third elected every two years); and it specifies the qualifications for voters and officeholders, leaving to the states and to Congress the determination of times, places, and manner of elections. It was the "Great Compromise" which determined that representation in the Senate would be *equal* (two senators to every state) and only that in the House be *proportional* to population, above the one representative guaranteed each state regardless of its population.[6] A "Congress" has a two-year life because of the House election cycle, so that the One-hundredth Congress will be elected in 1986 and assume office in January 1987. The Senate, however, is a "continuing body" by reason of the overlapping terms of its members, two-thirds of whom always hold their tenure.

A number of the changes that have been made in the Constitution since its ratification in 1789 relate to elections and formally express the major tendency in the history of American politics to expand the franchise and make the original constitutional government of the country democratic government as well. Today the president continues to be elected by *indirect* popular vote with members of the Electoral College, themselves representing the majority party *favored in each state* and the District of Columbia, subsequently casting ballots for the party's candidates on a winner-take-all basis. Electors in each state equal the sum of representatives plus senators, for a grand total of $435 + 100$ or 535 electors for the 50 states, plus 3 for the District of Columbia. A majority of the electoral vote (270) is necessary to secure election to the presidency and vice presidency.

The Twelfth Amendment (ratified in 1804) modified the operation of the Electoral College by requiring separate votes for president and for vice president. This was done to avoid the kind of situation that arose in 1800 when Aaron Burr and Thomas Jefferson tied in the electoral vote for president on the Democratic-Republican ticket because originally each elector was merely required to vote for two persons, without indicating which was his choice for president and for vice president. It took 36 ballots (and the support of Alexander Hamilton) for Jefferson finally to be elected by the House of Representatives as president. Already in 1800 the electors had become puppets of the parties, so the system of the Electoral College—conceived as the embodiment of the combined wisdom of the nation by the founders—had modified radically. And so it continues today, when political parties in national conventions choose their candidates, and the voters cast ballots for the party's electors on the first Tuesday after the first Monday in November. The winning electors are morally bound to support their party's candidates and, so, give faithful effect to the wishes of the majorities (or pluralities!) in each state.

The development of the two-party system in the United States (as contrasted with the multi-party systems of many other nations of the world) enhances the probability that one party's candidates will gain a majority of electoral votes. Only one election since ratification of the Twelfth Amendment has had to be decided by the House. In 1824, when the "second" party system was just coming into being and neither Andrew Jackson, John Quincy Adams, nor William Crawford had a majority of the electoral vote, the younger Adams was elected in the House, voting by states. The Senate has elected a vice president only once, in 1837. Because the choice in a two-party system normally is either one or the other ticket, the vote is not scattered, and an electoral majority for one set of candidates or party in a national election is virtually assured. Third and splinter parties alter this normal situation, of course.

Other constitutional amendments secured voting rights for the newly emancipated blacks after the Civil War (Fifteenth Amendment, adopted in 1870, and later expanded through judicial construction to prevent discrimination in voting more generally); provided for popular election of senators (Seventeenth Amendment, adopted in 1913); enfranchised women (Nineteenth Amendment, 1920); extended presidential voting rights to the residents of the District of Columbia, who choose three electors (Twenty-third Amendment, 1961); prohibited the poll tax as a device for depriving persons of voting rights (Twenty-fourth Amendment, 1964); extended voting rights to eighteen-year-olds, setting a record in the process by being ratified only five weeks after it was proposed by Congress (Twenty-sixth Amendment, 1971).

In this striking record of constitutional activity to foster participation in elections, we glimpse the background of a vast amount of litigation and legislation whereby the national foundation of the election processes in the United States has steadily expanded over the past two centuries. Elections originally were in state hands, and the only phrase in the Constitu-

tion that requires them is in Article I, where it states that
members of the House must be chosen by the "people of the
several states." Today elections are very largely in federal
hands or are at least governed by federal standards. A great
part of this development came little by little until the major
legislative breakthrough of the Voting Rights Act of 1965 and
thereafter. The securing of the civil rights of the Black American was the primary purpose of this legislation as of so much
else done to secure access to electoral processes in previous
decades. But the Congress can paint with a much broader
brush than can the courts, a Supreme Court justice once
remarked. And the 1965 act suspended the use of literacy
tests and authorized federal examiners empowered to order
registration of voters in those states and counties (in the
South, mainly) where fewer than 50 percent of the voting-age
population had voted or were registered during the previous
national election. Criminal sanctions were authorized for in-
terfering with persons seeking to vote.

In 1932 the Supreme Court stated that state legislatures,
under provision of Article I, Section 4, Clause 1, possessed
"authority to provide a complete code for congressional elections, not only as to times and places, but in relation to
notices, registration, supervision of voting, protection of voters, prevention of fraud and corrupt practices, counting of
votes, duties of inspectors and canvassers, and making and
publication of election returns; in short, to enact the numerous requirements as to procedure and safeguards which experience shows are necessary in order to enforce the fundamental
rights involved."[7] But this authority is subject to congressional oversight and revision since "Congress may at any
time by Law make or alter such Regulations." The result
of several Supreme Court decisions[8] and various congressional enactments has been to extend federal standards over
primaries and preprimaries in which candidates for the House
and Senate are nominated; to require the single-member district system for election of representatives and voting by
secret ballot; to place limits on expenditures for candidates;
and to issue regulations to curb fraud and corruption in connection with elections. In addition, as we have seen, most aspects of voter eligibility are governed by national standards:
every person eighteen years old or older is eligible to vote;
literacy tests and poll taxes have been outlawed; states cannot

require more than 30 days of residency before a person becomes eligible to vote; Spanish-speaking citizens and others incapable of reading English are entitled to ballots in their own languages if they comprise a substantial portion of the population; and federal registrars and poll watchers can be summoned to places where discrimination or voter harassment is evident from data in the previous presidential election.

Despite all of this attention to insuring the right to vote, voter participation in United States elections has steadily declined as the inclusiveness of the potential electorate has expanded. Of course, getting out the vote can be overdone. In the state of West Virginia in the last century (1888), 147,408 eligible voters cast 159,440 votes in the presidential election for a remarkable 108 percent "turnout"![9] But our national elections today suffer from a different problem. From a 1960 high of 65.4 percent of the potential electorate, voting turnout in presidential elections has declined steadily until it reached 54.3 percent in 1980, apparently to rebound slightly in 1984 to 55.0 percent. Only Switzerland among major Western nations has a lower average turnout than does the United States (53 percent). The implications and details of voting will be of concern in later pages. But the anomaly of enormous activity and substantial constitutional change through the cumbersome process of formal amendment of the fundamental law itself, side by side with tepid interest by the qualified citizenry in participating in elections, is a puzzle that lends credence to some scholars' startlingly simple conclusion that *most Americans are not interested in politics!* In the words of Richard Scammon and Ben Wattenberg: "The fact is this: *Most voters, most often, are not primarily political beings.* Thus, neither New Politics, nor Old Politics, nor malaise, nor hatred is the most important thing in the lives of most American voters. In shorthand, the American voter is typically unyoung, unpoor, unblack, *and* unpolitical."[10]

Political Parties and Realignment

If the Constitution is the foundation of all our government, including the electoral processes, the two-party system that sprang into being spontaneously by 1800 has been government's animating force. The development seems not to have been anticipated even by the remarkable men who framed the Constitution and came as something of a surprise—and an unwelcome one at that—and a sign to them that the evils of "faction" were even more insidious than they had feared. E. E. Schattschneider has tellingly characterized the relationship between our historically grown party system and our Constitution:

> The parties are bound to come into close and continuous contact with the Constitution because the parties were formed to control the government established by the Constitution. . . . If the parties are the river of American politics, the stream of the living impulse to govern, the Constitution is the river bed, the firm land whose contour shapes the stream. In the long run the river can transform the landscape, but it is also the prisoner of the land.[11]

As this language suggests, so far from being an evil to be minimized, the parties in our political system now are regarded as institutions to be fostered as very nearly essential to the operation of government at all levels.

Five great party systems typically are identified in American political history, and the question before the house is whether the sixth one has dawned with Ronald Reagan's back-to-back landslide victories in 1980 and 1984. More likely, it dawned when the so-called silent majority first made itself heard in 1968 and 1972 in the successive victories of Richard M. Nixon, only to abort into the stunned silence of Watergate and its aftermath to live in the underground of American politics. I believe something like this has, in fact, occurred, even if we do not as yet fully comprehend it. By his own unique analysis, Walter Dean Burnham generally concurs in this view (Chapter 8), although other contributors to this volume are more dubious or reject the notion of a Nixon-Reagan political era and realignment. But let us briefly glance at the earlier profile of electoral history.

The five periods are identified with "grand coalitions" welded together by dominant presidential personalities. (1) Thomas Jefferson (elected in 1800 and 1804) and succeeded by James Madison (1808 and 1812) established the Democratic-

Republican party as the supreme political force in the country by triumphing over the Federalists, who had dominated the first decade of politics under the Constitution in the presidencies of George Washington and John Adams. (2) Under the leadership of Andrew Jackson the Democrats emerged in the elections of 1828 and 1832 based on a massive coalition of perhaps 80 percent of the population of the country. It embraced farmers, frontiersmen, the rising "common man" generally, and slave-owners, all distributed over the South, the West, and along the frontier. An anti-Jackson coalition of National Republicans became the Whig party of the 1830's which eventually elected two presidents (William Henry Harrison and Zachary Taylor), but the Democrats remained dominant generally before this system shattered completely on the issues of secession and slavery. (3) The new Republican party began in 1854 and was consolidated by Abraham Lincoln (1860 and 1864) and the Civil War as the party of the Union. This broad-based coalition consisted of the Northern wealthy, the new freedmen of the South, farmers, and workers. The minority Democrats managed to stay alive largely in exile in the South among the white population, but not until Grover Cleveland's first term (1884) did the Democrats elect a president. (4) A new realignment occurred with the presidency of William McKinley (1896 and 1900) whose recast Republican coalition reacted against the social and economic impact of industrialization and the influx of foreign Catholic labor into the Northeast; the winning coalition brought together Northern businessmen, middle-class Protestants, and Midwest farmers. The only Democrat in this century elected president before Franklin D. Roosevelt was Woodrow Wilson (1912 and 1916). (5) The Roosevelt coalition emerged out of the social and economic chaos of the Great Depression with his election on the Democratic ticket in 1932 and 1936—and then in 1940 and again in 1944, for unprecedented third and fourth terms. This coalition dominated American politics for a half-century and was broadly based, bringing together Southerners, labor, farmers, unemployed middle-class persons, Blacks, and other ethnic minorities. Whether this coalition still exists is doubtful, at least to the extent of fielding a winning ticket in the Democratic party: Republicans have won four out of the last five presidential elections, and six out of the last ten elections in the period since the end of World War II (Harry S Truman in 1948 through Ronald Reagan in 1984).

A chief purpose of political parties, in the jargon of political science, is to act as "aggregators of national interest" and, so, bridge the differences among individuals and groups.[12] Their reason for being is to win elections, or "to select the personnel of government."[13] Some kind of consensus or intelligible unity may exist in a party, but ideological coherence is a rarity that always is sacrificed to pragmatic considerations and compromise—if a winning coalition is to be fashioned. The objective of gaining and retaining public office is the cardinal goal of partisan politics. *If* there is a vision of the common interest of the nation that galvanizes the jangle of conflicting interests and groups composing a political coalition, *then* the forceful articulation of that vision by a persuasive personality who is in tune with the humor of the country can give rise to a success at the ballot box that may outlast his own presidency. This is why American parties and winning coalitions seem to be anchored to the vision and personality of great men of American history, as we have just suggested: Jefferson, Jackson, Lincoln, McKinley, and Roosevelt—and some scholars doubt that McKinley belongs in the list. We do not have strict discipline in our political parties as do the British. Nor do we have a conservative party facing off against an equally discrete liberal party. Rather our parties are centrist and nonideological, indefinable conglomerates of groups in considerable conflict with one another but sharing beyond mere utilitarian or pragmatic purposes of power in a vision of the good of the country and its symbolic meaning. A partisanship born of interests, ideas, and convictions can succeed in aggregating public opinion and mobilizing the electorate in presidential campaigns and on national Election Day if it is a synthesis of common sense and credible patriotism—and only then. It was not by chance that the 1980 Reagan election theme chosen as the thread running through all the speeches and advertisements was: "America can do!"[14] The same upbeat message continued through the first term and into the reelection campaign.

Some Elements of a Presidential Landslide

Some of the *contextual* elements of Reagan's 1984 land-slide victory can be mentioned by way of completing our introduction. These factors will be considered without any attempt to evaluate either their impact or relative weight in the election's outcome: (1) the breakup in the 1960's of the New Deal coalition's liberal ideology; (2) the rise of the conservative right in America; (3) the Democrats' loss and Republicans' seizure of the political middle ground; and (4) the Reagan phenomenon.

1. The ideas characteristic of the New Deal coalition, and sometimes equated with the "liberal idea" itself, disintegrated through the self-inflicted wounds of the excesses of the Great Society. This disintegration, even though full of lofty intention and noble purpose, revolved around the conviction that it is government's role to devise and fund programs that address all the ills of modern society as the pathway to social and economic justice for all and to achievement of the kind of liberty and equality announced by the Declaration of Independence as the American creed. By Theodore H. White's analysis of the breakup of this reading of the American creed, three factors were instrumental in the process of disillusionment and collapse of the Rooseveltian political consensus.[15]

First, there was the Democratic party's translation of the age-old American vision of equality and justice in terms of the rabble-rousing slogans of "participation and entry." The effect was to splinter American society into its ethnic, age, and sex components as the labels for privileged place in public processes, welfare, and government service distinguishing the new American system. The society was beset by quotas, burgeoning bureaucracy, and regulation.

The *second* factor was the notion of America as a people of plenty, a bottomless cornucopia of material abundance and technological innovation that could be distributed generously both at home and throughout the world. In a paroxysm of goodwill, the United States set out to free all of its citizens and as many other people in the world as it could reach and ended up making a nation and world of dependents instead. In a devastating paragraph White writes:

By 1980, 36 million Americans received their monthly Social Security checks; 22 million drew Medicaid benefits; 26 million more, Medicare; 18 million added to their budgets by food stamps; 11 million received general welfare payments; 15 million received veterans' benefits; 27 million children were nourished by school lunch programs; 11 million drew from the Aid to Families with Dependent Children (AFDC) programs. Most of these categories overlapped. . . . All in all, much more than half the population of the United States depended in whole or in part on federal aid or protection.[16]

The economic impossibilities of this situation were of little concern to the clientele of the system of dependency, who only knew to clamor for more.

There was, *third,* the advent of television, a development of more profound impact than anything since Gutenberg invented printing. It nationalized public opinion by creating for the first time a truly unified audience to be manipulated for profit and power by the enormously influential medium of immediate visual and auditory communication with a large portion of the country at any given instant. Political reporting became both entertainment and an exercise in raw power through tailoring events along the biased lines of networks and of an intellectual establishment that White acknowledges to favor the liberal web of federal control associated with New Deal politics. This was, indeed, the basis of the upheaval in the country that finally led to the 1980 election of Reagan, "the most resolute ideologue in the modern presidency."

At the heart of the upheaval was the liberal idea, and guiding it was liberal dominance, in Congress, in academia, in the press, on television, in the great foundations and "think tanks." Under Republican Presidents, as under Democratic Presidents, the liberal idea prevailed—that the duty of government was to conceive programs and fund them so that whatever was accepted as right and just, at home or abroad, would come to pass, whatever the cost, whatever the contradiction between good intentions and prevailing reality.[17]

First Nixon and now Reagan represent the flash points in a major movement of rejection and demolition of a worthy enterprise run amok and careening toward collapse under its own grotesque weight. Kevin P. Phillips wrote the obituary: "Unrepentant liberalism having exhausted its credibility by the 1980s, the United States turned to a transformed, radicalized conservatism—and crossed its national fingers."[18]

2. That radicalized conservatism covers a hodgepodge of intellectual, activist, business, religious, and political personalities and groups scattered widely throughout American society and not necessarily on speaking terms with one another. If there is a noteworthy characteristic of the so-called "right" in our politics, it is a sense of purity of purpose accompanying hard-eyed zealotry that is antagonized by proposals of compromise as immoral and that can only awkwardly combine efforts to form coalitions to achieve objectives shared with kindred souls and groups. There is something of a siege mentality, sometimes tinged with paranoia, that often makes doing business, going along for half-a-loaf, a great obstacle to cooperation and concerted action. This syndrome suggests the atomism of the self-righteous dogmatist who has been in the opposition too long to know how to play the game, even when he is winning, with grace and civility.

This noteworthy characteristic is not universal, of course, and there are many urbane as well as canny operators among Phillip's "radical conservatives." And most conservatives are not "radical" but centrist. The most visible divisions of the conservative grouping includes the neoconservatives, free marketeers, and supply-siders in economics and business circles, the political new right elections activists who launched NCPAC (the National Conservative Political Action Committee) with such resounding effect in 1980, and the religious right—the traditional, antiabortion Catholics, the Mormons, the evangelical Protestants and the fundamentalist Protestant right, especially those groups identified with the Reverend Jerry Falwell's "Moral Majority." The political potency of the religious groups alone is suggested by the estimate that there are 75 million "right leaning Christians" in the United States, the most religious of all Western nations.[19]

While it is not possible accurately to characterize the sweep of beliefs of all these groupings in a few words, it can generally be said that the considerable part of the American citizenry embraced under the "radical conservative" label are patriotic and even nationalistic politically; they venerate the

Constitution but side with law and order over permissiveness in civil rights and liberties; they believe in the free enterprise capitalist system with as little intervention by government as is practicable; they are God-fearing and hardworking and have little patience with welfarism, which they equate with socialism (if not covert communism) as an evil to be fought against tooth and nail; they are strongly anticommunist and condemn "secular humanism"; they believe that poverty is not a governmental problem but one to be overcome by hard work and individual initiative; they believe in less government domestically but a strong military security system as the best defense against expansive world communism; they are anticrime and believe that the criminal element should be dealt with firmly as a major concern of state and local governments; they tend to be noninterventionist if not outright isolationist in foreign affairs and would be glad to observe Washington's warning against entangling alliances, if only that were possible.

The great upsurge in public effectiveness of the conservatives in recent politics arises, on one hand, from the strength and clarity of their several convictions and, on the other hand, from the high proficiency attained in what Richard Viguerie calls the marketing of ideas, especially the fine art of direct-mail fund-raising and salesmanship.[20] When Theodore White calls Reagan "the most resolute ideologue" in the modern history of the presidency, he is imputing to the president substantial parts of the views just summarized. This may or may not be entirely accurate. At any rate, the eagerness to attribute Neanderthal properties to conservatism constantly tempts liberal intellectuals into misplaced snobbery, not fairly directed toward the Reagan administration. A balanced statement of Reagan's orientation goes something like the following:

> The Reagan administration has wanted to bring about a change of assumptions about the role of government in American life. By signaling a determination to cut the growth of federal expenditure in areas other than military expenditure, by signaling a hostility towards the civil rights policies of previous administrations, and by signaling a more militant attitude towards the defense of American and Western interests internationally, President Reagan has cre-

ated a distinctive synthesis of conservative economics, populism, and nationalism which has no exact counterpart in the politics of the right in Europe.[21]

Indeed, a great surprise of the Reagan first term was the degree to which he proved to be the great compromiser and abandoned ideology for pragmatism when events frequently demanded such flexibility to the distress and outcry of his conservative friends. There are plenty of Neanderthal types around, of course, but they are no conservative monopoly. As Morton M. Kondracke grudgingly wrote in February 1985: "The simple fact is that . . . Reagan has put able people into important posts in his administration, and most of the incompetents, firebreathers, and misfits . . . are gone." Kondracke concluded: "After 20 years of saying one thing and doing another—and doing rather well at both—Reagan deserves a little credit from his friends. His enemies probably will never understand."[22]

3. If anything is obvious about the 1984 election it is that the Democrats lost big because they could not draw the great center that forms the heartland of American electoral politics. The data we cited in the beginning of this introduction suffice to demonstrate this fundamental fact, and more detailed analysis in chapters to come confirm and amplify its truth. The question is why. Again, a good part of what follows directly or indirectly addresses that mysterious question. It is roundly agreed that Mondale-Ferraro drew the minority vote, that Jesse Jackson's "Rainbow Coalition" turned out in the general election to be mainly black, with a goodly number of Hispanics supporting Reagan, especially because of his anticommunist appeal to refugees from Cuba and Central America, and that even a sweep of minority voters (something that did not take place in 1984) cannot win a presidential election in this country. You have to have the center, and the appeal of the Democrats to the center fell seriously short in 1984.

The question that must be pondered is this: What is the "center" of the American electorate? There is no doubt that elections analysts on the Democratic side are rechecking their answers to that question and probably trying to find out what the Republicans already seem to know. And, of course, the second question is how to make Democratic candidates—

especially the national candidates—more appealing to the constituency that has turned away from them in four out of the last five presidential elections.

While it is scarcely possible to admire Richard Nixon after his debauchery of the presidency and the Constitution that he swore to uphold, no one doubts his political acumen. And Nixon knew where the center lay: it lay in the silent majority that elected him in a squeaker in 1968 and in a thunderous landslide over George McGovern in 1972. The American center was then, and is now, this *silent majority* whose betrayal and humiliation at the hands of Richard Nixon have been put behind them and who now form the cutting edge of what President Ronald Reagan calls "The Second American Revolution."[23] One does not have to believe in unicorns to also believe in the silent majority. Perfectly sound elections experts—*psephologists* they call themselves[24]—clearly analyzed the matter in 1970 and, as credentialed Democratic intellectuals should, Richard Scammon and Ben Wattenberg tried to warn their party of the shifting nature of the American political center. Scammon and Wattenberg, perhaps as a ploy to sell books to readers (who are mainly Democrats), renamed the beast the "Real Majority." Now the *real majority* in Scammon-Wattenberg terms believe most of the things described in the preceding section of this chapter: the *real majority* is conservative America, in short. They are vastly concerned with what Scammon-Wattenberg called the "Social Issue," which, they wrote fifteen years ago, is a voting issue emergent in American politics so powerful "that it may rival bimetallism and depression in American political history, an issue powerful enough that under certain circumstances it can compete in political potency with the older economic issues."[25] In other words, they claimed it is an issue sufficiently powerful to realign the American political consensus and be the foundation of a new coalition for a sixth period in our electoral history. Within limits, I think they were right. I even imagine Ed Rollins and his comrades in the White House with Scammon and Wattenberg occupying a privileged place on their desks, side by side with Machiavelli's *The Prince*.

The silent or real majority are those strange Americans who work for a living, decry violence in the streets, corruption in political office (the traumatizing center that silenced them again after Nixon was forced from the presidency under threat of certain impeachment), aimlessness among the youth, anxiety among the elderly, hate the dope traffic, despise the communists, value their property and want it and their own lives and limbs to be safe at home, in the churches, schools, playgrounds, mall parking lots, workplaces, and even in the subways of the great cities. Scammon and Wattenberg warned that if the Democrats ignored the "Social Issue" they would commit political suicide. Maybe they were on to something, after all. Political scientists were properly skeptical about such a sweeping and commonsensical explanation of voting behavior (in so readable a book) and rated the thesis as unproven and the factors identified as only marginally important in our politics.[26] Kevin Phillips, the author of *The Emerging Republican Majority* (1968), for his part, decoded the Scammon-Wattenberg message by writing that they were "quite logically . . urging elected Democratic officials to ride around in police cars and to duck identification with permissivism and welfarism."[27]

If it is true that simplistic explanations of American voting behavior have only limited utility, there nonetheless appears to be a center to the American electorate, and it includes the Social Issue and the concerns so loudly voiced by the coalition of conservatives that we have been attending to. Again, a single factor or even a range of identifiable views provide only partial "explanations" of such complex phenomena as elections and why the voters decide as they do: there is an inarticulate depth that plays its part, not just in seemingly autistic seven-year-olds but in "We the people." On the other hand, the frustrations of the intellectual elite in this country have found expression in Haynes Johnson's gibe at Reagan that he is proving Lincoln wrong, for in this age of packaged candidates, it very well may be possible to fool all the people all of the time. This cry of rage against an electorate that votes in the bad guys like Ronald Reagan—not just once but twice—against all liberal advice, and even when there is a strong choice as an alternative with experience and integrity, like Fritz Mondale—leads to a strange posture in some enlightened quarters. As political scientist Austin Ranney well puts it, the intellectuals in their despair have decided that the American voters "are a bunch of jerks," and not the "good peasants and yeomen" of yore.[28]

4. The Ronald Reagan phenomenon is more than the merely celluloid presidency it sometimes seems to be. Perhaps there never was a silent majority, and maybe the real majority is as mythical as the unicorn. At any rate, it can only be a *real plurality* (statistically), since only 55 percent of the potential voters voted in 1984 (92.6 million out of 168.3 million), and only 59.1 percent of these voted for Reagan-Bush (53.5 million). This means they were elected by less than one third of the eligible voters in the country, *or* that nearly 70 percent of the people (or 114.8 million potential voters) either voted against them or did not bother to vote at all.[29] So much for the "real" or any other kind of majority.

Ronald Reagan is indubitably real, however. And what we may call the political-minded members of our citizenry who take politics sufficiently seriously to vote in our elections for president overwhelmingly approve him and his policies. The so-called issueless campaign in 1984 was conducted as a test of political America's view of first-term policy and performance. Reagan went into the campaign with the "Four P's" going for him: *Prosperity, Peace, Patriotism,* and *Personality.* He only faltered in the first televised debate when old age seemed to be taking its toll. After that stumble, it was back to stride. Mondale-Ferraro could not ignite the voters on any issue to the point of making a close race of it. The Reagan campaign strategy was vintage, textbook stuff for a candidate who is miles ahead and knows it: How do you campaign? "Safely." "Don't rock the vote." The Reagan record for four years was respectable, to the liking of the voters, and the American people liked the man. Nobody could have beaten Reagan in 1984. Walter Mondale and Geraldine Ferraro are not to be faulted for a gallant try.

The general reasons why Reagan was unbeatable are fairly clear: the Four P's. But everyone also has conceded that Reagan has made a difference in the country. He took something hooted at by all informed people, called *Reaganomics,* and somehow made it work to a considerable degree. He sought simultaneously to balance the federal budget, increase defense spending, slash personal income taxes by 30 percent, cure inflation, and reduce interest rates so as to restore prosperity. Lou Cannon calls this concoction "less of a program than a joyous secular theology."[30] Except for the small matter of a budget deficit that ran up $538 billion during the first term, and his having to settle for a mere 23 percent reduction in income taxes (partially offset by Social Security increases), Reaganomics *worked*—to the visible eye of the voter, anyway. The economists may have the last say, of course, but Reagan has become his own economist (see the discussion in Chapter 6). There he sits, sporting his B.A. in economics and sociology from little Eureka College, ignoring and confounding his own distinguished board of Harvard-trained economists, the President's Council of Economic Advisers.

This fits with the Reagan phenomenon. He is the best-liked figure in American public life in memory, as Speaker O'Neill remarked. He identifies with the little man, even though his policies have adversely affected the poor, and "fairness" ought to be the political Achilles' heel of the Administration. Moreover, the people identify with him. A cabdriver remarked that "Reagan is the only politician I can understand."[31] This is why the journalists call Reagan "The Great Communicator." But scholarly analysis concurs that Reagan's speeches reflect a unique command of "presidential rhetoric," and he proves to be the only "master speaker" among modern presidents.[32] The warmth of feeling is not sentimental, however. It arises from a regard for effectiveness and leadership that the electorate *believe* Reagan actually possesses and that makes him deserve to take credit for the achievements of his Administration. This, in turn, is the basis for the confidence and pride Americans *want* to take in their nation and (for the first time in a decade) now feel they are entitled to take.

Perhaps the chief substantive element in the Reagan phenomenon is that he obviously loves the country and has tried to do what he promised to do when he was elected in 1980—within the limits of common sense and the possible. There are many, of course, who by reason of a different reading of Reagan, or because of the kind of intense partisanship that comes to the surface especially in transitional periods in national politics, see only broken promises, duplicity, and a smile that masks gross inconsistency. Such segments of the citizenry supported Mondale-Ferraro despite the candor that promised a tax raise—a very damaging ploy for the ticket, in general—and against all other liabilities besetting the Democrats in 1984 (see Chapter 2 for a discussion of the campaign). But the majority of those who voted appeared to reflect the estimation of Reagan of one journalist who distinguished him from Richard Nixon in these words: "Reagan sought to be president in order to do something and Nixon sought to be president in order to be something."[33] And the positive reaction to Reagan as a unifying leader was expressed by a retired brewery worker in San Antonio this way: "He really isn't like a Republican. He's more like an American, which is what we really need."[34]

That observation pinpoints a key element in Ronald Reagan's success with the American people. By his ability to disarm political criticism and even frontal attack with a humorous "aw shucks," and "there you go again," and a boyish smile that somehow looks authentic on the face of a septuagenarian, Reagan slides by substantive issues and criticisms as the "Teflon President" (see the discussion in Chapter 3). In the process, he also turns the tables. It is the Democrats who have abandoned that party's true principles, the Franklin Roosevelt and John Kennedy party. It is government in the hands of those who have forsaken the policy of compassion mixed with regard for family values and individual initiative: the Democrats have gone off and left their own tradition and are seeking to block Ronald Reagan's return to it as the *true* America. Humor and masterful co-optation is the recipe for the Reagan stew. This is extremely savvy politics. Scammon-Wattenburg counseled the Democrats to find the center of American politics and both play to it and also *listen* to what it teaches. The Republicans got the message. As John Naisbitt tersely writes: "Ronald Reagan is riding the horse in the direction the horse is going."[35]

However one regards President Ronald Reagan, we study his reelection in this volume in the attempt to understand more clearly what happened in 1984 and why; what the Republicans did right and to what depth and effect, and what went so badly awry for the Democratic party and its national ticket, even as it held its own elsewhere in the elections. Our task is to understand the election as the expression of the will of the people in our constitutional democracy, all the while bearing in mind the timeless truth for our country's politics of Gouverneur Morris's statement of our First Principle to his colleagues in the Federal Convention on July 20, 1787. In America, he said, *"The people are king."*

Notes for Chapter 1

1. This story is told by Richard M. Scammon and Ben J. Wattenberg, *The Real Majority* (New York: Coward-McCann, Inc., 1970), p. 274.

2. See Ellis Sandoz and Cecil V. Crabb, Jr., eds., *A Tide of Discontent: The 1980 Elections and Their Meaning* (Washington, D.C.: Congressional Quarterly Press, 1981).

3. Data taken from *Time* (November 19, 1984); *The World Almanac, 1985* (New York: Newspaper Enterprise Association, Inc., 1984); and the Appendices below.

4. *The Washington Post* (November 8, 1984), p. A1.

5. D.W. Brogan, *Politics In America* (New York: Harper & Row, 1954), p. 1. Italics added.

6. See Max Farrand, *The Framing of the Constitution of the United States* (New Haven: Yale University Press, 1913), p. 105; also *The Federalist,* Nos. 59 and 60.

7. Smiley v. Holm, 285 U.S. 355 (1932).

8. See, for example, United States v. Classic, 313 U.S. 299 (1941); Smith v. Allwright, 321 U.S. 649 (1944); Terry v. Adams, 345 U.S. 461 (1953); also, Wesberry v. Sanders, 376 U.S. 1 (1964) and Oregon v. Mitchell, 400 U.S. 112 (1970). For a general overview see Ellis Sandoz, *Conceived In Liberty: American Individual Rights Today* (North Scituate, Mass.: Duxbury Press, 1978), pp. 197–206.

9. Morton Keller, *Affairs of State* (Cambridge: Harvard University Press, 1977), p. 524.

10. Scammon and Wattenberg, *The Real Majority*, p. 225. Italics as in the original.

11. E.E. Schattschneider, *Party Government* (New York: Holt, Rinehart & Winston, 1942), p. 124.

12. Charles G. Mayo and Beryl L. Crowe, eds., *American Political Parties: A Systematic Perspective* (New York: Harper & Row, 1967), p. 487.

13. Hugh A. Bone, *American Politics and the Party System,* 4th ed. (New York: McGraw-Hill Book Co., 1971), p. 20.

14. Kathleen Hall Jamieson, *Packaging the Presidency: A History of Presidential Campaign Advertising* (New York: Oxford University Press, 1984), p. 429.

15. Theodore H. White, *America In Search of Itself: The Making of the President 1956–1980* (New York: Harper & Row, 1982); also the perceptive review article by Kenneth S. Lynn, "Declaration of Dependence," *Times Literary Supplement* (June 10, 1983), p. 595.

16. White, *America In Search of Itself*, p. 135.

17. Ibid. p. 6.

18. Kevin P. Phillips, *Post-Conservative America: People, Politics, and Ideology in a Time of Crisis* (New York: Random House, 1982), p. 241.

19. Ibid. pp. 184–91.

20. Gillian Peele, *Revival and Reaction: The Right in Contemporary America* (Oxford: Clarendon Press, 1984), p. 56. Viguerie publishes *Conservative Digest, New Right Report,* and *Political Gun News*.

21. Ibid. p. 194.

22. Kondracke in *The New Republic* (February 4, 1985), pp. 11, 12.

23. The phrase is from Reagan's *Inaugural Address*, reprinted in the Appendix.

24. Scammon and Wattenberg, *The Real Majority*, p. 16: "psephology . . . is defined as 'the study of elections,' and it derives from the Greek word *psephos* which means 'pebble.' The derivation comes from the custom of ancient Greece for citizens to vote by dropping colored pebbles into the Greek equivalent of our ballot box."

25. Ibid. p. 40.

26. See the discussion and cited literature in Stanley Kelley, Jr., *Interpreting Elections* (Princeton, N.J.: Princeton University Press, 1983), pp. 111–114.

27. Phillips, *Post-Conservative America*, p. 56.

28. Quoted and paraphrased from Hugh Sidey, "When the Elite Loses Touch," *Time* (November 19, 1984), p. 69.

29. For details and analysis, see below Table 8–2 and the Appendix.

30. Lou Cannon, *Reagan* (New York: G. P. Putnam's Sons, 1982), p. 323.

31. Quoted ibid. p. 372.

32. Jamieson, *Packaging the Presidency*, pp. 414, 444, 451.

33. Cannon, *Reagan*, p. 410. The journalist quoted is Marty Nolan of *The Boston Globe*.

34. *Time* (November 19, 1984), p. 45.

35. Scammon and Wattenberg, *The Real Majority*, p. 305; John Naisbitt, *Megatrends: Ten New Directions Transforming Our Lives* (New York: Warner Books, 1984), p. 109.

References and Further Reading

Binkley, Wilfred E. *American Political Parties: Their Natural History*, 4th ed., enlarged. New York: Alfred A. Knopf, 1962.

Burnham, Walter Dean. *Critical Elections and the Mainsprings of American Politics*. New York: W. W. Norton & Co., Inc., 1970.

Cannon, Lou. *Reagan*. New York: G. P. Putnam's Sons, 1982.

Jamieson, Kathleen Hall. *Packaging the Presidency: A History and Criticism of Presidential Campaign Advertising*. New York & Oxford: Oxford University Press, 1984.

Kelley, Jr., Stanley. *Interpreting Elections*. Princeton, N.J.: Princeton University Press, 1983.

Naisbitt, John. *Megatrends: Ten New Directions Transforming Our Lives*, Rev. ed. New York: Warner Books, 1984.

Palley, Marian Lief. "Reaganomics and Class Cleavages in the United States." *Journal of Politics*, Vol. 46, No. 3 (August 1984), pp. 938–46.

Peele, Gillian. *Revival and Reaction: The Right in Contemporary America*. Oxford: Clarendon Press, 1984.

Phillips, Kevin P. *Post-Conservative America: People, Politics and Ideology in a Time of Crisis*. New York: Random House, 1982.

Sandoz, Ellis. and Cecil V. Crabb, Jr., eds. *A Tide of Discontent: The 1980 Elections and Their Meaning*. Washington, D.C.: Congressional Quarterly Press, 1981.

Scammon, Richard M. and Ben J. Wattenberg. *The Real Majority*. New York: Coward-McCann, Inc., 1970.

White, Theodore H. *America In Search of Itself: The Making of the President 1956–1980*. New York: Harper & Row, Pubs., 1982.

2

The Presidential Election of 1984

Thomas E. Cronin

The 1984 presidential election triumph by Ronald Reagan ranks with the most impressive landslides in American politics. He won a record 525 electoral votes and increased his popular vote of four years earlier by an important 8 percent in his 59 to 41 margin of victory over Walter Mondale.

Reagan won in every region. He won all age groups. He won 55 percent of the female vote and about 63 percent of the male vote. The elderly gave 61 percent of their vote to him, as did nearly half of those in union households. Democrats won only Minnesota and the District of Columbia and came close only in three states: Maryland, Massachusetts, and Rhode Island.

He helped Republicans recapture 14 seats in the House of Representatives. More important, with Reagan at the top of the ticket, Republicans scored heavy upset victories in several legislative elections at the state level (notably in Connecticut, West Virginia, North Carolina, Texas, and even in Mondale's home state of Minnesota).

Much was made in the month or so after Reagan's victory of the fact that his coattails did not appear to be long, or as one analyst put it, "his coattails seemed to lack Velcro." Democrats consoled themselves that the Congress was not much changed, and indeed that two important seats were gained in the U.S. Senate. One or two Democratic wags even pointed out that if ours were only a parliamentary system, Walter Mondale could be elected prime minister by the House.

But ours is not a parliamentary system. More important, to compare Reagan's victory to Franklin Roosevelt's victory in 1936 is wrong. Members of Congress nowadays have so many perquisites (free mailings, free travel, large staffs, seemingly unlimited stationery, and telephone resources) that it is near impossible to unseat incumbents. Thus 96 percent of

House members and about 90 percent of U.S. senators who sought reelection were returned to office. They won in part because of their experience and party ties—also because state legislatures frequently protect incumbents by crafting "safe" noncompetitive districts. They are also able to win reelection because of the constituency services and high visibility they are able to achieve. Nowadays, these campaigns have less and less connection (less than ought probably be the case) with the presidential elections waged in the fall every four years.

Reagan had an appeal in 1984 that only a handful of presidents have had during the past hundred years of the Republic. While it was an impressive personal victory for President Reagan, it was not just a matter of style and acting ability. Reagan, to be sure, realized that national leadership requires symbolic and ceremonial and patriotic leadership gestures. He performs these splendidly. But these alone would not have enabled him to win so well.

Reagan's fundamental message about the size of government and the role of government aided him in victory. Most Americans who voted agree with him and prefer that the private sector or local governments should play a larger role in the management and delivery of services in this country. At best we want only a conservative or limited welfare state. Most voters also want to see the national bureaucracy and all its regulations loom somewhat less large in their lives.

A key factor, probably the key factor, as I shall explain later, is that voters in every democracy almost always reward incumbent administrations when the economy is thought to be improving. While economists debated whether the economy (especially in light of deficits, trade imbalances, and increasing trade protectionism, bank bankruptcies, etc.) was genuinely in good condition, the political reality in the fall of 1984 was that the American voters believed the economy had improved, and they were quite prepared to attribute much of that improvement to Reagan and his Administration.

Some voters were voting more against Mondale—and perhaps even still voting against Jimmy Carter and George McGovern—rather than casting an enthusiastic pro-Reagan vote. Mondale was, for the most part, unable to project a vision of America, a vision of a more effective and competitive economy, that excited people—or that convinced people he was the person to lead us toward that more desired state of affairs. He was also, as I shall explain, a wounded challenger. The primary battles crippled Mondale. President Reagan, with considerable help from the improved economic picture, turned his own incumbency to his advantage. He adroitly turned Mondale's former White House ''incumbency'' to Mondale's disadvantage. The Reagan reelection strategy seized this advantage early and never let up on Mondale and the Democrats.

With the momentary exception of a few favorable polls immediately after the somewhat unifying Democratic convention in July, Mondale badly trailed Reagan throughout the summer and autumn months.

An unusually high number of voters made up their minds during the summer and in early September. The accompanying table 2–1 suggests that by the time of the October debates less than 20 percent of the electorate said they might change their minds. This is often the case in elections, more than is generally appreciated, but it was even more so in 1984.

Both the Republicans and Democrats engaged in feverish efforts to register voters and get out the vote. In the end, the Republican efforts appeared to be better organized and more effective. Still, there was less than a one percent increase in turnout of eligible voters in 1984. About 47 percent of those

Table 2–1
When Voters Made Up Their Minds—1984

Q. "Is your mind made up, or do you think you might change your mind before the election?"

	June 1984	Aug. 1984	Sept. 1984	Early Oct. 1984	Late Oct. 1984
Mind made up	69%	69%	68%	75%	77%
Could change	18	20	21	15	18
No choice	12	9	9	9	3
Don't know/ No answer	1	3	2	1	1

SOURCE: The New York Times-CBS News National Surveys, (N = 1,400+). Responses from registered voters.

Table 2–2
Reasons for Not Voting—1980 & 1984

Q. "What was it that kept you from voting?"

Reason	1980	1984
Not registered	42%	31%
Didn't like candidates	17	10
Not interested in politics	5	8
Working	3	7
Illness	8	7
Not an American citizen	5	6
New resident	4	6
Traveling, out of town	3	5
No way to get to polls	1	3
Didn't get absentee ballot	-	2
Other/No reason	12	16

SOURCE: Gallup Poll, 1980, 1984.

eligible to vote stayed home. What were the reasons for not voting? Pretty much the same as the reasons given in 1980. See Table 2–2.

For those who voted, the image of strong leadership and experience helped Reagan. The debates, the vice presidential candidates, and even party ties and ideology seemed to play a lesser role in this election. *The New York Times-CBS News* Election Day poll asked over 5,000 voters as they left their polling places both what general factors mattered most and what issues mattered most and their responses are instructive.

Reagan won support because of the improving economy, his tax cuts, and his pro-strong-defense stances. Mondale's chief issues were the nuclear freeze and fairness, but he was not able to build a large enough coalition around those two issues.

Mondale came across as a traditional liberal. Reagan came across as a conservative to conservatives and a moderate to moderates. Although he came into prominence as a spokesman for conservative causes, his record and reputation as president softened his image as a politician of the far right. As the election neared, he traveled to the People's Republic of China, he pledged to protect Social Security, he invoked the

Table 2–3
Factors and Issues That Mattered

Q. "Which of these factors mattered most?" (Respondent is asked to check up to 2 boxes.)

	Total	Voted Reagan	Voted Mondale
Experience	27%	35%	16%
Traditional values	19	21	15
My party's candidate	9	6	14
His vision for the future	29	23	37
The vice presidential candidates	10	7	13
He's a real conservative	4	6	1
Dislike other party's candidate	17	14	22
The debates	8	3	16
Strong leadership	32	41	19

Q. "Which issue mattered most in deciding how you voted?" (Check up to 2 boxes.)

	Total	Voted Reagan	Voted Mondale
Arms control, threat of war	29%	17%	45%
Reducing federal deficit	24	22	26
Policy toward Central America	4	2	6
Fairness toward poor	20	7	39
Strong U.S. defense	25	39	5
The economy	40	51	24
Abortion	8	9	6
None of these	3	3	3

SOURCE: *The New York Times-CBS News* Election Day Poll, November 6, 1984 (N = 5,051).

names and legacy of several Democratic presidents and heroes (Roosevelt, Truman, Kennedy, and Henry Jackson). Even liberals began to view him as merely conservative rather than as an extremist.

Mondale gained most of the John Anderson support from 1980. But Reagan won a great many former Carter voters and a healthy majority of those voting for the first time. Reagan made his strongest gains among men, younger voters, Catholics, independents, moderates, white voters in general, and Southern white voters in particular.

Of considerable help to Reagan was the reality that twice as many American voters now view themselves as conservative as opposed to liberal. Had liberals equaled conservatives in gross numbers, the election would have been close. See Table 2-4.

Table 2-4
More Conservatives Than Liberals

Q. "On most political matters do you consider yourself:"

	Total	Voted Reagan (59%)	Voted Mondale (41%)
Liberal	17%	8%	29%
Moderate	44	40	51
Conservative	35	47	16

SOURCE: *The New York Times-CBS News* Election Day Poll, November 6, 1984 (N = 5,051).

Economy the Key Issue

Reagan had won the White House in 1980 in large part because of his effective and stinging attacks on President Carter's inability to provide economic leadership. His clever question "Are you better off today than you were four years ago?" helped him enormously in 1980; it helped even more in 1984 as Americans generally viewed the economy as in better shape than it had been four years earlier. Table 2-5 indicates the public's response to Reagan's question on Election Day.

Mondale ran an issues campaign. He could hardly run against Reagan's personality or against the failure of Reagan to make the presidency work. He challenged Reagan to spell out his tax and economic plans for the future. This backfired

Table 2—5
Are You Better Off Today . . . ?

Q. "Compared to four years ago, is the U.S. economy:"

	Total	Reagan Voters	Mondale Voters
Better today	57%	83%	19%
Worse today	19	3	41
About the same	21	11	36

SOURCE: The New York Times-CBS News Election Day Poll, November 6, 1984 (N = 5,051).

as Reagan merely danced around the question of what he would do in a second term. It was not so much that Reagan was being deceptive or dishonest—although he was a little of both—as it was a case of his directing public attention to the Mondale pledge to raise taxes. Reagan generally refused to say what he was going to do. Sometimes, however, he would say he was not going to raise taxes, once even saying that taxes would be raised "over my dead body."

Although Mondale tried to project a "new realism," his approach to economic issues nearly always seemed strikingly close to the old New Deal something-for-everybody strategy. One of the ironies of the campaign was that the very New Deal programs of the past Mondale praised and wanted to continue have succeeded. "The success of the New Deal in expanding the middle class," write Germond and Witcover, "has come back to haunt the Democratic Party; the 'fairness issue' raised by Mondale fell on deaf ears among a middle class that is better off but now feeling somewhat put upon."[1]

The single greatest influence on voter preference throughout the 1984 campaign turned out to be the traditional pocketbook concerns of under which president would the voter be better off financially. People cared about the leadership issue, and issues of fairness and war and peace, but again and again they told pollsters and, later voted, with the economy most on their minds. In September of 1984, The Washington Post-ABC News telephone poll asked: "Regardless of how you might vote, I'd like you to compare Reagan and Mondale in some ways."

	Reagan	Mondale	No Opinion
Would make me better off financially	53%	37%	10%
Would do a better job in coping with the budget deficits	52%	40%	8%

A few weeks later those who were deemed as probable voters were asked whether they believed the economy would get better or worse in a Reagan second term and only a quarter of the population thought it might get worse. That was an important vote of confidence for Reagan—only two weeks before the election. See Table 2–6.

Table 2–6
Ronald Reagan and the Economy

Q. "Do you think that if Ronald Reagan is reelected this fall, the economy will get worse?"

No (will not get worse)	62%
Yes (will get worse)	12
Don't know/No answer	26

SOURCE: *The New York Times-CBS News* National Survey, October 23–25, 1984 (N = 1,463). Responses from "probable voters" only.

Throughout the campaign voters acknowledged the economy was their chief concern and would be the subject most important to them as they decided how to vote on November 6. And the record 6.8 percent growth in the GNP in 1984 doubtless reinforced the public's positive outlook.

In short, Reagan's reputation as a fiscal conservative, his tax cuts, his pledge not to raise taxes, and his general commitment to shrink the role of government in domestic and social programs won endorsement from the American voters. A growing number of Americans, especially in their 30s and 40s, favor tax relief of any kind and are positively turned off by traditional welfare programs. Their attitude was typified by voters who said, "Let's send a message to those who don't work that they'll have to begin earning their way the old-fashioned way—by working." Reagan himself reinforced this appeal to the middle and upper classes when during the

Table 2-7
Policy Concerns of Voters—1984

Q. "When you vote for president in November, what will be more important in deciding how you vote—the economy of this country, or U.S. military and foreign policy, or something else?"

Economy	55%
Military and foreign policy	18
Both (volunteered answer)	10
Something else	8
Don't know/No answer	8

SOURCE: *The New York Times-CBS News* National Survey, October 23–25, 1984 (N = 1,463). Responses from "probable voters" only.

final days of the campaign he said the differences between the two parties boiled down to this: The Democrats were *the party of April fifteenth*, while the Republicans were *the party of July Fourth*—it was a choice between, he simplistically suggested, taxes and liberty. Overstated, yes. Simplistic, woefully so, but effective politics and effective cue-signaling to those few who hadn't yet made up their minds.

The Leadership Issue

One of the paradoxes of the Reagan presidency is that while Americans view Reagan as a strong leader, they also view him as a semidetached chief executive, an executive who lets several of his key advisers make most of the important decisions in the White House. Jimmy Carter delegated little and worked long into the night. He almost gave hard work a bad name. Reagan, in contrast, loves to delegate. He often seems to have only limited information requirements, matched by limited curiosity.

"We are looking at a political puzzle here," writes Barry Sussman of *The Washington Post*. "If someone were to run for office and pledge to have advisers make the important decisions, he or she wouldn't get very far. But Reagan was

Table 2—8
Who's In Charge at the White House?

Q. "Who do you think makes most of the important decisions in the White House, Reagan or the advisers around him?"

Reagan	33%
Advisers	58
Both equally	5
No opinion	4

SOURCE: *The Washington Post-ABC News* Telephone Poll, April 8–12, 1983 (N-1,516).

Q. "Do you think that most of the time Ronald Reagan is in charge of what goes on in his Administration, or do you think that most of the time other people are really running the government?"

Other people running the government	45%
Reagan in charge	45
Don't know/No answer	10

SOURCE: *The New York Times-CBS News* National Survey, October 23–25, 1984 (N = 1,463). Responses from "probable voters" only.

seen as acting that way in office, and it did not hurt his reelection bid at all."[2]

Former Vice President Walter Mondale tried to make "leadership" a central issue in the campaign. "It's time for America to find new leadership," he said in the second debate. He blasted Reagan for not offering the bold leadership needed to negotiate a significant arms control treaty. He faulted Reagan for lack of fairness and compassion. He criticized Reagan's lack of vision for the future of America. He declared Reagan had not mastered the details of foreign policy situations needed by a chief executive. He called it "leadership by amnesia."

By several usual standards of presidential leadership performance, Reagan might be judged a failure. He often lost track of his facts, or simply got them wrong. He once mistook his secretary of Housing and Urban Development for just another visiting mayor. One of his aides, his chief public relations aide, told an NBC television reporter that the President sometimes dozes off and finds it difficult staying awake in Cabinet meetings. Many of his aides and Cabinet members proved mediocre, and some were forced out for conflicts of interest. Moreover, his budgets were way out of balance; he had few, if any, real foreign policy accomplishments, and his policies were shown to have hurt the poor.

Despite all that, Americans said Reagan was a strong leader. It is not exactly clear why voters felt this. Perhaps it was the force of personality, the firmness in national security matters, the John Wayne toughness and patriotism. Perhaps his success with Congress. Perhaps his standing up to the Soviets. Perhaps his invasion and rescue mission in Grenada. Perhaps his continual personal celebration of America and freedom and traditional values. He never flinched from speaking out, often with emotion and flair, about his love for his country.

A poll for *Time* magazine in August of 1984 found Americans saying Reagan was a more effective leader than Mondale by a 58 to 24 percent margin. It also reported that Reagan was likely to be better in times of crisis by a 57 to 22 percent margin. Who was the more dynamic and exciting candidate? Again, Reagan won by a 52 to 26 percent margin over Mondale.

Mondale never gained much ground. Nearly every poll conducted by every pollster indicated Reagan was viewed as a leader. Next to the improved economic situation this was probably the most important factor in this campaign, as illustrated in Table 2–9.

Table 2–9
Presidential Candidates as Leaders?

Q. "Do you think Ronald Reagan or Walter Mondale is a strong leader?"

	Ronald Reagan	Walter Mondale
Yes	70%	40%
No	24	45
Don't know/No answer	5	14

SOURCE: *The New York Times-CBS News* National Survey, October 23–25, 1984 (N = 1,463). Responses from "probable voters" only.

Mondale, in a postelection interview, acknowledged he was unable to make the "leadership" issue work for him. He said he was unable to appeal to the moderates and independents who were so crucial to any chances for his victory. "I was unable to make the case . . . that the long term, tough problems of our nation can only be solved by a president who masters the essential details and who's in command . . ." Mondale also suggested these additional reasons that made it extremely difficult for him to portray Reagan as ineffective.

> It is also the case that I was running against an incumbent President . . . who . . . is very popular personally—very well liked—in the midst of what is perceived as good economic times and with diminished international tensions . . . We've had this long history of one-term Presidents, and I believe the American people were strongly inclined to give the benefit of the doubt to the incumbent.[3]

Reagan had developed an uncanny rapport with the American people. Sometimes this was referred to as the skills of "the great communicator." Sometimes he was called our "Teflon president" because most of the problems or failings of his administration seldom stuck to him—at least for long. But, more probably, it was his ability to simplify the priorities of his administration. Reagan's chief strength was to concentrate on a few transcendent themes, and leave the details to his aides. This plus his career-long communications training made him one of the few national politicians average Americans could easily understand. He had a contagious self-confidence and an optimism about himself and his hopes for America, and seemed to be able to make the institution of the presidency work. Although he often delegated tasks, ultimately, however, he seemed in charge and demonstrated time and again that he liked the job, liked the American people and loved the fight to make things better. For this and for the ease with which he seemed to tackle each problem that came his way, a majority of Americans decided to "stay the course" with him for yet another term. The burden had been on Mondale to project an alternative vision of a more competent, more dynamic, more reassuring leader—and Mondale proved unable to make that case.

One further observation. Reagan's detachment from parts

of his job and his leaving details to others has often served him well. One of his long time biographers notes that one benefit for Reagan is that since Reagan seems so distanced from events of his own administration and so essentially unpolitical many people are often apt to blame his surrogates or deputies rather than him when things go wrong. His detachment leaves him free to come in and turn some of the lemons into lemonade. The above-the-battle stance also enhances some of the magic and mystique of his national renewer and symbolic leadership efforts.

Divided Democrats and a Wounded Challenger

The Democratic nomination battle was about as bruising as primary and caucus campaigns can get. Mondale was the front-runner from the outset. All the others aimed their barbs at him. From mid-1983 all the way up to the Democratic convention in July of 1984, Mondale's record and leadership style were exposed and criticized, especially by John Glenn, Alan Cranston, Gary Hart, and Jesse Jackson. Glenn said he was too liberal. Cranston said he was not enough of a leader for the nuclear freeze. Hart said Mondale was far too cautious and too much the captive of the establishment special interests. Jackson's charismatic star quality always made Mondale look dull in contrast.

Mondale won most of the more important endorsements. Ironically, however, the endorsements became as much a burden as a blessing. Speaker Thomas P. "Tip" O'Neill's endorsement carried with it the image of an old-style "tax and spend" Democrat. The AFL-CIO endorsement carried with it the message that Mondale favored trade protectionism. The National Educational Association's endorsement and similar public employee support tagged Mondale as perhaps too much the friend of bureaucrats and public employee pensions. The endorsement won from the National Organization of Women associated Mondale with aggressive affirmative action policies. Jimmy Carter endorsed Mondale as well and that carried more liabilities than benefits. The list was long, but the overall impression was left that Mondale was less an independent, fresh challenger than a creature and spokesman for a host of Democrats and single-issue groups whose time had passed.

One of the sharpest attacks on Mondale came in a debate with Gary Hart. Senator Hart asked Mondale to point out even a single issue where he differed from the leadership of the AFL-CIO. Mondale failed to respond. Hart had made his point. Hart won enormous support from the so-called neoliberals who wanted to move away from government bailouts and subsidies and toward newer market incentive systems that might spur competition and greater trade.

Mondale won the Iowa caucuses but was badly upset in the New Hampshire primary and throughout New England. Indeed, had Mondale won just a few thousand votes less in Georgia's "Super Tuesday" election in March, he probably would have been forced out of the nomination race. As it was, Hart continued to pound on Mondale right up until the final primaries in June.

Mondale, although an experienced and able politician, came across as a dull, cautious, traditional Democrat. Hart won the reputation as the candidate of new ideas. Jackson won the reputation as the bold, passionate candidate who truly cared about minorities and the poor. Both Hart and Jackson used television more effectively.

Democrats were also divided when it came to the issues. Many wanted to stress Reagan's unfairness to the poor and the elderly. Others wanted to make the nuclear freeze issue the major issue. Some wanted to make defense spending the central issue. Still others wanted to confront Reagan on all the social issues and raise the question of who would control Supreme Court nominations for the next four years. U.S. involvement in Central America was yet another issue. So also was the deficit.

A rather sizable chunk of Democrats seemed to want to move away from the traditional issues and talk about the need for new economic strategies. Divisions and fights in the final sessions of the Democratic Platform Committee typified these splits. Young professionals on the committee wanted greater emphasis on Gary Hart's policies. The Jackson and Mondale delegates wanted to stick to traditional social-programs approaches, and they especially wanted to protect all existing federal domestic programs.

The impression was often conveyed—in the Platform Committee, at the convention and throughout the campaign—that the Democrats were unclear about their priorities. They could criticize Reagan. But their own positive program was less than clear. Mondale's speeches and interviews reflected this tentativeness and unsureness. He would focus on one issue for a while only to drop it and take something else up a few days later. His honest admission that he would raise taxes turned out to be hurtful not helpful to his election chances. Ultimately, even the Mondale campaign stopped running their tax-increase television ads. His blasts at Reagan's failure to serve as a leader were ineffective, especially in light of the fact that most voters felt Reagan was an effective leader. His focus on Reagan's failure to work well with the U.S.S.R. was undercut by Reagan's meeting with Soviet Foreign Minister Andrei Gromyko and by Reagan's earnest pledge to concentrate more on arms control efforts in his second term.

In short, both Mondale and the Democrats were unable to project a positive vision of America that won appeal. Mondale emerged from the hard-fought and often bitter Democratic primary season as very much a *wounded* challenger. Mondale was *wounded* in at least four ways. *First,* his ties to Jimmy Carter and many of the unsuccessful policies of the late 1970's (Iran, interest rates, inflation, etc.) were voiced in primary contests, setting the stage for Reagan strategists to conduct a rerun of their 1980 defeat of the Carter-Mondale Administration. *Second,* his image as a candidate of the special interests, an image his Democratic rivals, not Reagan, had successfully pinned on him, hurt him immeasurably. *Third,* he had failed to win widespread support in his own party. His winter and spring failures among independents, younger voters, in New England and in the West, came back to haunt him as he in vain tried to unify Democrats in the fall. *Finally,* the Democratic party organization was in poor shape at the national level and in most of the states. Mondale had tried to fire the national chairman—an act that backfired on him. He had tried to appoint Bert Lance, as a representative of the South, to a key party and campaign post—and that backfired. More important, the Democrats had failed to do much fund-raising that would help to register voters, get out the vote, and so on. Outspent, outorganized, and deeply divided, the Democrats gave little help to their standard-bearer, while the Republican party provided ample financial and organizational support to their unanimously and enthusiastically backed national ticket.

The Ferraro Factor

Geraldine Ferraro, as the first woman ever nominated for the vice presidency by a major party, brought considerable excitement and controversy to the 1984 campaign. Although relatively unknown before her nomination, she developed a star quality that attracted large crowds, helped raise funds, and almost certainly altered forever the role women will play in American politics.

On balance, however, Ferraro appears to have hurt Mondale's chances more than she helped. Reagan did surprisingly well with women, winning at least 55 percent of the women's vote. If there was a gender gap, it appeared to be a male one. Men backed Reagan over Mondale by 63 percent to 37 percent.

Voters do not ordinarily decide to vote for a president because of the choice of vice presidential running mates. Fewer than 10 percent of the voters in any election cite vice presidents as one of the major factors explaining their vote. This was also the case in 1984. Conventional wisdom holds that vice presidential running mates can hurt a presidential candidate but usually can't help. On occasion, in 1960 for example, a vice presidential running mate like Lyndon Johnson can help balance a ticket geographically and ideologically. But that case was probably an exception to the general rule.

Ferraro's nomination doubtless helped to encourage Democratic support among feminists, supporters of the National Organization of Women, and among countless working and professional women. Most of these people, however, would ordinarily have voted for Mondale and against Reagan. Ferraro probably did more to reinforce their inclination than to convert many voters.

On the other side of the ledger, however, Ferraro's candidacy hurt Mondale on several counts. *First,* her own financial disclosure problems and some of her husband's real estate tax problems surfaced in a way that badly damaged her credibility and perhaps even her integrity. More important, these questions dominated the news through most of August—making it difficult for Mondale to make his views known. *Second,* her regional accent and style probably hurt Democratic chances (which were already slim) in the South and Southwest. *Third,* her lack of experience on foreign and national security policy matters concerned even her own supporters. *Fourth,* according to survey data, she lost her debate with George Bush. *Finally,* Congresswoman Ferraro, also the first Italian American to be on a national party ticket—a fact little written about in the campaign—may have lost some additional votes because of discrimination against that ethnic group.

Table 2—10
Evaluations of Bush and Ferraro

Q. "Which candidate do you think did the better job, George Bush or Geraldine Ferraro?"

Bush	47%
Ferraro	31
A tie, both, neither	17
Don't know, No answer	5

SOURCE: *The New York Times-CBS News* Post-Debate Survey, October 11, 1984 (N = 790). Responses from "probable voters" only.

Q. "Do you have confidence in Geraldine Ferraro's/George Bush's ability to deal with a crisis, or would you feel uneasy about her/him?"

	Geraldine Ferraro	George Bush
Confident	38%	55%
Uneasy	54	35
Don't know/No answer	8	10

SOURCE: *The New York Times-CBS News* Poll, September 12–16, 1984 (N = 1,546). Responses from "probable voters" only.

It is probably true that an unfair standard is still placed on women candidates for high public office. This different kind of scrutiny involves expecting a woman to be better than comparable men who have run or served in office in the past. For example, Ronald Reagan had little or no foreign policy experience, and he won election anyway. If women talk tough, they are apt to be called loud or mean, or worse. If they speak with feeling, emotion, and compassion, they are apt to be called soft or naive.

In a poll taken the week after the 1984 election, half of the American people surveyed said it hurt the Democrats to have had a woman on the ticket. And very few people said it helped that Ferraro was the woman candidate.

The postelection polls probably overstate her as a liability. She was also hurt by being teamed up with Mondale, and he most surely had a lot of negatives—even more so as voters looked back after the lopsided defeat.

All in all, Ferraro probably cost some votes. Plainly she was not a major plus. Her own district in Queens voted for Reagan. Mondale, however, couldn't have won if his running

Table 2–11
A Woman on the Ticket: What Impact?

Q. "In general, do you think it helped or hurt the Democrats to have a woman on the presidential ticket?"

Hurt	50%
Made no difference	29
Helped	18
Don't know/No answer	3

Q. "Did it help or hurt for that woman to have been Ferraro?"

Hurt	34%
Made no difference	46
Helped	16
Don't know/No answer	4

SOURCE: Media General-Associated Press Survey, November 12–19, 1984 (N = 1,476).

mate was Walter Cronkite, Michael Jackson, or Mary Tyler Moore—or any combination of celebrity running mates. Nor would John Glenn or Gary Hart have added much to the ticket. He was going down to defeat anyway. Most people had made up their minds on the basis of issues and the two top-of-the-ticket candidates. The Reagan Administration neutralized the Ferraro factor by calling attention, time and again, to their three women in the president's Cabinet and to the Reagan nomination of Sandra Day O'Connor as the first woman appointed to the U.S. Supreme Court. Ultimately, Ferraro helped a little here, hurt a little there, but had virtually no impact on the overall election outcome.

Candidate Reagan

Several observers called Reagan's victory a triumph of personality over substance. Elizabeth Drew, writing in *The New Yorker*, called it "above all a testimony to the man as a political phenomenon."[4] She credited much of his victory to his natural talents, his ability to help create and reflect the mood of the times, and the good luck that generally characterizes his political career.

As president and as candidate, Reagan exuded optimism. Nearly everyone saw him as a strong and positive person. If, on occasion, his message was harsh, it was always said in soft and genial tones. He never looked mean-spirited.

There is an old aphorism in politics that it helps a lot if you like and enjoy people. It obviously helps even more if people know you like and enjoy them. Reagan benefits on all scores. He likes himself (high self-esteem). He likes people. He likes his job. And he positively loves his country. All this comes across.

Over the course of his first term, Reagan had advocated policies or acted in ways that endeared him to some of the most powerful blocs in American politics. An illustrative list would go like this:

Major Tax Cuts
Major Reduction in Inflation

Fired PATCO Union Air Traffic Controllers
Lessened Governmental Regulations
Doubled Military Spending
Invaded Grenada
Got "Tough" with Soviet Union
Championed Balanced Budget Constitutional Amendment
Championed the Olympics of 1984
Championed Prayer in School
Championed Get-Tough-With-Criminals Positions
Honored both Vietnam and World War II Veterans
Nominated First Woman to Supreme Court
Helped Refinance Social Security Program
Championed Volunteer Groups and Volunteer Spirit
Advocated a Go-Slow Approach to Affirmative Action
Championed an End to Corporation Tax
Got Rid of Grain Embargo with Russia

Reagan may be an enormously effective ceremonial and symbolic leader, but he also took stands and fought for his programs. Not everything won passage, but in taking strong positions the President reinforced the political support that had won him the White House. Reagan has shown himself quite able, on a number of occasions, to outline in an appealing way conservative positions to large numbers of voters who in the past did not view themselves as particularly conservative. In Reagan, many moderates or neoconservatives found conservative viewpoints at least temporarily acceptable. As he headed into the 1984 campaign, he could count on strong support from a number of key groups: business leaders, upper-income individuals, conservatives, Republicans, military leaders, the defense and space contractors, the Moral Majority, orthodox religious groups, and those who believed minorities were being unfairly advantaged at the expense of the broad middle class. That gave the President a fine head start.

What he needed to do in the campaign was to encourage more support from Southerners, Catholics, women, and younger voters. He needed to appeal to the moderates, the independents, and to conservative Democrats. He and his strategists knew well that the only extreme that wins in American politics is the extreme middle.

Reagan and his strategists set out, therefore, to run on his record of achievements and reinforce his promises to conser-

Table 2–12

Voters' Concerns and Skepticism about Reagan

Q. "Does the Reagan Administration try hard enough to reach diplomatic solutions, or is it too quick to get American military forces involved?"

Too quick with military	42%
Tries diplomacy	39
Both	2
Neither	2
Don't know/No answer	16

Q. "Do you think the United States government should provide military assistance to the people trying to overthrow the government of Nicaragua, or not?"

No, do not help	44%
Yes, help	30
Don't know/No answer	26

Q. "Do you think the United States has done everything reasonable to try to reach agreement with the Soviet Union about controlling nuclear weapons, or should the United States do more?"

Should do more	60%
Has done everything	31
Don't know/No answer	9

Q. "Some people have proposed developing a defense system in space to protect the United States from nuclear attacks, the concept called 'Star Wars.' Do you think this would make us more secure, or would it just speed up the arms race?"

Speed up the arms race	48%
Make us more secure	31
Both	3
Neither	2
Don't know/No answer	16

SOURCE: The New York Times-CBS News National Survey, October 23–25, 1984 (N = 1,463). Responses from "probable voters" only.

vatives while at the same time moderating some of his more "hard-line" positions. His trip to the People's Republic of China in the spring of 1984 helped to portray him as both a moderate and an international leader. Time and again, however, he would be pressed to demonstrate that diplomatic solutions were preferable to military escalation. Note that even in October, the chief voter concern about Reagan revolved around his reputation as somewhat "trigger-happy" and as perhaps overly hawkish.

One of the ways Reagan tried to improve his image—especially with moderate and conservative Democrats—was to claim that he was in the Franklin Roosevelt, Harry Truman, and John F. Kennedy tradition. He participated in Roosevelt and Truman anniversary ceremonies and even held election-year receptions at the White House in honor of Hubert Humphrey and Henry Jackson. He often invoked their names, quoted them, and would point out that he too had been a Democrat. But, he would add, the Democratic party had shifted too far to the left. It had, in more recent years, weakened our defense preparedness. It lacked a firmness of resolve in dealing with the Soviets. Reagan doubtless succeeded in these efforts. Curiously, he never invoked the Harding, Coolidge, Hoover, Nixon, and Ford legacies.

The President, who was often accused by Democrats of bellicose language in talking about the Soviets, sought in his second debate to stress his realistic approach to the U.S.S.R. While saying he would not retract past statements, he also said the two superpowers, who have it in their power to destroy civilization, must live together and thus should reduce their nuclear armaments. He said the Soviets had broken off the talks on intermediate nuclear forces. And he stressed that his commitment to peace would always be matched by his commitment to military strength.

Reagan would try, and sometimes succeed, in moderating his positions on national security. He would not let up, however, in painting Mondale as weak on defense issues. Illustrative in this Reagan rebuttal in the middle of the second debate: "He [Mondale] was against the F-14 fighter; he was against the M-1 tank; he was against the B-1 bomber; he wanted to cut the salary of all the military; he wanted to bring home half of the American forces in Europe. And he has a record of weakness with regard to our national defense that is second to none. Indeed, he was on that side virtually throughout all his years in the Senate, and he opposed even President Carter when, toward the end of his term, President Carter wanted to increase the defense budget."[5]

Reagan held almost no press or news conferences during the campaign. He gave set campaign speeches to well-organized throngs of admirers, and he visited places that were ideal for television news bites. He also benefited from extremely well produced television ads that featured Reagan proudly hailing the economic recovery, the reduction in international tensions, the renewal of faith and optimism and patriotism in America, and his firm commitment to traditional values. Reagan was very convincing when he looked moved, and it was, on such occasions, difficult to view him as hard-hearted or extremist.

In short, Reagan—with the help of a regular stream of poll data and campaign strategy advice—stressed all his positives, harped on Mondale's and the Democrats' "tired-old-failed policies," and kept cleverly mum about what his own economic or tax policies would be in a second term. He was perhaps least persuasive when he claimed the budget deficits would just fade away with economic growth. Mondale plainly scored some points in that first debate when the President seemed hesitant, vague, and ill at ease as Mondale disputed the President's facts and figures. If Mondale could have continued to unsettle and upstage the President in the second debate, the election would have been a little closer. This was not to be. Even Mondale recognizes he failed to convince people in that second debate. "After the first debate, I thought we had a chance. . . . My chances of winning probably disappeared at the end of the second debate. . . . The President did sufficiently well . . . that I think it reassured Americans, and they did what I think they were planning to do all along."[6] Namely, to stick with Reagan. Notice how virtually no shift in voter attitudes was occurring throughout the eight weeks of the general election campaign. See Table 2–13.

The Debates and Television

The League of Women Voters organized and sponsored three formal televised debates in 1984. Two were between

Table 2–13
Mondale Gained No Ground

Breakdown of Voter Support

	Sept. 7–9	Sept. 21–23	Sept. 28–30	Oct. 15–17	Oct. 26–28	Nov. 1–3
Reagan-Bush	55%	57%	56%	58%	57%	57%
Mondale-Ferraro	40	39	39	38	40	39
Others/Undecided	5	4	5	4	3	4

SOURCE: Gallup Poll National Surveys, 1984.

Mondale and Reagan, and one between vice presidential candidates Bush and Ferraro. The debates did not appear to play an important role in this election—certainly not as important as they had been in 1960 or 1976. Most voters had already made up their minds. Although Mondale was viewed as the winner of the first debate, Reagan was viewed as the winner of the second presidential debate. Bush won, albeit narrowly, the Bush-Ferraro "contest."

Poll results after the first debate found probable voters saying Mondale was more impressive than they thought he would be. Nearly half the respondents said Reagan was not as sharp as he was four years ago. Mondale clearly won the debate, according to the people polled—and the issue of Reagan's age was raised anew—but it did not appear to change how they planned to vote. The data are striking. See Table 2–14.

Two weeks later the presidential candidates met again, this time discussing and answering questions about foreign and defense policy. This time Reagan was viewed as the victor, although some surveys suggested it was more of a draw. Twice as many people told *The New York Times-CBS News* poll it was a tie in the second debate than had said so after the first debate. Reagan had slipped a little in the polls but still enjoyed a comfortable lead.

What of the impact of the debates? At best it can be said that Mondale impressed some voters and may have gained a few undecided voters. Reagan voters had pretty much already made up their minds. Economic issues such as lowered inflation, lower interest rates, rising employment figures, and an

Table 2–14
After The First Debate

Q. "Which candidate do you think did the best job—or won—Sunday night's debate, Ronald Reagan or Walter Mondale?"

Reagan	17%
Mondale	68
A tie/Both/Neither	10
Don't know, No answer	7

Q. "If the 1984 presidential election were being held today, would you vote for Ronald Reagan for president and George Bush for vice president, the Republican candidates, or for Walter Mondale for president and Geraldine Ferraro for vice president, the Democratic candidates?"

Reagan/Bush	56%
Mondale/Ferraro	37
Wouldn't vote	1
Don't know, No answer	7

SOURCE: The New York Times-CBS News Post-Debate Poll, October 9, 1984 (N = 515). Responses from registered voters.

improved stock market all had far more of an effect than anything Mondale got to say in these debates. They were, to be sure, a possible trap for the President. Challengers always have a greater chance to gain in such encounters. With virtually nothing to lose, Mondale gained in that first debate as he came across relaxed, forceful, informed, and articulate. The President barely survived the first debate but gave a reassuring performance in the second debate—sufficiently reassuring to keep his supporters solidly behind him.

"Modern politics," Mondale said on the day after the election, "requires mastery of television." He said he had never really warmed up to television. He implied that he didn't come across well and that he was ill at ease. He worried, too, that too much of politics is the 20-second snippet on the evening news. He said he was scared Ameri-

Table 2–15
Evaluations after Second Debate

Q. "Which candidate do you think did the best job—or won—Sunday night's debate, Ronald Reagan or Walter Mondale?"

Reagan	39%
Mondale	26
A tie/Both/Neither	21
Don't know/No answer	13

Q. "Well, as of today, do you lean more toward Reagan and Bush, or more toward Mondale and Ferraro?"

Reagan/Bush	52%
Mondale/Ferraro	43
Wouldn't vote	1
Don't know/No answer	4

SOURCE: *The New York Times-CBS News* Post-Debate Poll, October 24–25, 1984 (N = 546). Responses from registered voters.

can politics is losing its substance, losing the depth needed to discuss and debate the tough problems facing the country.

Reagan, not surprisingly, has not made similar complaints. He likes television and is about as adroit in using it as any politician has ever been. Indeed, except for his first debate, he was a master television performer throughout the campaign. His memorable quip in the second debate that "I will not make age an issue of this campaign. I am not going to exploit for political purposes, my opponent's youth and inexperience" did more than anything else to dispel concerns about his age and to disarm Mondale's efforts to upstage him.

Mondale's comments about television are doubtless sincere. Far more important than the role of television in the 1984 election, however, was the near impossible challenge Mondale had in trying to devise a surefire strategy to beat a peace-prosperity-and-strong-leadership incumbent president.

Paradoxes of the 1984 Campaign

The 1984 Reagan reelection was almost as full of paradoxes and puzzles as the American presidency itself.[7] One of these paradoxes has already been noted—namely that nearly half of the people believe Reagan doesn't make the decisions at the White House, and yet they believe he is a strong leader.

Reagan abounds with paradoxical characteristics. Even after twenty years in politics, he still is able to portray himself as above politics and, at worst, as just a citizen-politician. He is also the first union leader to become president—although he shifted parties and some ideology in the process. And ever since he has been a national figure, he has been ridiculed as a B-grade movie actor who has simplistic or naive views of both the past and the future. Yet by 1984 Reagan had shown himself to be far more than the "amiable dunce" Washington elder statesmen had thought him to be. He has proven to be a complex and contradictory amalgam of ideology and pragmatism, of optimism and realism.

So also his 1984 reelection campaign was full of paradoxes.

> Ronald Reagan has contrived to be President of the United States for four years and still to run as if he were the challenger rather than the incumbent. From his White House lair, he has campaigned against Washington. Perched on a mountain of debt, he has canvassed against the big spenders. With a giant Madison Avenue budget, he has denounced the East Coast media. As the man who "lost" Lebanon, he has attacked the craven bureaucrats who surrendered to the Islamic foe. It was the best underdog campaign the country had ever seen.[8]

Another Reagan campaign year paradox is that he simultaneously is able to strike a pose as both a *programmatic ideologue* and as an artful *compromiser* (as pragmatic and flexible). His Grenada invasion, his "Star Wars" defense system, and his fulsome embrace of the Moral Majority suggest he is an ideologue. His trip to China, his embrace of the Social Security system, and his evolving position on relations with the U.S.S.R. all suggest he is flexible. In one sense, Reagan has been able to have it both ways—to appear firm and fixed in his views and also able to compromise when this is necessary. Despite the tough rhetoric, he usually acted pragmatically. In the end he has earned a reputation as a "cautious ideologue."

Another Reagan paradox is that he ran a decidedly *issues-oriented campaign when he was the challenger in 1980*, but he seemed to run a *personality/strong leader oriented campaign in 1984*. He made it perfectly clear what he would do in 1980—slash taxes, curb social programs, raise military spending. In 1984 he sometimes made things perfectly opaque. He was very vague about tax reform. He was even less clear about economic programs. Even the friendly *Wall Street Journal* began to chide him for apparently working "on the theory that he can't be hurt by what the voters don't know."[9] He hedged some on military spending, and he was hazy too about his plans for negotiations with the leaders in Moscow.

He loved to talk about being in favor of *a balanced budget*, yet his budget deficits soared to unimaginable highs. His tax cuts and defense spending increases, in fact, made him the biggest spender of them all—*the great budget unbalancer*. He talked often in 1984 of wanting an item veto for presidents—but he failed to produce and send Congress a proposed balanced budget, he failed to use his existing general veto authority to fight deficits, and he failed to take much advantage of other technical powers and authority (such as deferrals and recisions) that are permitted a president through the Budget and Impoundment Control Act of 1974. It often was as if Reagan wanted the reputation as an awesome fiscal conservative, yet he also didn't want (or politically was afraid) to go after the waste and excesses in the current budget. If the truth be known, Reagan differed only slightly with the Congress in the overall budget expenditure patterns in his first four years. U.S. Senator Daniel Patrick Moynihan speaks directly to this Reagan paradox this way:

> A law of opposites frequently influences the American presidency. Once in office, presidents are seen to do things least expected of them, often things they had explicitly promised not to do. Previous commitments or perceived inclinations act as a kind of insurance that protects against any great loss if a President behaves contrary to expectation. He is given the benefit of the doubt. He can't have wanted to do this or that, he must have *had* to do it. . . .

Something of this indulgence is now being granted President Reagan. Consider the extraordinary deficits, $200 billion a year and continuing . . . as far as the eye can see. This accumulation of serious debt . . . is all happening without any great public protest, or apparent political cost.[10]

It is as if Reagan-the-Conservative could not really be doing this—after all, he is a right-wing Republican. But he did.

Another puzzle of the Reagan presidency is that while he is *a great defender of the American political system, he also has championed more proposed amendments to our U.S. Constitution* than any president in memory. He wants to change it as it speaks to, among other things, prayer, abortion, death penalty, exclusionary rule, item vetoes, a balanced budget, and more. One assumes he would like an amendment to prohibit corporation taxes, as one additional example.

Reagan is perceived *as a strong leader,* and he is, on certain issues he cares about. Yet, at the same time, *he has ducked many of the critical issues* of the day: industrial policy, tax reform (until 1985), arms control, world hunger, human rights (especially in South Africa), civil rights, women's rights, environmental standards, and more. Ultimately, he has been a kind of "restoration leader"—he has restored a respect for traditional values, for private sector initiative, for business, for military strength, for a more limited role for government (along the McKinley, Coolidge, and Eisenhower lines). He has been a strong leader, but for selective goals, for matters he cares about.

A personal paradox typified by Reagan is that he *champions orthodox family and religious values,* yet he is the first divorced person to win the presidency. And he seems *distant if not cool to some of his own children* and rather *aloof too from any formal religious practices* for himself.

Another paradox, discussed earlier, is that Reagan rather remarkably gets away with the clashing sentiments of *loving his country* but *hating government.* He is one of the all-time great morale-builders and cheerleaders we have ever had—yet he is also a symbol of bashing the bureaucrats, slashing taxes, and opposing Congress and the courts. This love my country/hate the government stance allowed Reagan to rerun for the presidency almost as if he was the outsider and challenger. He was able to portray Mondale as the friend of big government and as the longtime Washingtonian, and that strategy played well with voters.

Still another paradox is raised by the image of Reagan as *anti-big government*. On the other hand, he favors and has helped to enact many programs that are very expensive. Reagan favors *big government conservative-style*. To double the defense budget in five years was to cause big government. To favor Star Wars is to bring about a bigger budget and more bureaucracy. He has favored a whole catalogue of new weapons systems. He wants new and more prisons. His tuition tax credits would cause greater budget deficits, as would his proposed elimination of the tax on corporations. He also has greatly expanded the CIA during his presidency. He also wants the national government to play a bigger role in prohibiting abortion and enforcing prayer in schools.

But he is not consistent. He simply likes to pose as a crusader against big government. Many of his actions, however, have measurably added to both bigger government and soaring deficits.

Finally, one of the fascinating paradoxes of the 1984 election was that *many of those who voted for Reagan voted for him even though they differ with him on some issues they care deeply about.* Ultimately, they voted for him because the economy had improved and they were not convinced that Mondale could do better. This included at least a third of those who had supported or favored Gary Hart in the spring of 1984.

A great many people voting for Reagan believe he is uncaring about the poor, uncaring about equal opportunities for women, and inadequately concerned about the arms race and the real possibility of nuclear war. Polls showed far more voters believe Mondale would be better than Reagan at: keeping us out of war, insuring that programs and policies are fair, caring about people "like me," and protecting the Social Security system.

A *Washington Post-ABC News* poll in September 1984 examined the other policy views of those who felt they personally will be financially better off under Reagan. It turned out that how they answered the question of their own economic well-being explained far more than anything else. Moreover, it drew them to Reagan despite their differences with Reagan on many other matters. See Table 2–16.

Table 2—16
Will Do Better Financially Under Reagan

But Differ With Him . . .

Of the 53 percent of all voters who say they personally will be better off under a Reagan second term, the table below shows they often differ with Reagan on other important issues.

"I will do better financially under Reagan, *but . . .*"

	Prefer Reagan	Prefer Mondale	Undecided
Disapprove Reagan's handling of the economy	63%	35%	2%
Disapprove his handling of foreign policy	66	32	2
Have the same views as Democrats on most issues	79	19	4
Feel the Republicans are more conservative than themselves on most issues	76	22	2
Feel Reagan sides with special interests	81	16	3
Feel Mondale sides with average citizen	86	13	1
Feel Mondale programs will be fairer to all people	71	27	2
Feel Mondale will reduce the threat of nuclear war more than Reagan will	68	31	1
Feel Blacks have been hurt, not helped, by Reagan	77	21	2

SOURCE: *Washington Post-ABC News* Poll, September 6–11, 1984 (N = 1,507). Responses from registered voters.

In short, many of those voting for him do not support him on many of the crucial issues of the day. Thus, many who voted for him want more thoughtful arms control negotiations and strong federal standards for clean air and clean water. Similarly, many who voted for him do not want to see another doubling of the military defense budget in the next four years. Many who voted for him also differ with him on his semi-interventionist policies in Central America. Unlike the man they voted for, many of his supporters also are concerned and worried about the soaring deficits, and they want more focused and honest leadership about a deficit reduction program.

This list could be continued. The point is that Reagan's win is not a broad and deep affirmation of his own brand of conservative domestic and foreign policy programs. Reagan probably realized and appreciated that—more than he publicly acknowledged. He shied away from claiming a mandate, other than to say that the voters don't want taxes to be raised. He was wise to deflate the notion of a mandate on other matters.

Implications of the 1984 Election

One major implication of the 1984 presidential election is that the Republicans seem to have a pretty good lock on the White House. They have won the White House six times in the past 32 years to only three Democratic victories. Further, five of those six wins were decisive lopsided victories (1952, 1956, 1972, 1980, and 1984). Only in 1964 did a Democratic win big.

This has led some analysts to describe the Electoral College as a Republican College. Others note an important demographic shift. The Northeast and Upper Middle West, long the home base of the Democratic party, continue to lose population while the South, Southwest, Rocky Mountain region, and Far West continue to surge with population increases. Democrats have failed to come up with issues and leaders that can appeal to these newer sections of the country. Until they can do so, the chances for the Democrats will be slim.

The deep South has de-aligned from the presidential Democratic party. Especially is this the case among white Southerners. Even Jimmy Carter lost the white South—in 1976 as well as in 1980. The Mondale-Ferraro ticket, widely viewed in the South as a Northern ticket, faired very poorly throughout the South, getting only 34 to 37 percent of the vote in many of the Southern states.

Much has been written about a fundamental party realignment taking place in American partisan loyalties. This may be slowly taking place in parts of the South. But much of the shifting may be temporary—and explained more by Reagan's enormous personal appeal, the upturn in the economy, and Mondale's lackluster campaign.

Party realignment takes a decade or more to see and is better seen from hindsight. It also has to alter how people vote for Congress and in governors' races. And that hasn't begun to change. We need to remember that analysts and pundits were prematurely writing the obituary for the Republican party soon after the 1964 Barry Goldwater defeat. But the Republican party rebuilt itself and came back strong in the 1970's and 1980's. Democrats are likely to do the same.

An examination of public attitudes toward the parties and toward Reagan over the course of the past four years suggests, and rather convincingly, that voters became increasingly more favorable toward the President while becoming only slightly more favorable to the Republican party. As the economy improved, so also did Reagan's stock improve. See Table 2–17. The Republican party has gained some new support, especially in the South and among some new, younger voters. But the Democratic party is still the plurality political party in America.

The Democrats will doubtless win the White House and possibly as soon as 1988 or 1992. To do so, however, they will again have to become the party of ideas and innovation and offer a vision of both a more revitalized and more equitable America. They will have a somewhat easier time when they don't have to campaign against Ronald Reagan. Indeed, if he was not on the ballot in 1984, one would imagine the election would have been much closer. But Democrats will have to rethink some of their economic and social policy positions. The realignment that may come about may be one inside the Democratic party itself. To win the White House, they will need to win support from middle-income, middle-class families, and they will have to do a better job of sensing the needs and aspirations of the moderates and the independents in the electorate. They will have to be more aggressive at cultivating the support of the rank and file of the unions, teacher associations, and women's groups, and not just the officials in these organizations. They will need a more regionally balanced ticket. Democrats will have to move away from the "preachy politics" of McGovern and Carter and concentrate more on straightforward economic growth and military preparedness issues. While they cannot diminish their concern for fairness and social justice, they have to realize the majorities on Election Day are white, middle-class, and business and professional working people. To the extent Democrats are viewed as the party of only, or even of primarily, the minorities or strident feminists or gay activists or of those on welfare, they will jeopardize forever their chances of winning the White House except on a "throw-the-rascals-out" occasion such as after Watergate.

Table 2–17
Evaluation of Ronald Reagan

Q. "Do you approve or disapprove of the way Ronald Reagan is handling the job as president?"

	June '81	Jan. '82	June '82	Jan. '83	June '83	Jan. '84	June '84	Sept. '84
Approve	59%	49%	43%	41%	47%	57%	58%	58%
Disapprove	23	38	44	47	39	32	33	29
Don't know/ No answer	18	14	13	12	15	11	8	13

Political Party Association

Q. "Generally speaking, do you consider yourself a Republican, a Democrat, an independent, or what?"

	Jan. 1981	Jan. 1982	Jan. 1983	Jan. 1984	June 1984	Jan. 1985
Republican	26%	22%	27%	24%	26%	28%
Democrat	37	37	38	38	41	37
Independent/Other	33	35	30	30	30	32
Don't know/No answer	4	5	5	8	2	4

SOURCE: The New York Times-CBS News Polls, 1981–1984.

The Democratic party can still champion the cause of the less privileged, as it should, but what it cannot afford to do is to be defined mainly as representing groups the mainstream voter rejects or resents. As several political analysts have suggested, the Democrats must take stands and recruit candidates that are seen as pro-working people as opposed to union officials, prowomen as opposed to feminists, pro-lower- and middle-income people as opposed to welfare recipients, and pro-an effective military as opposed to a "weak on defense" stance. Two especially important blocs of voters need to be courted—white males and younger voters. Reagan, while winning 59 percent of the vote, won over 66 percent of the white male vote. In the South he won 74 percent of the white male vote, in the West 68 percent. He won 70 percent of the white male vote between the ages of 18 to 24. He even won about 55 percent of the white males earning less than $10,000 a year! If Democrats can count, these basic figures tell them most of what they need to know about what needs to be done.

Finally, the Democrats will have to learn far more than they have from the impressive Republican party renewal efforts. The Republicans are ten years ahead of the Democrats in knowing how to raise funds, use direct mail, computerize their organizational efforts from the national down to congressional district levels, and combine local and national polling and media spots to maximum advantage. The Democrats doubtless will learn; they have no alternative. It is just a matter of when.

The implications for the Reagan second term are less obvious. Can he move from his rank as an "above average" president into the ranks of the "near great" or "great"? This is possible. It would require, probably, that he secure a significant arms control treaty with the Soviets. He would have to make considerable progress at reducing the budget deficits. He will have to win some fights with Congress, perhaps in the tax reform area. And he will also have to display some form of leadership in improving the quality of life in America. During his first term, he seemed indifferent toward matters such as civil rights, environmental protection, clean air and water, and other concerns expressed by the unemployed, the elderly, students, and scientists—just to name a few groups that have felt at times left behind by this Administration. Most of the presidents we elevate in the direction of Mount Rushmore were presidents during crises and were also champions of expanding the suffrage, or expanding equal opportunities for all. Like Franklin Roosevelt or Harry Truman, they took seriously the need to move toward a second Bill of Rights, a set of principles that revolve around equity and social justice.

Reagan, in his own way, is a reforming president. But the chief beneficiaries of his self-reliance and rugged individualism themes are the upper and upper middle classes. He may well achieve the applause of later generations and even of historians as the kind of president we needed to balance the goals of liberty and individual freedoms against the growing, centralized welfare state. If he achieves retrospective evaluations of greatness, it will be because he will be viewed as a fighter who restored respect for the basic and traditional American Dream and he fought to keep government in its proper place. That is not the usual presidential "moral leadership" that the historians and political scientists write about—but it may just be accepted as what the times required. There is a lingering feeling, however, that a president must somehow not just reflect the times, but also represent and contribute to the best enduring and most generous impulses of the American Experiment.

The potential minefields that could trip Reagan up or derail him from his currently favored status are many. Failure to lessen the likelihood of a nuclear war will probably earn Reagan considerable disfavor. He will be facing a tougher Congress than he enjoyed back in 1981 and 1982, and this will make it more difficult to win congressional support for some of his economic measures and tax reform proposals. Unwanted U.S. involvement in Central America, the Middle East, or in the Philippines would obviously prove costly as well. An inability to turn around the problems of the national debt and the budget deficits will also earn him wrath rather than wreaths.

We hold presidents to high standards. If the economy or other things sour and go wrong, we will almost surely blame the President. The plight of the farmers is illustrative. Landslide victories, as Lyndon Johnson and Richard Nixon learned, do not guarantee long-term public affection and approval. These have to be earned on a day-to-day basis. Doubtless we ask more of presidents than we should ask, but that is what we have always done, and we are very likely to continue to do so. Few second-term presidents have enjoyed an easy time of it, and the Twenty-second Amendment hardly makes it any easier these days. Reagan will have plenty of problems, plenty of challenges, and as he matures into his late 70s, he will need all the good luck, best wishes, and support he can muster. The glow of his 1984 victory will fade, but it surely was one of the most notable votes of confidence a president ever received. It may not have been a resounding mandate for all his beliefs, but it provides a splendid opportunity for him to continue some of what he was doing and, in addition, to tackle some of the other pressing issues facing the nation.

Notes for Chapter 2

1. Jack W. Germond and Jules Witcover, "On Reagan's Second Term Plans . . ." *National Journal* (November 10, 1984), p. 2176.

2. Barry Sussman, "If Reagan Is Not In Charge, That's Fine With the Public," *The Washington Post National Weekly Edition* (January 21, 1985), p. 33.

3. Walter Mondale, excerpts from news conference the day after the election in St. Paul, Minnesota, reported in *U.S. News and World Report* (November 19, 1984), p. 37.

4. Elizabeth Drew, "A Political Journal," *The New Yorker* (December 3, 1984), p. 100.

5. Transcript, Reagan/Mondale Foreign Policy Debate (October 21, 1984).

6. Mondale at postelection news conference, St. Paul, Minnesota (November 7, 1984).

7. For a discussion of the paradoxes and clashing expectations that affect the presidency, see Thomas E. Cronin, *The State of The Presidency* (Boston: Little, Brown & Co., 1980), Chapter 1.

8. Christopher Hitchens, "Reagan's Morning Break," *Spectator* (November 10, 1984), p. 8.

9. Kenneth Bacon, *The Wall Street Journal* (October 29, 1984), p. 1.

10. Daniel P. Moynihan, "Reagan's Bankrupt Budget," *The New Republic* (December 31, 1983), p. 18.

References and Further Reading

Barrett, Laurence I. *Gambling with History: Reagan in the White House*.Garden City, N.Y.: Doubleday, 1983.

Cannon, Lou. *Reagan*. New York: Putnam, 1982.

Cronin, Thomas E. *The State of the Presidency*, Boston: Little, Brown and Co., 1980.

Cronin, Thomas E., ed. *Rethinking the Presidency*. Boston: Little, Brown and Co., 1982.

Greenstein, Fred I. *The Reagan Presidency: An Early Appraisal*. Baltimore: Johns Hopkins University Press, 1983.

Kessel, John. *Presidential Parties*. Homewood, Illinois: Dorsey Press, 1984.

Polsby, Nelson and Aaron Wildavsky. *Presidential Elections*, 6th Ed. New York: Scribners, 1984.

Pomper, Gerald, et al. *The Election of 1980*. Chatham, N.J.: Chatham House, 1981.

Salamon, Lester M. and Michael S. Lund, eds. *The Reagan Presidency and the Governing of America*. Washington, D.C.: Urban Institute, 1984.

Sandoz, Ellis and Cecil V. Crabb, Jr., Eds. *A Tide of Discontent: The 1980 Elections and Their Meaning*. Washington, D.C.: Congressional Quarterly Press, 1981.

Tufte, Edward R. *Political Control of the Economy*. Princeton, N.J.: Princeton University Press, 1978.

Wayne, Stephen J. *The Road to the White House*, 2nd Ed. New York: St. Martin's, 1984.

See also, various essays in *Presidential Studies Quarterly* and *Public Opinion*.

3

Ronald Reagan's Presidential Leadership

Fred I. Greenstein

The 1984 election returns were barely in when I received a macabre-sounding query from a leading metropolitan newspaper. "I'm updating President Reagan's obituary," my caller explained, "and I want to know what the historians and political scientists of the future will conclude about his presidency."

Since it is well known that news organizations make a practice of maintaining "obits" of leading public figures, and since my questioner's tone of voice was matter-of-fact, I knew that he and his editor had not suddenly received dire news about the health of the oldest incumbent ever to have occupied the presidency. Rather, they genuinely wanted a long-run judgment of the sort we traditionally expect from scholars about the legacy of the thirty-ninth president.

I commented, as it were, from the front of my mind, because I had a back-of-the-mind impulse to say: "Call me back in the year 2010, and I will have a answer." My suppressed impulse was an unhelpful way of saying that "final" scholarly assessments cannot be made in the short run. My choice of 30 years from the 1980 election campaign stemmed from my own recent experience. In 1982 a book of mine had appeared analyzing the leadership of a president (Dwight D. Eisenhower) based on what I was able to make of his presidency three decades after he was initially elected.[1]

It was obvious to me that I could not have assessed Eisenhower's leadership adequately any time *during* his two terms as president. In part, like any participant in the politics of an era, I would have lacked detachment. By the 1980's, I had not come to regret my 1952 and 1956 votes for Eisenhower's opponent, Adlai Stevenson. Nevertheless, I was now remote from the passions of the day and could disentangle my policy preferences from my ability to analyze the operating procedures of a presidency.

More important, like all but a few inevitably self-involved Eisenhower administration insiders, I simply did not have, in the 1950's, the necessary information to characterize significant aspects of the man and his presidency. In the 1970's a cascade of previously classified Eisenhower papers and other primary sources had become available, much of which revealed dramatically different features that would have been evident in any account of his presidency based on public sources.

In the 1950's, however, I would have been under an added impediment, which is now so much reduced that the resources scholarship *can* be used to put the leadership of an incumbent president such as Ronald Reagan in comparative perspective. Eisenhower was only the third chief executive in the era of what can conveniently be called the modern presidency. Indeed, if he had not kept and expanded on institutions and practices that took shape in the Roosevelt and Truman years, there might have been no modern presidency.

There now have been nine presidents since the landslide, realigning 1932 election in which Herbert Hoover was overwhelmingly defeated. With the sweeping 100 Days legislative program Roosevelt drove through Congress immediately after taking office, and his electrifying inaugural address, the job of the chief executive began to acquire (and has maintained) a distinctive new form. Enough is known about the similarities and differences in the performances of Franklin Roosevelt, Harry Truman, Dwight Eisenhower, John Kennedy, Lyndon Johnson, Richard Nixon, Gerald Ford, and Jimmy Carter within that form to identify ways in which successive incumbents have (a) resembled all of their modern predecessors, (b) resembled some more than others, and (c) been distinctive and perhaps innovative.

The Modern Presidency

The presidential leadership of Ronald Reagan needs to be assessed in terms of the requirements and challenges faced by modern chief executives, not those that confronted a Millard Fillmore or a Chester Arthur. The much expanded—and much more complicated—chief executive's role that took shape during the long tenure in office of Franklin Roosevelt has been marked by four quantum changes in the presidential job from that of the presidents from George Washington to Herbert Hoover. How the president handles these changed job requirements is central to his success or failure as a leader.

First, the modern president has come to be expected to initiate policy, not simply to respond to congressional initiatives. Throughout the year, but especially in the annual State of the Union and budget messages each January, presidents now present the Congress with proposed legislative programs. Presidential programs are by no means rubber-stamped, but they set the basic agenda for congressional debate and action. Before Roosevelt, it was only the rare activist president who even *had* a legislative program. The most assertive of the premodern activists, Woodrow Wilson, put forth programs only in his early years in office.

Second, as the domestic and international role of American government has increased, there has been a vast expansion in the number and significance of the policies and other actions that can be carried out on the president's personal initiative. The limiting case of potential unilateral exercise of power is the president's capacity in principle to unleash the nuclear arsenal if he concludes that the nation faces immediate attack. In practice, the unilateral powers he most often uses are the provisions for exercising executive discretion in the thousands of laws passed since 1932 that are necessarily stated in general terms and need to be interpreted and applied by the executive branch and, therefore, if he desires, by the president himself.

Third, presidents in the modern era are able to meet the first two requirements of their job because they have at their disposal a staff of about 2,000 civil servants and personal appointees—the members of the executive office of the president—as well as virtually unlimited power to ''borrow'' personnel and resources from the rest of the executive branch. The last premodern president, Herbert Hoover, worked with a handful of clerks as aides, and even adhered to the nineteenth-century ritual of holding a New Year's Day reception line in which he shook the hand of any citizen who cared to line up outside the White House.

Fourth and especially important for the Reagan approach to leadership, the president has become the nation's single most visible and publicized celebrity. Before the modern period, the press typically devoted more coverage to the doings of Congress than to the president. Now the president is so centrally visible to citizens that he often receives credit for outcomes he has not brought about and blame for matters that were not his fault—for example, favorable or unfavorable fluctuations of the economy.

Much of the complexity of contemporary presidential leadership stems from tensions implicit in the changes in the president's job. Each provides a potential lever for successful leadership, but at least as significant an opportunity for disaster. At the core is the conspicuousness of modern presidents, which enables them to take credit for favorable states of the nation, but also to be the most handy scapegoat when things go wrong. The modern president's capacity to frame the national legislative agenda and his ability to make unilateral decisions also are instruments that can yield effective leadership, but they may weigh the president down. If his program does not go through, he raises expectations that he fails to satisfy. And if it *does* go through, but fails to have acceptable effects, he again garners hostility. The unilateral powers of the president work the same way. John F. Kennedy, for example, campaigned in 1960, stating that much racial segregation could be abolished by executive order ("a stroke of the pen"). Once in office, he found he needed the support of Southern Democratic segregationists more than that of Blacks. He disappointed Blacks and their liberal allies by delaying the promised pen stroke.

Even the massive increase in presidential staff is a mixed blessing and poses additional leadership demands. Now the president must manage his own aides as well as the rest of the executive branch. Failure to keep aides in line can lead to such difficulties as the corruption scandals which weakened Harry Truman's leadership and the forays by Nixon aides into political espionage that initiated the sequence of events summarized by the term "Watergate" which drove Nixon from office.

Reagan's Leadership Style and the American Public

The very fact that there *is* an occasion to bring out a book like this one on a president's reelection and the advent of his second term highlights the area in which Ronald Reagan has the most obvious lessons to offer future modern presidents. By now we have enough perspective on the modern presidency to see how profoundly vulnerable it is to political disaster.

In 1956, when the third modern president was reelected, the only novelty in this event seemed to be that it marked the first occasion in which a president was about to be limited to only two terms by the Twenty-second Amendment. But between Eisenhower and Reagan, presidents have been birds of passage.

Kennedy's thousand days were ended by an assassin. Thereafter, presidents were consistently rejected by the public and other national leaders. Johnson felt forced not to run again in the face of probable defeat. When Nixon resigned, he knew that otherwise he would be impeached and convicted. The voters removed Ford and Carter from office. It therefore is challenging to seek to account for the reason Ronald Reagan enjoyed so much support in the fourth year of his first term that he collected almost 60 percent of the popular vote.

President Reagan's great popularity leads to two observations and a caveat concerning what the Reagan first term teaches us about how presidents in the modern era can win strong backing.

Observation *one* is that it obviously helps to have a president who is a professionally skilled communicator and whose staff also includes highly skilled professionals in the same enterprise. It is easy to deprecate a chief executive who has devoted much of his adult life to employing and perfecting his ability to come across in public. And I will comment on why a president whose special gifts are in dramatic presentation of self may present problems as a national leader. It also is easy to deprecate a staff that includes people who are career speech writers, that makes extensive use of expert market research, and that is continually preoccupied with coming across in the mass media. Nevertheless, Reagan's critics would prefer to be able to emulate than to deprecate him.

Much of the derision of Reagan as The Great Communicator reflects ill-concealed envy. After all, the debate within the leadership of the Democratic party over the suitability of Walter Mondale as a candidate dwelled on his "lackluster" impression before the television cameras. And it is as much oratorical effectiveness as substance that led Democrats to begin speaking of New York Governor Mario Cuomo as the party's most promising candidate for 1988 after his address at the 1984 Democratic convention.

In retrospect, it is less difficult to see how a professional communicator like Ronald Reagan became president of the United States in the modern era than to account for the lateness of this development. The modern presidency had been launched by Franklin Roosevelt, whose oratory and presentation of self through the new auditory (radio) and pictorial (newsreel) means of communication had been a major force in his ability to win election four times. Yet, with the exception of Kennedy, no other president until Reagan was even as gifted as a run-of-the-mill broadcast announcer in mastering modern mass communications.

"By the time he got to the White House," Laurence Barrett writes, "Reagan had spent more than fifty years using every communications medium save Morse code and smoke signals. He had been a successful stage actor in high school and college, a pioneer in the young radio business, a journeyman screen performer, a television personality, a speechmaker to audiences of every description, author of a syndicated newspaper column."[2] What should be added to Barrett's account is that from quite early in his adult career Reagan began to move toward becoming an explicitly political communicator. In the late 1930's he became an activist in the Screen Actors Guild (he likes to note that he is the first president who was a labor union leader); in the 1940's, still a liberal Democrat, he campaigned in national and state elections; by the 1950's he was "selling" free enterprise in his capacity as General Electric spokesman; his speech at the 1964 Republican convention launched him as the most articulate GOP conservative; then he served for eight years as governor of the largest state in the nation, using the media with great effect; and he was consistently before political audiences from the end of his governorship, in 1974, to his nomination and election in 1980.[3]

Reagan is second to Franklin Roosevelt (and possibly John F. Kennedy) among modern presidents in his ability to convey himself and his message to the public effectively and reassuringly. The Reagan presidency is second to none in its capacity to function as a team composed of the president and highly media-wise aides.

Pollsters such as Richard Wirthlin maintain what is in effect a daily sequence of interviewing in order to keep track of the "market" and how it is responding to chief Administration salesman Reagan. White House aides hold daily staff meetings to determine the "theme of the day," playing down announcements and events that would provide the media with alternatives to the story most likely to present the president positively, and focusing on conveying the message most likely to put him in a favorable light. Reagan's public appearances are carefully crafted in order to occur in locations that enhance the image he conveys of strength, confidence, and assurance that the nation is in good hands.

"No previous administration has had such a keen understanding of television, whose hunger for presidential pictures sometimes clouds journalistic judgment and gives the president's handlers powerful leverage over what is aired," *The Wall Street Journal* reporter Jane Mayer notes.[4] But overall it is not the specific techniques, but rather an overall strategy of *constantly* being alert to effective display of the President that makes Reagan and company so well equipped to appeal to a broad cross section of Americans. And at the core of this is the extraordinarily attractive persona of a president who is constantly alert to the image he conveys and who seems to view selling himself and his policies as perhaps the greatest single priority for use of his time.

The *second* observation that arises from observing the Reagan team's approach to maintaining support for the top man is summarized by what Reagan's media lieutenants sometimes call "damage limitation" and what frustrated or bemused outsiders have dubbed the "Teflon effect." Countless surveys show public criticism of many aspects of the Reagan presidency and of many of Reagan's associates, but most of what is viewed as bad about the Administration seems not to stick to the President himself.

Efforts to convey positive messages about the president have not been unique to the Reagan presidency. There simply has been greater skill on the part of the Reagan team in accomplishing an end all presidents have sought to achieve. But Reagan's consistent efforts to allow subordinates to "take the heat" for controversial policies and pronouncements has a distinct precedent in the practices of President Eisenhower.

Reagan is like Ike in putting great emphasis on making the types of pronouncements and even comporting himself physically in ways that convey him as a warm embodiment of universally admired values. Both of them also conveyed the impression of being leaders who sketch the broad outlines of policies but make extensive delegations of power to their subordinates, who then implement specifics.

In principle, a president who delegates broadly might seem to be vulnerable to charges that he is not minding the shop. But if the bulk of Americans were preoccupied with whether a president put in long working hours and became involved in the detailed operations of the government—in short, if they had time-and-motion-study criteria for deciding whether a president is doing a good job—Jimmy Carter might well have been the most (rather than the least) popular modern president.

During the Eisenhower years, controversial farm policy was blamed on Agriculture Secretary Ezra Taft Benson, complaints about foreign policy were addressed to Secretary of State John Foster Dulles, and most other complaints were directed at the White House staff chief, Sherman Adams. At least for Eisenhower, this use of political lightning rods was not accidental. Years after Eisenhower was out of office, his press secretary James Hagerty reminisced about conversations he and the President would have about statements Eisenhower asked Hagerty to make in the press secretary's daily conferences with White House correspondents:

> President Eisenhower would say, "Do it this way." I would say, "If I go to that press conference and say what you want me to say, I would get hell." With that he would smile, get up and walk around his desk, pat me on my back and say, "My boy, better you than me."[5]

Reagan has had his own lightning rods in the form of people like Interior Secretary James Watt and Office of Management and Budget Director David Stockman. Moderates in his constituency have blamed hard-line conservative policies on presidential aide Edwin Meese, and conservatives have attributed what they did not like to Meese's pragmatic compatriot James Baker. Reagan may be less self-conscious than Eisenhower was about using associates to take the heat. However, at one point, when James Watt issued a particularly controversial order, he was presented on television receiving the White House award for shooting oneself in the foot—a plaster cast of a foot penetrated by an arrow.

"Later it was learned that David R. Gergen, director of communications at the time, had commissioned the making of the foot four weeks before, with the thought that it would come in handy if someone in the Administration happened to make a gaffe."[6] Gergen was no stranger to the Eisenhower lightning rod technique—indeed, as editor of *Public Opinion* magazine he had reviewed and published an article discussing it just before he joined the White House staff.[7]

Perhaps the most striking (or blatant) use by the Reagan Administration of the Teflon approach came shortly after the 1984 reelection, when as a trial balloon and possible eventual bargaining chip, a highly controversial "tax simplification" plan was sent forth—a plan which had in it major costs for a large number of interest groups, some of them central in the Reagan constituency. The plan was unveiled not by *Rea*gan, however, but *Re*gan—then Treasury Secretary Donald Regan. The explanation was that the President had been too busy campaigning to review the plan, but that in order to save time and encourage public debate, it was being released before he could make a judgment on it. Thus every reportorial question about tax simplification directed to the President was dismissed with an amiable presidential shrug of the shoulder, and Regan was left on the firing line.

The *caveat* about the skill and Eisenhower-like guile through which Reagan works to maintain his broad appeal is that technique, no matter how smooth, will not win support for a president by itself. Technique is necessary, especially when a president's goals are controversial. But it is not sufficient. Reagan's high fourth-year popularity would not have been present if the economy had not been dramatically improved—an improvement which many economists hold to have been due largely to the tendency of an economy to rebound back after a steep recession. And the recession in

Reagan's second and third year was the sharpest since World War II.

Reagan's popularity, as measured by a question the monthly Gallup Poll has been asking Americans since late in Franklin Roosevelt's presidency ("Do you approve or disapprove of the way X has been doing his job as president?"), began slipping by the time he signed into law in the summer of 1981 the most distinctive enactment of his presidency. I refer to the reduction of domestic expenditures and the far more substantial tax reduction, based on the "supply-side" economics theory that lower tax rates in the upper income brackets would lead to increased investment and a surging economy. His first-year high of 68 percent "approve," 21 percent "disapprove," 11 percent "Don't know," came in May 1981, following his dramatic post-assassination attempt address to a joint session of Congress. By December, as the economy began its downward slide, his support declined to 49–41–10. By April 1982, with the recession well under way, marginally more Gallup respondents expressed disapproval than approval: 45–46–9.

In general, approval of Reagan's performance as president continued to slip through 1982 and well into 1983. At his low point, in January 1983 (35 percent "approve," 56 percent "disapprove," 9 percent "no opinion"), his support was lower than that of any president Gallup had polled at the same point in his presidency—lower than that of Truman, Eisenhower, Kennedy, Johnson, Nixon, or Carter. (Gallup traditionally shifts from approval-disapproval ratings to assessments of voting intentions after the nominating conventions, and Ford had not served for a full two years by the time the 1976 nominations had been made.)[8]

It was not until September 1983 that, with a rising economy, Reagan's approval ratings began consistently to exceed disapprovals; by early 1984 his approval was solidly in the mid-50-percent range, disapproval was in the upper-30-percent range, and he was a handy winner in the "trial heat" polls setting him against the array of Democrats who were contesting with one another throughout the bloody primary season. The pyrotechnic Reagan performance in managing his public appearances and media coverage, including staged events such as a media-oriented trip to China, a meeting with the pope, and an emotional celebration of the anniversary of

D-Day at the site of the Normandy invasion made it seem as if no Democrat could have beat him under any circumstances. But one reason why so many Democrats were running in the primaries was that even as late as October 1983, Walter Mondale and the man then perceived as Mondale's strongest contender for the nomination, John Glenn, were running *ahead* of Reagan in responses to the Gallup question "Suppose the 1984 election were held *today*. If President Reagan were the Republican candidate and X were the Democratic candidate, which would you prefer to see win?"[9]

Reagan Leadership Style and the Washington Community

Even though the president—especially in the modern era—is the single most important actor in shaping the policies of the federal government, American government continues to be a pluralistic universe in which the constitutional division of powers is reinforced and complemented by multiple centers of extra-constitutional power and influence. As Richard Neustadt points out in *Presidential Power*,[10] the classical account of the conditions under which presidents are more or less likely to achieve their political aims, the increased legal powers to take unilateral action that accrued to presidents beginning in the 1930's did not eliminate the need for bargaining, persuasion, and exercise of strategic skills on the part of presidents who seek to transform their goals into policies. Noting the ways in which seemingly arbitrary unilateral presidential policy-making may be self-defeating, Neustadt stresses the importance for presidents of winning backing in the "Washington Community," a phrase that refers to the legislators, administrators, party activists, nongovernmental groups and associations, and other power wielders who are the president's policy-making counterparts.

Reagan's operating style within the Washington Community, like the ease and relish with which he turns to oratory to seek widespread national support, displays striking resemblances to that of his first political hero—the recipient of his vote in the first four presidential elections of his adult years,

FDR. The Hudson Valley patrician and the son of a ne'er-do-well Illinois shoe salesman could not have had more different social origins. And Reagan and Roosevelt are not clones in political psychology. Roosevelt, for example, was a sponge for political information, and Reagan's aides acknowledge that he lacks curiosity about the details of policies and political tactics. Roosevelt fostered political intrigue and conflict among his colleagues, whereas Reagan seeks (but, as we shall see, fails to get) collegiality.[11]

Both men, however, display a quality that the pioneering political psychologist Harold D. Lasswell identified as central to the political motivations and operating style of a type of political leader found in virtually every kind of institution—that is, self-dramatization.[12] The existence of such individuals no doubt accounts for the presence in political discourse of such theatrical terminology as "role" and "stage." Reagan, like Roosevelt, appears to flourish in the presence of audiences. He appears to share Roosevelt's pleasure in face-to-face camaraderie. Like Roosevelt he is not a book reader, and if he has a reflective subjective life, he does not exhibit it to those with whom he regularly associates. Most significantly from the standpoint of leadership, both men appear to have stepped into the role of president with utter ease and self-confidence. Of Roosevelt it has been said that the presidency fit him as comfortably as a well-worn carpet slipper. Steven Weisman contrasts Reagan with his predecessor, Jimmy Carter, who "wore the burdens of office like a cross," remarking that Reagan "positively enjoys the job. . . . No matter how grave things look, his attitude is invariably upbeat and reassuring."[13]

Even on the matter that would seem to most sharply divide Roosevelt from Reagan, the former's lack of commitment to clear-cut political dogmas and the latter's distinctive association with a comprehensive conservative ideology, the propensity of both to engage in role-playing seems to provide a common denominator. Roosevelt was a master at changing positions and compromising; and Reagan's commitment to principles has not prevented him from shifting ground sharply when he cannot achieve an aim and exercising the well-known pragmatism that marked his performance as California's governor as well as his presidency.

Whatever the merits of applying Lasswell's construct to

Reagan and Roosevelt, it is fascinating to note three major common elements in their political styles as Washington operators and a fourth that neither helped them accomplish their own aims, nor served the nation well.

One Roosevelt-like quality that helps Reagan with the modern presidential role is his impressive capacity to be personally ingratiating. Such a capacity might, on first impression, simply be dismissed as the typical coinage of professional politicians. The counterexamples among modern presidents are numerous, however. Kennedy sometimes simply did not take the time to maintain personal contacts with Washington Community counterparts, especially wavering members of his own party whose votes would have helped him on key roll calls. Lyndon Johnson's famous hard sell could backfire because he was overly aggressive. Nixon, in spite of his long career as a professional politician, tended to be reclusive and did not even make the acquaintance of a number of key legislators who could have helped him with his program. And Jimmy Carter could be a positive irritant. A congressman interviewed by Allen Schick compared a session he had with Carter and one with Reagan.

In meeting with Carter on a legislative matter, the congressman reported, "We had barely got seated when Carter began lecturing us about problems he had with one of the sections of the bill. He knew about the details better than most of us, but somehow that caused more resentment than if he had left the specifics to us." The congressman remembered a similar mission to Reagan in the Oval Office far more positively. Although he had only been with the President "a couple of minutes," he "didn't feel rushed. . . . A photographer shot the usual roll of pictures; the president gave me a firm, friendly handshake. He patted me on the back and told me how much he needed and appreciated my vote. He said I should call if I needed anything."[14] Visitors to Roosevelt had similar reports of being charmed, won over, but later not being able to remember points of substance that had persuaded them to back the president.

A *second,* rather surprising, similarity between Reagan and Roosevelt is that both men managed to surround themselves with intensely loyal subordinates and principal associates, many of them able, selfless, hard workers. In each case, there was bickering and animosity within the ranks of the president's subordinates, tensions that the president did not intervene to settle. Nevertheless, each of the presidents managed to harness these energies, uniting their aides in the conviction that they were working for a president who was leading the nation on the path of major policy reform.

The aides Roosevelt used for negotiations and planning are now the topics of doctoral dissertations and are recorded by historians. They have names like Rexford Guy Tugwell, Thomas Corcoran, Benjamin Cohen, and Harry Hopkins. At the time when records are available for historians of the Reagan presidency, there will be detailed accounts of Reagan's use of Edwin Meese, James Baker, and Michael Deaver as his top White House aides. Perhaps the most interesting innovation in presidential leadership is the legislative strategy group, a White House command post, linking the president to Capitol Hill and engaging in sophisticated brokering and bargaining, doing whatever is feasible to win for the President results that are as consistent as possible with his ideology. The group is effective due to the willingness of all of the key people within the Administration who are needed to agree on policy recommendations to the president to serve on it and to the subtle appreciation of Washington Community mores that informs its operations.[15]

Just as Reagan's skill at presenting himself to the general public was not in itself sufficient to win him support in the absence of a prospering economy, the strategy group is far from all powerful. There have been no repetitions of the profoundly sweeping spending and tax cut enactments of the summer of 1981. And even in 1981 the administration would not have succeeded if the 1980 election had not led to Republican control of the Senate for the first time since the Congress that was elected in 1952. As the recession grew and deficits mushroomed, Reagan's strategists found it more and more necessary to compromise in their dealings with Congress, especially after the Democratic majority in the House of Representatives increased in the 1982 mid-term election. Nevertheless, the legislative team performed excellently, within the boundaries of political feasibility.

Loyal Reagan subordinates also have performed in ways that greatly increased the impact of the President's policy goals at the administrative level. Richard Nathan has shown how imperfectly most American presidents have used the executive branch, including the appointments process and application of administrative rules, in order to advance presidential policy. Richard Nixon was about to proceed on this front in his second term, but became enmeshed in Watergate. Reagan, Nathan argues, has picked up where Nixon left off in using his aides to seek maximum advantage from "the administrative presidency."[16] Nathan and his associates carefully documented the Reagan effects on the federal-state mix in policy-making,[17] Kraft and Vig[18] have shown how administrative procedures have been used by the Administration to change environmental policy, and others have documented changes brought about by Reagan appointees in additional domestic spheres.[19]

The *third* Reagan-Roosevelt parallel brings us back to presidential preoccupation with and professionalism in mass communications, but relates to how this affects the Washington Community rather than the general public. A president who is a master of rhetoric may garner an indirect advantage in his dealings with other leaders, above and beyond his capacity to reach directly to the public and to shape reports of his performance in the media. Even in bad times, when Reagan was not doing well in the polls, other politicians took him seriously as a potentially powerful electoral force and as someone who might go over their heads to their own constituents. They did this in part because they had periodic signs from constituent mail and other representations that their supporters were favorably disposed to the President. But in part, the political professionals *themselves* were so impressed by Reagan's skill in communicating to the public that they took it for granted that he appealed to mainstream Americans.

The *fourth* and least happy Reagan-Roosevelt parallel poses major threats and challenges for Reagan's second term. Like Roosevelt, Reagan has been more impressive in placating and inspiring the public and in pressing for the enactment of policies than in analyzing policies for their *coherence* or anticipating their *consequences*.

The New Deal was full of inconsistencies which led policies to cancel one another out. Many New Deal policies simply had negative effects on the functioning of the economy. It was not New Deal policies, but the advent of military production beginning in 1939 that ended the Great Depression.[20]

The most striking Reagan parallel was the doctrinaire supply-side tax cuts instituted in 1981. In spite of occasional efforts to remedy the shortage of funds to operate the government (under such euphemistic headings as "revenue enhancement"), the national debt increased by over $600 billion during Reagan's first term, an outcome that seemed not to disturb him, although one of his campaign promises had been a balanced budget. The consequences of this massive debt are too complex to explore here. But they begin with a massive annual tax bill simply for interest on the debt, which limits the potentiality for lowering overall expenditures and encourages foreign investment in government securities rather than American industrial growth.[21]

It also was hard to see signs of systematic planning in foreign policy-making during the Reagan first term. Relations with the Soviet Union were unfavorable. There was no evidence during much of the Reagan first term that arms control agreements were being pursued effectively. The foreign policy establishment of the Administration was (in contrast to the public relations and policy enactment establishments) far from being a team. Reagan "went through" three White House assistants for national security. None was able to quell tensions between the State Department (first under Alexander Haig and then under George Shultz) and Defense Secretary Caspar Weinberger. Reagan succeeded in getting much larger military appropriations than anyone would have thought feasible, but there was no evidence that they were being used effectively or subordinated to any overarching strategic views. In spite of more American military hardware, it would have been hard to say that the world was more secure on Election Day 1984 than four years earlier.

Summary and Prospect

Reagan has been more effective than any president other than Roosevelt in the modern era in his communications to the larger public. He has innovated in the use of skilled communications technicians. His often feuding policy-making aides have helped him advance his purposes in the Washington Community with outstanding skill. Further, to a striking degree, and despite playing musical chairs between the White House staff and the Cabinet, he has kept his core team together and promises to continue holding it together at least into the early years of his second term.

The substance of his policies, however, has often been problematic—most obviously in the case of the debt. Wall Street conservatives and traditional as well as liberal economic commentators share the view that the debt is a time bomb that needs to be defused. And if any "bomb" needs even more to be defused, it is the explosive East-West relationship.

In a second term it is logical that a president will seek to avoid leaving the "final" judgment of history to chance and the vagaries of his obituary writers and biographers. Shortly after the election Reagan was showing more substantial interest in reaching accommodations with the Soviet Union than he had before. The tax and spending situation was in limbo, since Reagan's initial stance was to seek to reduce the deficit by slashing domestic programs which have strong constituencies. But Reagan's pragmatism, the advice of aides who see the need to correct policies enacted on flawed premises, and the need for a Reagan legacy may lead this President and his associates to produce surprising and interesting second-term results.

Notes for Chapter 3

1. Fred I. Greenstein, *The Hidden Hand Presidency: Eisenhower as Leader* (New York: Basic Books, 1982).

2. Laurence I. Barrett, *Gambling with History: Reagan in the White House* (New York: Penguin, 1984), p. 33.

3. Lou Cannon, *Reagan* (New York: Putnam, 1982).

4. Jane Mayer, "Best 'Spin Control' Ever: How Reagan Staff Manages News," *The Wall Street Journal* (October 12, 1984). Also see her "Searching for Substance: Reagan, in China, Focus on TV," ibid. (April 27, 1984); Fay S. Joyce, "2 Approaches to Candidate's Image: Showing the Message or Speaking It," *The New York Times* (November 1, 1984); and Steven R. Weisman, "The President and the Press: The Art of Con-

trolled Access,'' *The New York Times Magazine* (October 14, 1984).

5. Quoted in Gordon Hoxie, ed., *The White House: Organization and Operations* (New York: Center for the Study of the Presidency, 1971), p. 4.

6. Steven R. Weisman, ''Can the Magic Prevail?'' *The New York Times Magazine* (April 29, 1984).

7. Fred I. Greenstein and Robert Wright, ''Reagan . . . Another Ike?'' *Public Opinion*, Vol. 3 (December/January 1981), pp. 51–55.

8. See the monthly reports of *The Gallup Report* (formerly known as *The Gallup Opinion Index*).

9. *The Gallup Report*, No. 219 (November 1983), pp. 26–28.

10. Richard E. Neustadt, *Presidential Power* (New York: Wiley, 1960).

11. The richest source presently available on Reagan's life, personality, and career in public life is Cannon's *Reagan* (note 3). The literature on Franklin Roosevelt is voluminous. Standard overviews include James MacGregor Burns, *Roosevelt: the Lion and the Fox* (New York: Harcourt Brace, 1956), and *The Soldier of Freedom* (New York: Harcourt, Brace, 1970), as well as the multivolume works in progress by Frank Freidel and Arthur Schlessinger, Jr.

12. Harold D. Lasswell, *Power and Personality* (New York: Norton, 1948), p. 62 and passim.

13. Weisman, ''Can the Magic Prevail?''

14. Allen Schick, ''How the Budget was Won and Lost,'' *President and Congress: Assessing Reagan's First Year*, ed. Norman Ornstein (Washington: American Enterprise Institute, 1982), pp. 14–43.

15. John H. Kessel, ''The Structures of the Reagan White House,'' *American Journal of Political Science*, Vol. 28, No. 2 (May 1984), pp. 231–58, and his *Presidential Parties* (Homewood, Ill.: Dorsey, 1984).

16. Richard P. Nathan, *The Administrative Presidency* (New York: Wiley, 1983).

17. See, for example, Richard P. Nathan et al., ''Initial Effects of the Fiscal Year 1982 Reductions in Federal Spending,'' *Reductions in U.S. Domestic Spending: How They Affect State and Local*, John William Ellwood, ed. (New Brunswick, N.J.: Transaction Books, 1982), pt. 3., and Richard P. Nathan and Fred C. Doolittle, ''The Untold Story of Reagan's 'New Federalism,' '' *The Public Interest*, No. 77 (Fall 1984), pp. 96–105.

18. Michael E. Kraft and Norman Vig, ''Environmental Pol-

icy in the Reagan Presidency," *Political Science Quarterly*, Vol. 99, No. 3 (Fall 1984), pp. 415–39.

19. Lester M. Salamon and Michael S. Lund, eds., *The Reagan Presidency and the Governing of America* (Washington, D.C.: The Urban Institute, 1984).

20. Stanley Lebergott, *The Americans: An Economic Record* (New York: Norton, 1984), pp. 444–52.

21. Hugh Heclo and Rudolph G. Penner, "Fiscal and Political Strategy in the Reagan Administration," *The Reagan Presidency*, ed. Fred I. Greenstein, pp. 21–47.

22. I.M. Destler, "The Evolution of Reagan Foreign Policy," Ibid., pp. 117–58; Strobe Talbott, *Deadly Gambits: The Reagan Administration and the Stalemate of Nuclear Arms Control* (New York: Knopf, 1984); I.M. Destler, Leslie H. Gelb, and Anthony Lake, *Our Own Worst Enemy: The Unmaking of American Foreign Policy* (New York: Simon and Schuster, 1984); and David Ignatius, "Man in the Middle: Foreign Policy Rows Make McFarlane's Job Unusually Tough One," *The Wall Street Journal* (August 10, 1984).

References and Further Reading

Barrett, Laurence I. *Gambling with History: Reagan in the White House*. New York: Penguin, 1984.

Cannon, Lou. *Reagan*. New York: Putnam, 1982.

Destler, I.M., Leslie H. Gelb, and Anthony Lake. *Our Own Worst Enemy: The Unmaking of American Foreign Policy*. New York: Simon and Schuster, 1984.

Greenstein, Fred I., ed. *The Reagan Presidency: An Early Appraisal*. Baltimore: Johns Hopkins University Press, 1983.

Greider, William. *The Education of David Stockman and Other Americans*. New York: Dutton, 1982.

Hamilton, Gary G., and Nicole Woosley Biggart. *Governor Reagan, Governor Brown: A Sociology of Executive Power*. New York: Columbia University Press, 1984.

Kessell, John. *Presidential Parties*. Homewood, Ill.: Dorsey Press, 1984.

Nathan, Richard. *The Administrative Presidency*. New York: Wiley, 1983.

Oye, Kenneth A., Robert J. Lieber, and Donald Rothchild.

The Eagle Defiant: United States Foreign Policy in the 1980's.
Boston: Little, Brown, 1983.

Salamon, Lester M., and Michael S. Lund, eds. *The Reagan
Presidency and the Governing of America.* Washington, D.C.:
The Urban Institute, 1984.

Talbott, Strobe. *Deadly Gambits: The Reagan Administration
and the Stalemate of Nuclear Arms Control.* New York: Knopf,
1984.

4

The Voters Say Yes: The 1984 Congressional Elections

Charles O. Jones

Postelection analysts concluded that the American people transmitted a confusing message in 1984. Ronald Reagan was reelected by a landslide in the electoral and popular vote. Yet, the Republican party failed to gain a majority in the House of Representatives and lost two Senate seats to reduce its majority to 53–47. These results were unsettling to those who seek a clear-cut mandate from our elections. Therefore, many postelection headlines focused on the issue of the mandate.

The idea of an election mandate is simple: candidates offer a program, voters approve or disapprove of this program by electing one or the other set of candidates to office, the winning candidates then claim a mandate, or command, to put their program into effect. The principal difficulty with this elementary formula is that it cannot be applied to our complex electoral and governmental system. Voting analyst Raymond E. Wolfinger is absolutely correct when he states that "Mandates are inherently implausible."[1] We don't vote for slates of candidates at the national level; we vote between individuals who are running for president, senator, and representative. Since voting is a voluntary act, some of us engage in it, some of us don't. And for those of us who vote, the rules are permissive—we can, and do, split our tickets however we please. Some voters base their choices on policy issues that are important to them, but they are not always well informed as to the candidates' positions on those issues. Further, as Wolfinger reminds us, the "candidates say a great many things, as well as running on a platform that is devoted to programmatic commitments. . . . As Chairman Mao might have said, 'many issues, one vote.' "[2]

What do our national elections produce, if not mandates? They legitimize a set of decision-makers who then populate the White House and Capitol Hill. These elected decision-makers may be expected, in turn, to read the returns to judge whether there is a definitive message for them. Typically there is no such message in regard to most of the issues they must face. Nor is it likely very often that those elected or reelected will find the same message where there is one to find on an issue. Occasionally, however, a policy command is identified by most decision-makers, and they act accordingly—as with the tax and budget cuts in 1981. Even then it may not be entirely correct to label their interpretation or subsequent action as a mandate. Politicians, too, misread election returns.

This brief discussion of the election mandate serves the important function of permitting me to dismiss it as an issue for purposes of this essay. I do not want to interpret whether or not the congressional election returns contributed to or detracted from a Reagan mandate. Rather I want to concentrate on what in fact happened in the House and Senate elections. What I will emphasize throughout is that the people said yes in this election. To an extraordinary degree, they approved of the existing government—its president and the partisan composition of the Congress. The chapter is organized to treat the following topics: the historical context for the 1984 congressional results; the nature of the 1984 congressional campaigns; a detailed analysis of the 1984 House and Senate results; and the organization and politics of the Ninety-ninth Congress.

Reelecting Presidents: The Historical Record

It is considered commonplace knowledge that no two presidential elections are ever alike. Yet it is possible to identify broad categories of elections that are bound to differ in various ways. Table 4–1 lists five such types. First there is the simple distinction between those elections involving an incumbent president and those where there is no incumbent in the race. The latter category is of least interest to us presently. It is the first listing in Table 4–1 and includes six elections in this century. If President Reagan serves out his second term, then 1988 will also be in this category. Of more direct interest are those more frequent cases when an incumbent president is running. Incumbents differ as to whether they have been previously elected or not. Those who have are identified in Table 4–1 in categories 2 and 3—divided simply by whether they won or lost. Finally there are the vice presidents who served as president and sought election on their own—four of whom won, one of whom lost.

Table 4–1
Types of Presidential Elections, 1900–1984

	Year	Winner
1. No incumbent	1908	Taft
	1920	Harding
	1928	Hoover
	1952	Eisenhower
	1960	Kennedy
	1968	Nixon
2. President reelected	1900	McKinley
	1916	Wilson
	1936	F.D. Roosevelt
	1940	F.D. Roosevelt
	1944	F.D. Roosevelt
	1956	Eisenhower
	1972	Nixon
	1984	Reagan
3. President defeated	1912	Wilson (over Taft)
	1932	F.D. Roosevelt (over Hoover)
	1980	Reagan (over Carter)
4. Vice president as president elected	1904	T. Roosevelt
	1924	Coolidge
	1948	Truman
	1964	Johnson
5. Vice president as president defeated	1976	Carter (over Ford)

SOURCE: Compiled by the author.

Next we consider the electoral fortunes of the president's party in Congress during these elections. In doing so, it seems rational to divide these presidents into two groups—majority party presidents (i.e., where the president's party is a majority among registered voters) and minority party presidents. There are four cases in each category. Table 4–2 shows the congressional results for these two sets of elections. For the majority party presidents the variation in House seats gained is slight—though, of course, the base number of seats varies considerably. The variation in Senate results is greater, due in part to the party split for any one year and the inevitable erosion in Roosevelt's coattails by the fourth term.

Among the minority party presidents, Wilson experienced a significant loss of House Democrats but, of course, he won reelection by a very narrow margin.[3] The three Republican presidents all won by huge margins, but Eisenhower experienced a slight loss of House Republicans, Nixon and Reagan both realized gains. The Senate changes were not greatly different for any of the four minority party presidents.

Taken together these presidential reelections do not show large changes in the congressional margins. Even when presidents win by a landslide, the shifts in House and Senate seats tend to be modest. The principal difference is in the base number of seats. The Democrats had commanding congressional majorities during the 1930's, and Roosevelt's landslide elections could not be expected to add significantly to those numbers. And the Republicans during the Eisenhower years had already reached the outer limits in the number of seats a minority party might normally expect to control. At minimum, these results seem to suggest that it would have been extraordinary for the Republicans to have realized large gains in congressional elections in 1984, despite Reagan's landslide win. The record simply shows that personal triumphs do not typically produce large turnovers in the House and Senate.

There is more to be learned from Table 4–2. The third set of presidential elections includes the three cases of incumbent majority party presidents being defeated for reelection. Here we have truly large changes in Congress. The combined House and Senate losses for the incumbent's party rank first, fourth, and fifth largest in this century for a presidential election year. In all three cases the new president's party captured control of the Senate (the Democrats already con-

Table 4–2

Congressional Results for President's Party in Presidential Reelection Years, 1900–1984

	House Results		Senate Results	
	Seats Gained or lost (Winner's Party)	Change in % of Seats Held	Seats Gained or lost (Winner's Party)	Change in % of Seats Held
1. Majority Party President Reelected				
1900 (McKinley-Republican)	+13 (R)	+4% (52 to 56)	+3 (R)	+5% (59 to 64)
1936 (Roosevelt-Democrat)	+11 (D)	+3% (74 to 77)	+6 (D)	+6% (72 to 78)
1940 (Roosevelt-Democrat)	+5 (D)	+1% (60 to 61)	−3 (D)	−3% (72 to 69)
1944 (Roosevelt-Democrat)	+21 (D)	+5% (51 to 56)	0 (D)	0 (59 to 59)
2. Minority Party President Reelected				
1916 (Wilson-Democrat)	−21 (D)	−5% (53 to 48)	−3 (D)	−3% (58 to 55)

1956 (Eisenhower-Republican)	− 2 (R)	−1% (47 to 46)	0 (D)	0 (47 to 47)
1972 (Nixon-Republican)	+12 (R)	+3% (41 to 44)	−2 (R)	−2% (45 to 43)
1984 (Reagan-Republican)	+14 (R)	+3% (39 to 42)	−2 (R)	−2% (55 to 53)
3. Majority Party President Defeated				
1912 (Taft-Republican—by Wilson)	+62 (D)	+9% (58 to 67)	+9 (D)	+7% (46 to 53)
1932 (Hoover-Republican—by Roosevelt)	+97 (D)	+22% (50 to 72)	+12 (D)	+13% (49 to 62)
1980 (Carter-Democrat—by Reagan)	+33 (R)	+7% (37 to 44)	+12 (R)	+12% (41 to 53)

SOURCE: Calculated by the author from data in Congressional Quarterly Weekly Report, October 23, 1982, p. 2742.

trolled the House in 1912 and 1932; the Republicans fell short of a majority in 1980).

It seems reasonable to interpret the data in Table 4–2 as supporting the following propositions:

1. When voters reelect a president, they tend as well to support the existing partisan division in Congress. Landslide margins in the reelection of the president do not produce high turnovers of House and Senate seats.
2. When voters reject a president, they tend as well to reject his party and thus defeat many House and Senate incumbents.

What these propositions amount to is simply that voters approve the government when they approve of the president. With the increase in split-ticket voting, that outcome is even more convenient for voters to arrange than in the past.

Placed in this historical context, the 1984 results are not in the least extraordinary. It is true that the president's party had fewer House seats going in to the 1984 election than any other president's party seeking reelection in this century. All that suggests is that he had more to make up in the election. It says nothing about the probability of his party gaining additional seats due to his own landslide victory. On the other hand, his party retained its majority in the Senate in spite of earlier predictions that the Democrats would probably regain control. And, in fact, the Republicans retained their majority for three consecutive elections—a feat the Republicans had not accomplished since the 1920's.

The Presidential and Congressional Campaigns

It was described as "an utterly predictable election" by *Time* magazine.[4] Though issues were discussed, the 1984 election was not basically about issues. It was about the reelection of Ronald Reagan—the confirmation of his leadership. Walter Mondale did identify many of the right questions: How can we reduce the deficit? achieve arms control?

manage the trade imbalance? But the voters were not in a mood to listen attentively. Basically, they were satisfied. They did not actively disapprove of Walter Mondale as much as they approved of Ronald Reagan.[5] On election eve the suspense was "not about who would win . . ." "Rather, the question was whether Ronald Reagan would win re-election by a historic landslide. The verdict came almost the moment the count began: a resounding yes."[6]

The character of the presidential race inevitably influences the congressional campaign. In most parts of the nation Republican candidates could be expected to run with the president, hoping to profit from the Reagan magic. House and Senate candidates do not necessarily believe that attaching themselves to the president will overcome a personal liability (as with Iowa Senator Roger Jepsen's indiscretion in applying for membership in a spa that turned out to be an illicit massage parlor), a strong and well-financed challenger (as was the case for Illinois Senator Charles Percy), or a policy record that is judged to be counter to constituency interests. Rather, most are in a position to run comfortably with the president, not having to detach themselves during the campaign (as, for example, many Democrats did in 1980 with Carter heading the ticket, and many Republicans did in 1964 with Goldwater heading their ticket). The presidential campaign did not create a special problem for Republicans in 1984.

The problem for incumbent Democrats running for Congress in 1984 was less that of detachment from the Mondale campaign than one of reemphasizing their service to the state or district. It was almost a matter of ignoring the national ticket, since they did not have to compensate for its negative character. Few Democratic challengers could expect to win in the face of approval voting by the American public (and few did—only three Democrats successfully challenged House Republican incumbents, two successfully challenged Senate Republican incumbents). The task for incumbents was simply to win approval too for their record.

In summary, given the inevitable outcome of the election, the presidential and congressional campaigns had less interactive impact than normal. For the Republicans, President Reagan had already created a positive mood for the party. It was unlikely that personal campaigning on his part for Republican candidates would contribute more (though that did not prevent criticism of his failing to do so—including postelection criticism from House Minority Leader Robert Michel).[7]

For the Democrats, the "utterly predictable election" meant that they could campaign throughout 1984 by emphasizing the advantages of their incumbency. They had ample time to prepare for survival. The dire circumstances for their presidential candidate could even be used as an excuse for urging voters to return a Democrat to Congress—separation of powers, checks and balances, and all that. These circumstances were also used by Democratic candidates to explain why a desperate Mondale had to support a tax increase but they did not. That is, Mondale had to propose something dramatic to draw public attention to the adverse effects of budget deficits. But Democratic incumbents were not in such desperate straits and therefore could rationalize separation from the presidential candidate on this sensitive issue. In fact, one Reagan White House adviser asked his staff "to list all Democratic House candidates who campaigned this fall on Mr. Mondale's tax-increase plan. So far, he says, he knows of only two. Both were incumbents, and both were defeated."[8]

This greater-than-normal separation of the two campaigns contributes to our understanding of the relatively limited congressional turnover in presidential landslides. When the White House outcome is inevitable due to approval voting, then all incumbents seek to accommodate the voters' positive attitude. They were unusually successful in accomplishing this goal in 1984. We turn now to the details.

Reelecting the House

The high return rate of House incumbents is a subject that has intrigued political scientists in recent years. A number of interesting explanations have been offered for this phenomenon—redistricting to favor the incumbent, increased perquisites that allow for more constituency service, increased campaign contributions to incumbents from special interests, and weak and under-financed challengers.[9] No doubt all of these factors have had some influence. Whatever the precise explanation, it is unquestionably the case that most incumbents are returned to office. The return rate of incumbents fell below 90 percent only four times in the last 18 elections. The range during this period (1950–1984) was from 86.6 percent returning in 1964 to 96.8 percent returning in 1968.[10]

Countering this trend has been an increasing number of retirements—a rather curious development given the increased safeness of seats. An average of 28 members per election retired, 1950–1970 (11 elections), compared to an average of 42 members per election, 1972–1982 (six elections).[11] Explanations for this trend were that pension benefits improved, the rewards for longevity were fewer with changes in the seniority system, the increase in congressional bureaucracy made the job more difficult, the increasing demands from interest groups made the job more hectic, and overall it just wasn't as much fun to serve as in the old days.[12]

House incumbents were returned in 1984 at one of the highest rates in the post-World War II period, and the number of retirements fell to the averages of the 1950's and 1960's. As shown in Table 4–3, only 24 members did not seek reelection. Of the 411 who did, only 19 were defeated—3 in the primaries, 16 in the general election. The return rate for Republicans was just over 98 percent, for Democrats, nearly 94 percent. And the combination of few retirements and even fewer defeats meant that overall return rate (i.e., as a percent of the whole House) was very high (90.1 percent)—the second highest in the post-World War II period.

Not only were incumbents being returned in near record numbers, but their margins of victory were large. Nearly 80 percent won by 60 percent or more, and 43 percent won by 70 percent or more. Only 29 incumbents (7 percent of those running in the general election) won in the 50–55 percent range that is normally identified as competitive.[13] The margins for House incumbents in 1984 were among the largest in three decades of elections. Unquestionably this was an election in which most voters endorsed the existing set of representatives.

Republican House candidates garnered 47 percent of the total popular vote cast for such races.[14] Yet with nearly half of the vote, Republicans won only 42 percent of the House seats. Why? The answer lies in part in the artful redistricting of Democratic state legislatures to favor their party and in the

Table 4–3

Return of House Incumbents, 1984, By Political Party

	Total Members	Not Seeking Reelection	Seeking Reelection	Defeated in Primary	Defeated in General	Returned	As a % of Total
Democrats	267	10	257	3	13	241 (93.8%)	90.3%
Republicans	168	14	154	0	3	151 (98.1%)	89.9%
House	435	24	411	3	16	392 (95.4%)	90.1%

SOURCE: Compiled by the author from election returns reported in the *Congressional Quarterly Weekly Report*, November 10, 1984, p. 2900.

large number of uncontested Democratic seats. Regarding the first point, the popular vote split in California for 43 contested House races was 51 percent Democratic, 49 percent Republican. Yet the Democrats won 26 contested seats (60 percent), the Republicans won 17 (40 percent). Regarding the second point, the Democrats continue to have a significant number of uncontested seats. There were a total of 66 House seats settled in advance of the election itself. Of these, 53 were held by Democrats, 13 by Republicans. If one subtracts these uncontested seats from the totals, then the ratio of popular vote to seats won is less distorted. The Democrats won 200 contested seats (54 percent); the Republicans won 169 (46 percent).

Second, the Republicans won a majority of the 27 open seats—that is, those districts in which an incumbent did not seek reelection or where the incumbent was defeated in the primary. There were 13 open seats previously held by Democrats, 14 previously held by Republicans. The Republicans were able to hold 13 of their 14 seats and win 5 previously held by Democrats—a net gain of 4 seats. Adding these 4 seats to their net gain of 10 among defeated incumbents produced the 14-seat gain for the Republicans.

A comparison of the incombents' margins of victory, 1982 and 1984, shows that a very high proportion of Republican incumbents increased their percentage of the vote. The results of this analysis are presented in Table 4–4. Nearly 80 percent of Republican incumbents in 1984 increased their margins of victory over 1982. This was a higher percentage than in 1980—also a good year for Republican candidates—when 64 percent of the incumbents increased their percentage over 1978. Of course, 1982 was not a good year for Republican House candidates—the Democrats had a net gain of 26 House seats. The point is that even though House Republicans did not gain back the seats lost in 1982, a huge proportion of them won by more handsome margins. In fact, of the 29 incumbents winning in the 50–55 percent range, only 5 were Republicans.

One House seat remained vacant for nearly four months while a House task force supervised a recount. Republican Richard D. McIntyre had been certified as the winner of the Indiana 8th Congressional District by Indiana election officials. But the task force, composed of two Democrats and one Republican, declared incumbent Frank McCloskey the winner by 4 votes. The task force report sparked a bitter debate on the House floor with cries of "stolen election" from the Republicans.

The Democrats also did somewhat better in 1984 by this measure of the change in margin of victory, further confirmation for the basic proposition of this chapter that the voters were saying yes in this election. A higher proportion of Democratic incumbents increased their margin of victory in 1984 than in 1980. Very nearly the same in absolute numbers had their margin decreased, though the proportion was smaller. It is also the case that several formerly safe Democratic seats became more competitive in 1984 (see below).

Republican candidates demonstrated growing strength in the South—and particularly in North Carolina and Texas. Figures 4–1 and 4–2 show what is happening. The first figure shows the proportion of Republicans from the region (for example, of the 150 total representatives from the South in 1984, 35 percent were Republicans). Note that Republican proportions from all regions declined in 1982—rather uni-

Table 4−4
Changes in Margin of Victory for House Incumbents, 1978–1980; 1982–1984

| | Total Incumbents* | Number and (Percent) of Incumbents Whose Margin of Victory | | |
		Increased	Decreased	Remained the Same
1978 to 1980				
Democrats	216	76 (35%)	101 (47%)	39 (18%)
Republicans	138	88 (64%)	32 (23%)	18 (13%)
1982 to 1984				
Democrats	235	100 (43%)	100 (43%)	35 (15%)
Republicans	149	117 (79%)	23 (15%)	9 (6%)

*Does not include Louisiana where members are declared elected if they receive over 50 percent of the vote in the primary.

SOURCE: Computed by the author from election returns reported in various issues of the *Congressional Quarterly Weekly Report.*

formly so. They increased substantially in the South and Northeast in 1984, only slightly in the West. The Midwest, formerly a Republican stronghold, showed no change.

The second figure shows the regional representation within the House Republican Party (for example, of the 182 total Republicans in the Ninety-ninth Congress, 29 percent were from the South). These data are particularly interesting. They

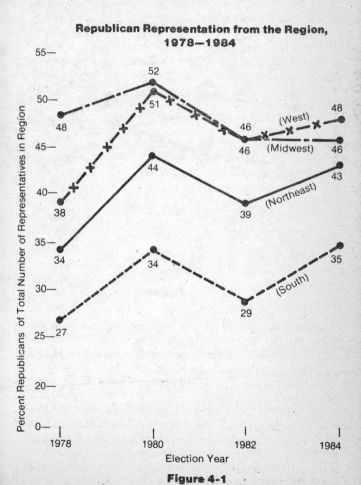

Republican Representation from the Region, 1978—1984

Figure 4-1

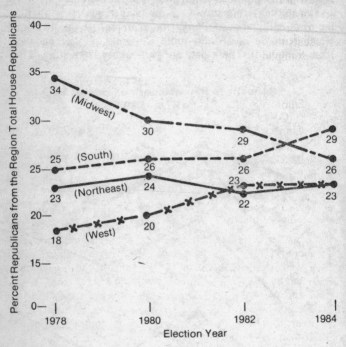

Regional Representation in House Republican Party, 1978—1984

Figure 4-2

show that the South now is the most heavily represented region in the Republican Party. The West also shows an increase. Representation from the Northeast has remained rather steady throughout the period, and the Midwest shows a steady decline—from a third in 1978 to just over a quarter of the Republicans in 1984.

The shifts in the South have occurred primarily in Florida, North Carolina, Texas and Virginia. These four states make up 28 of the 52 Southern seats presently held by Republicans. In 1984, the Florida Republican delegation increased by 1 seat—that of Andy Ireland, who switched parties, ran as a Republican, and won. The other switches came in Georgia (1 seat), Maryland (1 seat), North Carolina (3 seats), and Texas (4 seats). The Texas Republican delegation is now one of the largest in the House Republican party—10 seats (equaling the size of the Ohio and Pennsylvania delegations). It is interesting to see the erosion of Democratic support in certain Southern seats that were considered safe not so long ago. Here are four examples, all of which are now held by Republicans:

	1978	1980	1982	1984
Elliott Levitas (Georgia-4th)	81%	69%	66%	47%
Clarence Long (Maryland-2nd)	66%	57%	53%	49%
Ike Andrews (North Carolina-4th)	94%	53%	51%	49%
Jack Hightower (Texas-13th)	75%	55%	64%	47%

There may be future potential for Republican gains in the South as indicated by the fact that 23 seats were won by Democrats by less than 60 percent of the vote, and nine of these were won by less than 55 percent. On the other hand, many of the Republican gains were by narrow margins in 1984 and are themselves vulnerable to being recaptured by the Democrats in 1986. The overall point remains valid, however: the Republicans are much more competitive in the South than before and are likely to be so in the future.

It is difficult to discuss individual House races due to their vast number. Certain races are worth mentioning, however, simply because they drew national attention:

Idaho-2nd: Republican George Hansen, a seven-term veteran, was convicted of filing false financial disclosure statements. He lost by the narrowest of margins after claiming a double standard had been employed—one that convicted him but was not applied to Geraldine Ferraro.

Illinois-19th: Republican Daniel Crane, a three-term member, narrowly lost his bid for reelection in the face of his House censure for sexual contact with a female congressional page.

Maryland-2d: Veteran Democrat Clarence Long, 11 terms, faced the same candidate, Helen D. Bentley, three elections in a row. She kept narrowing the margin and finally defeated him in 1984.

Massachusetts-10th: Democrat Gerry Studds was also censured by the House for sexual contact with a congressional page—in his case a male page. The six-term representative successfully fought off primary and general election challenges to win a seventh term.

Michigan-10th: Three-term Democrat Donald Albosta chaired the subcommittee investigation of the so-called Carter debate papers controversy. He was defeated for reelection by a well-financed Republican opponent.

Mississippi-2d: Freshman Republican Webb Franklin faced a rematch with Robert Clark. Clark was again seeking to become the first black member of Congress from Mississippi in this century. Franklin won by fewer than 3,000 votes in 1982; he won reelection by just over 4,000 votes.

New York-9th: Attention here focused on whether Geraldine Ferraro's district would remain in Democratic hands. It did. Democrat Thomas Manton won with 53 percent of the vote. Reagan, however, won the district handily.

New York-15th: The interest in this district was primarily due to the large amounts of money spent (nearly $2 million—see below). Third-term Republican Bill Green faced Andrew Stein. Green won with 56 percent of the vote.

Oklahoma-1st: The Republicans mounted a strong campaign to oust James Jones, a six-term veteran and chairman of the House Committee on the Budget. Their effort failed, and Jones was reelected with 52 percent of the vote.

Pennsylvania-7th: Democrat Robert Edgar, seeking a seventh term, is a true survivor, always winning by narrow margins. He survived again by a margin of fewer than 1,000 votes despite a supreme effort by Republicans, including a visit to the district by President Reagan.

Early analysis of campaign costs for House races in 1984 showed a leveling off after significant growth in recent years. Michael Malbin and Thomas Skladony of the American Enterprise Institute found that House candidates in the general election had raised $160 million by October 17—"about 10 percent more than at a comparable time in 1982."[15] This growth rate was modest in comparison with that of other recent elections (40 percent, 1976–1978; 35 percent, 1978–

1980; 48 percent, 1980–1982). Contributions from Political Action Committees (PACs) also increased at a much slower rate than in the past—21 percent as compared to 56, 57, and 61 percent for the earlier elections. Still, PAC contributions were important for House candidates—particularly incumbents and Democrats, according to Malbin and Skladony. And as has been the case before, if a candidate can somehow establish that he or she has a good chance of winning, then the money becomes available. PACs like to support those candidates who have a high probability of actually showing up on Capitol Hill.[16]

The Republican party continued to outspend the Democratic party in supporting both House and Senate candidates. In fact, the party was able to provide the maximum allowed by law ($50,800) to 75 House candidates; the Democrats could do this for only 2 candidates.[17] In addition, the well-heeled National Republican Campaign Committee financed other forms of support for candidates—polling, issues research, media advice, etc. The Democratic Committee was in better shape than in the past, however—giving out almost $2 million to candidates—and the fund-raising for the national party overall showed a significant increase over the recent past.[18]

The combined receipts for each of 11 House races exceeded $1 million (reports as of October 17, 1984). Several of these races were those referred to earlier as meriting national attention. Two of these races were particularly costly. The aforementioned Green-Stein contest in New York's 15th district had receipts of nearly $2 million and was therefore the most expensive of the year. Stein spent nearly $1.2 million, or about $15 per vote received. The second most costly campaign was that for the Oklahoma 1st—between James Jones and Frank Keating. Total receipts were approximately $1.8 million—70 percent of that available to the victorious Jones.[19]

Reelecting the Senate

A great deal of research was directed to the question of why senators lose following the record number of defeats for

the 1976, 1978, and 1980 elections.[20] The average return rate
for incumbents for those three elections was slightly less than
60 percent. In 1980 four incumbents suffered primary defeats, another nine were defeated in the general election. In
analyzing these results, I quoted Senator John Heinz, then
chairman of the National Republican Senatorial Committee,
who observed: "Being an incumbent Senator is increasingly
hazardous to one's political health."[21]

All of that has changed. To paraphrase the advertisement
for the movie *Jaws II*, "Just when you thought it *wasn't* safe
to seek reelection to the Senate. . . ." Table 4–5 shows the
incumbent return rate for 1984. Only three were defeated—
one Democrat and two Republicans—and a shift of a very
few votes in two cases (Kentucky and Illinois) would have
reduced the number to one. The 90 percent return rate is the
third highest in the post-World War II period. Further, the
combined return rate for the two most recent elections—1982
and 1984—is the highest for any two consecutive elections in
that same period. Only five incumbents were defeated in
these two elections—a return rate of 91.5 percent.

The 1984 election featured the 1978 class of incumbents.
The 1978 class was a particularly interesting one since it
contained such a large number of first-termers—a total of 20.
In fact, it was the second largest freshman class since the
popular election of senators in 1914. As reported at the time:
"The most obvious characteristic of the class of 1978 is its
youth. . . . Youth means inexperience."[22] These young, aggressive senators did not miss the political lessons taught to
them by their own election and two years later in the 1980
election (when turnover was almost as high). It was very
obvious that they could not wait until their fifth or sixth year
to campaign for reelection. Like their House colleagues, senators had to run a perpetual campaign.

Given its youth, one would not expect many retirements
among the 1978 class. Two senior Republicans retired—John
Tower, Texas, and Howard H. Baker, Jr., Tennessee, the
majority leader. One senior Democrat—Jennings Randolph,
West Virginia—and one junior Democrat—Paul Tsongas, Massachusetts, also retired. Tsongas stepped down for health
reasons. Thus, there were four open seats in states where the
Democrats could be expected to do well. In addition, national
attention focused on three other races judged to be very close:

Table 4–5

Return of Senate Incumbents, 1984, By Political Party

	Total Members in Class	Not Seeking Reelection	Seeking Reelection	Defeated in Primary	Defeated in General	Returned
Democrats	14	2	12	0	1	11 (91.7%)
Republicans	19	2	17	0	2	15 (88.2%)
Total	33	4	29	0	3	26 (89.7%)

SOURCE: Compiled by the author from election returns reported in the *Congressional Quarterly Weekly Report*, November 10, 1984, p. 2905.

Illinois, where Republican Charles Percy, Chairman of the Committee on Foreign Relations, was being challenged by Representative Paul Simon; Iowa, where Republican Roger Jepsen was vulnerable to a vigorous campaign by Representative Tom Harkin; and North Carolina, where Republican Jesse Helms, the arch-conservative in the Senate, faced a stiff battle from the popular incumbent governor, James Hunt. If the Democrats captured all of these seats, and lost none of their own, they would realize a net gain of five—not enough to organize the Senate, since each party would have 50, and the tie would be broken by the vice president if Reagan were reelected.

Table 4–6 shows the outcome. The Democrats held their two open seats, won one of the Republican open seats, and defeated incumbents Percy and Jepsen. In a totally unforeseen outcome, Senator Walter Huddleston (D-Ken) lost in a very tight race to his Republican opponent, Mitchell McConnell, and thus the Republicans retained an absolute majority in the Senate, 53–47. The light turnover produced the second smallest freshman class since the popular election of senators (the smallest having been in 1982). Only seven new senators came to Washington for the Ninety-ninth Congress.

The reduction in the Republican majority got most of the attention following the election. Detailed analysis of the results produces some interesting and surprising findings, however. In fact, if one was unaware of the net gain for the Democrats, the following facts would suggest a Republican victory in the 1984 Senate races.

1. In the contested seats, the Republicans outpolled the Democrats—gaining 50.2 percent of the total popular vote. In 1980, when the Republicans gained 12 seats, the Democrats actually won a majority of the popular vote cast for Senate candidates.

2. A review of individual races shows that most Republican winners had very comfortable winning percentages (see Table 4–6). A total of 8 Republicans won with vote totals of 70 percent or more. Figure 4–3 shows the extraordinary nature of this result. Only 15 Republican senators have won by 70 percent or more in the last ten elections—thus over half of those were elected in 1984. In fact, only 25 percent of Republican senators in this period were elected by more

than 60 percent (compared to 50 percent of Democratic senators elected by 60 percent or more). Yet in 1984, 70 percent of the Republican senators won by 60 percent or more.

3. The average winning percentage of Republican senators in 1984 was higher than that for Democratic senators

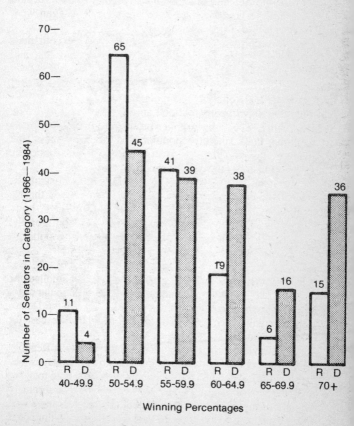

Winning Percentages of Senators 1966—1984, by Party

Figure 4-3

Table 4-6
1984 Senate Results (with Comparisons to 1978)

State	% of Vote Winner	% of Vote in 1984		% Change in 1978		1978–1984	
		R	D	R	D	R	D
Alabama	*Heflin (D)	37	62	-	94	+37	-32
Alaska	*Stevens (R)	71	29	76	24	-5	+5
Arkansas	*Pryor (D)	42	58	16	77	+26	-19
Colorado	*Armstrong (R)	64	35	59	40	+5	-5
Delaware	*Biden (D)	40	60	41	58	-1	+2
Georgia	*Nunn (D)	20	80	17	83	+3	-3
Idaho	*McClure (R)	72	26	68	32	+4	-6
Illinois	Simon (D)	49	50	53	46	-4	+4
Iowa	Harkin (D)	44	56	51	48	-7	+8
Kansas	*Kassebaum (R)	77	22	54	42	+23	-20
Kentucky	McConnell (R)	50+	50	37	61	+13	-11
Louisiana	*Johnston (D)	-	100	-	100	-	-
Maine	*Cohen (R)	74	26	57	34	+17	-8
Massachusetts	Kerry (D)	45	55	45	55	-	-

Michigan	*Levin (D)	47	53	48	52	−1	+1
Minnesota	*Boschwitz (R)	58	42	57	40	+1	+2
Mississippi	*Cochran (R)	61	39	45	32	+16	+7
Montana	*Baucus (D)	41	57	44	56	−3	+1
Nebraska	*Exon (D)	47	53	32	68	+15	−15
New Hampshire	*Humphrey (R)	59	41	51	49	+8	+8
New Jersey	*Bradley (D)	35	65	43	55	+8	+10
New Mexico	*Domenici (R)	72	28	53	47	+19	−19
North Carolina	*Helms (R)	52	48	55	45	−3	+3
Oklahoma	Boren (D)	23	76	33	66	−10	+10
Oregon	*Hatfield (R)	66	34	62	38	+4	−4
Rhode Island	Pell (D)	27	73	25	75	+2	−2
South Carolina	*Thurmond (R)	67	32	56	44	+11	−12
South Dakota	*Pressler (R)	74	26	67	33	+7	−7
Tennessee	Gore (D)	34	51	56	40	−18	+21
Texas	Gramm (R)	59	41	50	49	+9	−8
Virginia	*Warner (R)	70	30	50+	50	+20	−20
West Virginia	Rockefeller (D)	48	52	50	500+	−2	+2
Wyoming	*Simpson (R)	78	22	62	38	+16	−16

*Incumbent
SOURCE: Election results taken from Congressional Quarterly Weekly Report, November 10, 1984, pp. 2923–2930; and March 31, 1979, pp. 576–582.

(excluding the one uncontested seat in Louisiana). In fact, as displayed in Figure 4–4, the Republican average was dramatically higher than for other recent elections. The explanation in part is that Republicans unseated only 1 Democrat. In 1980, they unseated 12—many by small margins. But another part of the explanation is simply that many seats had become safe for Republicans—a new phenomenon.

4. Most Republican incumbents improved their winning

Average Winning Percentage, Republican and Democratic Senators, 1978—1984 (Contested Seats)

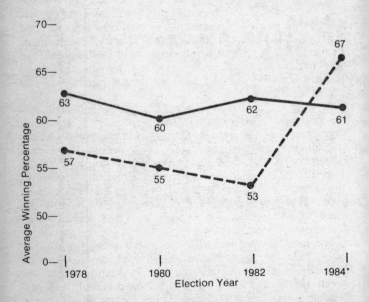

*Excluding the uncontested seat in Louisiana

Figure 4-4

percentage over 1978—13 of the 15 who were reelected (see Table 4–6). The range was from a 1 percent increase to 23 percent. Of the 10 Democratic incumbents (again excluding the one uncontested seat), only 5 increased their winning percentage.

It is very difficult to provide definitive interpretations of Senate elections. By design they are all different. Bearing this caveat in mind, it is particularly important to make comparisons with other elections—particularly that for the class of senators up for reelection (1978 in this case). When these comparisons are made for the 1984 senatorial elections, one is impressed with the strong showing of the Republican incumbents. This finding may deserve equal attention to that of the net loss of two seats to the Democrats, yet it went virtually unnoticed in postelection commentary.

Another feature of the 1984 senatorial elections was the record number of women candidates. The Democrats ran six, none of whom was victorious; the Republicans ran four, one of whom was victorious (an incumbent, Nancy Kassebaum of Kansas). The number of women running in 1984 matched the total number that had run in the three previous elections. Table 4–7 shows that Republican women candidates have tended to do better than their Democratic counterparts. Three have been elected—Kassebaum twice and Paula Hawkins, Florida, once. Three other Republicans and one Democrat have come close by getting 47 percent of the vote or more. Overall, the average percentage received by the Republican women is 45.8 (42.3 if Kassebaum's 1984 lopsided win is dropped out) compared to 36.5 for the Democratic women. In 1984, the showing of Democratic women was particularly weak. They averaged only 32.5 percent of the vote, compared to 46.5 percent for Republicans (36.3 percent when Kassebaum's percentage is dropped).

The most interesting Senate campaigns were, not surprisingly, among the most expensive. National attention focused primarily on the aggressive campaign in North Carolina between Helms and Hunt. It was believed initially that the popular governor would defeat Senator Helms. But Helms is an energetic campaigner with access to huge sums of money from various right-wing groups. As of October 17, he had raised over $14 million. Meanwhile Hunt also demonstrated a capacity to raise money, reporting receipts of over $8.5 mil-

Table 4–7
Women Candidates for Senate, 1978–1984,
Ranked by Percentage of Vote

Candidate	Party	Year	State	Percentage of Vote
1. Kassebaum	R	1984	Kansas	77
2. Kassebaum	R	1978	Kansas	54
3. Hawkins	R	1980	Florida	52
4. Woods	D	1982	Missouri	49+
5. Buchanan	R	1980	Colorado	49
6. Fenwick	R	1982	New Jersey	48
7. Hoch	R	1984	Nebraska	47
8. Holtzman	D	1980	New York	44
9. Growe	D	1984	Minnesota	42
10. Eskind	D	1978	Tennessee	40
11. Gojack	D	1980	Nevada	37
12. Dick	D	1984	Colorado	35
13. Mochary	R	1984	New Jersey	35
14. Foust	R	1980	Kentucky	35
15. Sullivan	R	1982	New York	34
16. Hendrickson	D	1984	Oregon	34
17. Harrison	D	1984	Virginia	30
18. Pratt	D	1984	New Mexico	28
19. Leonard	R	1984	Rhode Island	27
20. Mitchell	D	1984	Maine	26

SOURCE: Compiled by author from election returns in several issues of the *Congressional Quarterly Weekly Report.*

lion. This total for the North Carolina race of nearly $23 million represented 18 percent of money raised for *all* national senatorial candidates!

Table 4–8 shows that in three of the four open seats (Texas, West Virginia, and Tennessee), the candidate with the spending advantage won. In Iowa the candidates spent equally, and in Illinois and Massachusetts the losing candidate spent more. The other race which resulted in the defeat of an incumbent was in Kentucky, which ranked twelfth in total expenditures. Here the losing incumbent outspent his challenger.

Table 4-8
The Top Ten Senate Races by
Election Receipts, 1984*

State	Candidates		Receipts (millions)		
	D	R	D	R	Total
1. North Carolina	Hunt vs. *Helms***		$8.6	$14.4	$23.0
2. Texas	Doggett vs. *Gramm*		4.9	7.9	12.8
3. West Virginia	*Rockefeller* vs. Raese		9.4	.8	10.2
4. Illinois	*Simon* vs. Percy		3.6	4.4	8.0
5. Minnesota	Growe vs. *Boschwitz*		1.2	5.4	6.6
6. Tennessee	*Gore* vs. Ashe		3.5	1.5	5.0
7. Massachusetts	*Kerry* vs. Shamie		1.5	3.5	5.0
8. New Jersey	*Bradley* vs. Mochary		3.9	.8	4.7
9. Iowa	*Harkin* vs. Jepsen		2.3	2.3	4.6
10. Michigan	*Levin* vs. Lousma		3.1	1.4	4.5

*Includes primary and general election receipts as of October 17, 1984
**Winner in italics
SOURCE: Compiled from data in Michael J. Malbin and Thomas Skladony,
"Campaign Finances, 1984: A Preliminary Analysis of House and Senate
Campaign Receipts," paper prepared for Public Policy Week, American
Enterprise Institute, Washington, D.C., December 3, 1984, pp. 1–3.

Note that in a few races one candidate had an enormous
spending advantage over the other. The greatest disparity
occurred in West Virginia, where Rockefeller outspent Raese
by nearly 12 to 1, yet garnered only 52 percent of the vote
(approximately $25 per vote received). Other disparities in-
clude the nearly 5 to 1 advantage for Boschwitz (Minnesota)
and for Bradley (New Jersey), not to mention the huge dollar
advantages for Helms (North Carolina) and Gramm (Texas).

Overall, the total money raised for Senate races continued
to increase at an impressive rate—33 percent more than was
raised in 1982. The growth rate exceeded that for 1980 and
1982 but was less than that in 1978. New records were set for
individual races—again with North Carolina and Jesse Helms
leading the way. In fact, the total receipts in that state were
not far from what was spent for all Senate races just ten years
ago ($28.4 million spent in 1974). The ten costliest races
accounted for 67 percent of the total receipts in 1984 and at
$84.4 million exceeded by $10 million the total spent for all

races in 1980. There is no doubt about it: Senate elections have become very expensive political affairs.

The Ninety-ninth Congress

The light turnover in House and Senate seats had different effects for each chamber. In the House no committee chairman either retired or was defeated. There were, however, several subcommittee chairmen who did not return—the most important being Clarence Long (D-Md.), chairman of the Subcommittee on Foreign Operations of the Committee on Appropriations (replaced by David Obey, D-Wis.) and Richard L. Ottinger (D-N.Y.), chairman of the Subcommittee on Energy Conservation and Power of the Committee on Energy and Commerce (replaced by Edward Markey, D-Mass.).

One major committee was likely to undergo a leadership change unless the Democratic Caucus altered the House rules. Membership on the Committee on the Budget is limited to three consecutive two-year terms. James Jones (D-Okla.) chaired the committee during the Ninety-eighth Congress but was ineligible to serve again under the term limitation. Efforts were made to change the rules, but all proposals were defeated, thus opening the chairmanship for others. William Gray, III (D-Pen.), a Black who also serves on the Committee on Appropriations, won the post. Proposals were also made in the Democratic Caucus to reform the congressional budgetary process yet again, but with one minor exception these were defeated.

A second important committee had a leadership change when House Democrats ignored seniority and ousted the sitting chairman of the Committee on Armed Services, Melvin Price (D-Ill.). Price's age (80) was a factor in his defeat. In a stunning move, the Democratic Caucus approved Les Aspin (D-Wis.) as chairman. Aspin is the seventh-ranking Democrat on the committee. Though three chairmen were removed in 1975, never in modern times had the caucus dipped so deeply into the seniority rankings on a committee.

Several ranking Republicans retired, leaving a number of vacancies in the committee and subcommittee leadership posts.

By far the most important of these shifts occurred in the Committee on Ways and Means, where senior Republican Barber Conable, Jr., New York, retired. Conable was among the most respected members of the House, considered by many to be a model legislator. John J. Duncan, Tennessee, moved up to take the ranking position on Ways and Means. Significant shifts caused by retirements also occurred in the Committee on Education and Labor (John N. Erlenborn, Illinois, being replaced by James M. Jeffords, Vermont), the Committee on Science and Technology (Larry Winn, Jr., Kansas, being replaced by Manuel Lujan, Jr., New Mexico), and the Subcommittee on Defense of the Committee on Appropriations (Jack Edwards, Alabama, being replaced by Joseph McDade, Pennsylvania). There were other less important subcommittee shifts.

There were two changes in the House Democratic leadership. Geraldine Ferraro, who resigned to run for the vice presidency, had been serving as caucus secretary. This post was won by Mary Rose Oakar, Ohio. And by Democratic party rules, the caucus chairman can only serve four years. Thus Gillis Long, Louisiana (who then died in January 1985, creating a vacancy to be filled by special election), had to step down. Richard A. Gephardt, a very promising young Democrat from Missouri, was elected to replace Long. Charles W. Stenholm, a conservative Democrat from Texas, threatened to oppose the renomination of Thomas P. O'Neill to the speakership. He withdrew this challenge before the caucus, however, and O'Neill was renominated by acclamation. Stenholm is the leader of a group called the Conservative Democratic Forum. He met with O'Neill before the caucus on December 3 and apparently received assurances that his group's views would be fully represented in party councils.[23]

On the Republican side, all but the conference vice chairman, Jack Edwards, Alabama, returned and were reelected to their posts. A woman, Lynn Martin, Illinois, was elected to Edwards's post. Table 4–9 lists the principal House Democratic and Republican leaders for the Ninety-ninth Congress.

Leaders in both parties found themselves pressured to respond to younger members after the 1984 election. Junior Democrats demanded more of a voice in shaping policy. They also expressed concern that the image of the Democratic

Table 4-9
Party Leaders, U. S. House of Representatives,
Ninety-ninth Congress

Democrats	Age	Term
Speaker; Thomas P. O'Neill, Massachusetts	72	17th
Majority Leader: Jim Wright, Texas	62	16th
Majority Whip: Thomas S. Foley, Washington	55	11th
Chief Deputy Whip: Bill Alexander, Arkansas	51	9th
Caucus Chairman: Richard A. Gephardt, Missouri	43	5th
Caucus Secretary: Mary Rose Oakar, Ohio	44	5th
Republicans		
Minority Leader: Robert Michel, Illinois	61	15th
Minority Whip: Trent Lott, Mississippi	43	7th
Conference Chairman: Jack F. Kemp, New York	49	8th
Conference Vice Chairman: Lynn Martin, Illinois	45	3rd
Policy Committee Chairman: Dick Cheney, Wyoming	43	4th

SOURCE: Compiled by author.

party was too much that of Speaker O'Neill. Mike Synar
(D-Okla.) expressed it this way:

> The American people have a perception that the Demo-
> cratic Party is Tip O'Neill. But 75 percent of the House
> was elected since 1974, the average age is about 45 and
> many of us grew up in the 1960s. This is the type of image
> we've got to project.[24]

Pressure on Speaker O'Neill emanated from all wings of the
party and resulted in a promise that the Caucus and Steering
and Policy Committee would be more active than in the
recent past so as to provide forums for junior members. The
removal of Price as chairman of the Armed Services Committee served as a warning to senior Democrats to be more
attentive to the wishes of their younger colleagues.

On the Republican side, the pressure came primarily from a
group of activist conservatives led by Newt Gingrich, Georgia. Gingrich and his colleagues have been promoting a

"conservative opportunity society" as a means for the minority to take initiatives in policy-making. In his acceptance speech, Minority Leader Michel sounded the principal theme of the young conservatives: "The most important thing we have done is rid ourselves of that subservient, timid mentality of the permanent minority. The Republican Party in the House is no longer content to go along. We want to go for broke."[25]

In the Senate the retirements and defeats were few but very important. The most crucial changes occurred among the Republicans. Senator Howard Baker, Jr., Tennessee, stepped down after 18 years in the Senate. A highly respected member, Baker had risen to assume the position his father-in-law, Everett McKinley Dirksen, had held before him. Senator John Tower, Texas, also retired. He had served in the Senate for nearly 24 years. Tower headed the powerful Committee on Armed Services. Senator Charles Percy, Illinois, sought reelection for a fourth term but was narrowly defeated. Percy was chairman of the Committee on Foreign Relations. The loss of these three veteran senators set in motion considerable politicking and committee shuffling.

The first matter to be settled was the majority leadership contest. Five senators were in the race: Robert Dole, Kansas; Ted Stevens, Alaska; Richard Lugar, Indiana; Pete Domenici, New Mexico; and James McClure, Idaho. The politics of selection were very complex, since they were inexorably linked to the committee chairmanships. Dole chaired Finance, Lugar would become chairman of Foreign Relations if Helms chose to remain as chairman of Agriculture (which he intended to do), Domenici chaired Budget, and McClure chaired Energy and Natural Resources. Only Stevens lacked a major committee post or the prospect of getting one. Balloting proceeded by eliminating the low person after each vote, and it took four ballots to elect a leader. The results were as follows:[26]

Ballot

	1	2	3	4
Dole	14	17	20	28
Stevens	12	14	20	25
Lugar	10	12	13	out
Domenici	9	10	out	out
McClure	8	out	out	out

The election of Dole was widely interpreted as a victory for the moderates and for those who prefer that Senate Republicans be more independent of the White House.

The rest of the Republican leadership team was also changed in what was "the largest turnover . . . in at least 40 years."[27] Table 4–10 provides the details. Both moderates and conservatives are represented in the new leadership team, but the principal characteristic appears to be that of pragmatism. A fresh and aggressive set of leaders has taken over as the Senate Republicans look ahead to the 1986 elections, when 22 of their number will be up for reelection (including Dole).

Table 4–10
New Republican Leadership in the Senate, Ninety-ninth Congress

Contest (Winner first)	Vote	Winner's Age	Term
Floor Leader			
Robert Dole, Kansas vs. four opponents	28–25 (4th ballot)	61	3rd
Whip			
Alan Simpson, Wyoming vs. Slade Gorton, Washington, and Robert Kasten, Jr., Wisconsin	31–22 (2d ballot)	53	2d
Conference Chairman			
John Chafee, Rhode Island vs. Jake Garn, Utah	28–25	62	2d
Conference Secretary			
Thad Cochran, Mississippi vs. Rudy Boschwitz, Minnesota	32–21	46	2d
Policy Committee Chairman			
William Armstrong, Colorado	Unopposed	47	2d
National Republican Senatorial Committee	27–26	46	2d
H. J. Heinz, Pennsylvania vs. Malcolm Wallop, Wyoming			

SOURCE: Compiled by author from information in Diane Granat, "GOP Overhauls Its Senate Leadership," *Congressional Quarterly Weekly Report*, December 1, 1984, pp. 3022–3023.

Committee changes were also numerous as a consequence of the shuffling that took place once the leadership issue was settled. New chairmen were selected for the following committees:

> Armed Services: Barry Goldwater, Arizona, for the retiring John Tower, Texas
> Commerce, Science and Transporation: John Danforth, Missouri, for Bob Packwood, Oregon, who chose to chair the Committee on Finance
>
> Finance: Bob Packwood, Oregon, for Robert Dole, Kansas, who was elected floor leader
> Foreign Relations: Richard Lugar, Indiana, for the defeated Charles Percy, Illinois
> Veterans Affairs: Frank Murkowski, Alaska, for Alan Simpson, Wyoming, who was elected whip

By comparison, the Democrats had few changes. Third-term Senator Lawton Chiles, Florida, challenged the reelection of Minority Leader Robert Byrd, West Virginia, in an unprecedented move. He lost by a wide margin, 36–11, as Byrd won his fifth term as Senate Democratic leader. The whip, Alan Cranston, California, and caucus chairman, Daniel Inouye, Hawaii, also won reelection. The only new leader was George Mitchell, Maine, who succeeded Lloyd Bentsen, Texas, as chairman of the Democratic Senatorial Campaign Committee. Bentsen voluntarily stepped down. The committee changes among the ranking Democrats were limited to two:

> Agriculture, Nutrition and Forestry: Patrick Leahy, Vermont, for the defeated Walter Huddleston, Kentucky
> Environment and Public Works: Lloyd Bentsen, Texas, for the retiring Jennings Randolph, West Virginia

From the President's perspective, the 1984 congressional elections produced a mixed message. The Republicans did realize a 14-seat gain in the House of Representatives and performed well in overall vote totals for contested seats. But the Democrats retained a sizable majority of 71 seats. The Senate results produced a slightly less conservative body. The three House Democrats who won seats (Gore, Tennessee;

Harkin, Iowa; and Simon, Illinois) all had higher liberal voting records than the Republicans whom they replaced. The two other Democratic freshmen (Kerry, Massachusetts, and Rockefeller, West Virginia) are reported to be liberal and moderate respectively, but they replaced Democrats similarly ranked. The two new Republicans (Gramm, Texas, and McConnell, Kentucky) do not represent significant changes over those they replaced (though McConnell will likely turn out to be more conservative than Huddleston). Thus, the composite result for the president who was particularly encouraging. Building majorities for his programs will require the special political skills this president reportedly possesses.

The agenda appears to be a presidential advantage in working with Congress. Once again the dominant issues tend to be more consolidative, if not downright conservative, in nature. Budget cutting, tax reform, the maintenance of a strong defense, and making government work better continue to be major themes that must be dealt with by liberals and conservatives alike. Members of Congress will differ with the President on how best to accomplish these goals but not over whether they should be accomplished. The President continues to manage the agenda.

Conclusion

In regard to the specific outcomes of the 1984 congressional elections, the following conclusions are warranted:

1. House and Senate turnover was not dramatically different from that for previous reelection landslides, particularly those by recent Republican presidents (Eisenhower and Nixon).
2. The incumbency return rates for representatives and senators were among the highest recorded in contemporary elections.
3. House Republican candidates were successful by several measures other than seats gained and demonstrated continuing strength in the South.
4. Winning Republican senators were reelected by record

margins, and incumbents in both parties appear much safer than in the recent past.

5. Campaign costs continued to escalate in Senate races with new records set for individual races. The cost of House races stabilized.

6. The high return rate of House incumbents contributed to unusual stability in party and committee leadership. The loss of a few key Senate Republicans led to the election of a new leadership team and significant changes in committee chairmanships.

7. The composite result from the 1984 congressional elections produced a Congress slightly less favorable to President Reagan's programs but one which must cope with an agenda essentially formulated by the President.

In his review of the election, elections analyst William Schneider concluded that:

> The behavior of American voters appears to be a product of two competing forces—partisanship and incumbency. While the balance of partisanship has been shifting in the Republicans' favor, incumbency has held back the rate of electoral change. It is therefore premature to describe the Republicans as the new majority party in American politics, as the weakness of Reagan's electoral coattails demonstrates. On the other hand, the Democrats' standing as the majority party seems to be sustained mostly by the inertial appeal of incumbency.[28]

Inertia was purposefully built into our system. The separation of elections allows Americans to vote yes to opposites. In 1984, the voters overwhelmingly approved of President Reagan and substantially approved of their representatives and senators. That this two-directional positive attitude has confused the pundits appears once again not to have bothered American voters. It is even possible that they like what they have done.

* * *

The author wishes to acknowledge the support of the John Simon Guggenheim Memorial Foundation, the White Burkett Miller Center of Public Affairs, and the research funds associate with the Robert Kent Gooch Chair in Government, University of Virginia.

Notes for Chapter 4

1. Raymond E. Wolfinger, "Dealignment, Realignment, and Mandates in the 1984 Election," paper prepared for Public Policy Week, American Enterprise Institute, Washington, D.C. (December 3, 1984), p. 27

2. Ibid. p. 28.

3. The Democrats were the minority party nationally at this time. They actually elected fewer House members than the Republicans in 1916, but a sufficient number of "independents" voted with the Democrats so that they could organize the House.

4. "Election '84," *Time* (November 19, 1984), p. 38.

5. Thus, this election was very different from 1980, when voters actively disapproved of President Carter, thus turning to Ronald Reagan as the alternative.

6. "Election, '84," op. cit.

7. The President did campaign for certain candidates in the final weeks of the campaign, but candidates in the states and districts where he campaigned were not notably successful. See Richard E. Cohen, "Unconventional Wisdom," *National Journal* (November 17, 1984), p. 2212.

8. As reported by Robert Merry, *The Wall Street Journal* (December 7, 1984), p. 31.

9. For details see Gary C. Jacobson, *The Politics of Congressional Elections* (Boston: Little, Brown, 1983), ch. 3.

10. See Norman J. Ornstein, Thomas E. Mann, Michael J. Malbin, Allen Schick, and John F. Bibby, *Vital Statistics on Congress, 1984–1985 Edition* (Washington, D.C.: American Enterprise Institute, 1984), pp. 49–50.

11. See Ornstein et al., pp. 49–50.

12. See Joseph Cooper and William West, "The Congressional Career in the 1970s," *Congress Reconsidered*, 2nd ed., eds. Lawrence Dodd and Bruce Oppenheimer (Washington, D.C.: Congressional Quarterly Press, 1981), pp. 83–106.

13. As reported in Michael J. Malbin and Thomas W. Skladony, "Campaign Finance, 1984: A Preliminary Analysis of House and Senate Campaign Receipts," paper prepared for Public Policy Week, American Enterprise Institute, Washington, D.C. (December 3, 1984), Table 5, and calculated by the author.

14. As reported in *Congressional Quarterly Weekly Report*, April 13, 1985, p. 687.

15. Malbin and Skladony, op. cit. p. 1. Later reports showed a slight decline in expenditures, but an increase in PAC contribu-

tions. See *Congressional Quarterly Weekly Report,* April 13, 1985, p. 701.

16. For details see Gary Jacobson, *Money in Congressional Elections* (New Haven, Conn.: Yale University Press, 1980) and Michael Malbin, ed., *Money and Politics in the United States: Financing Elections in the 1980s* (Chatham, N.J.: Chatham House Publishers, 1984).

17. As reported by Thomas B. Edsall in "Democratic Fund-Raising Strong," *The Washington Post* (November 12, 1984), p. A6.

18. Reported by Edsall, ibid. See also a report by Adam Clymer in "Democrats Gain in Business PAC Funds," *The New York Times* (November 6, 1984), p. A22, on the increase in business PAC contributions to Democrats.

19. As reported in Malbin and Skladony, op. cit. pp. 1–26.

20. For example, see my own report in "The New, New Senate," *A Tide of Discontent: The 1980 Elections and Their Meaning,* eds. Ellis Sandoz and Cecil V. Crabb, Jr. (Washington, D.C.: Congressional Quarterly Press, 1981), pp. 92–100.

21. Ibid. p. 90

22. Steven V. Roberts, "Senate's New Class Reflects Changing Political Standards," *The New York Times* (November 15, 1978), p. A18.

23. Diane Granat, "Democrats and GOP Leaders Named for the 99th Congress," *Congressional Quarterly Weekly Report* (December 8, 1984), p. 3053.

24. Ibid. p. 3054.

25. Ibid. p. 3053.

26. As reported in Diane Granat, "Dole Elected Majority Leader," *Congressional Quarterly Weekly Report* (December 1, 1984), p. 3025.

27. Ibid. p. 3022.

28. William Schneider, "Incumbency Staved Off Disaster for Congressional Democrats in 1984 Elections," *National Journal* (December 8, 1984), p. 2364.

References and Further Reading

Davidson, Roger H. and Walter J. Oleszek. "Changing the Guard in the U.S. Senate." *Legislative Studies Quarterly,* Vol. 9 (November 1984), pp. 635–664.

Hinckley, Barbara. *Congressional Elections*. Washington: Congressional Quarterly Press, 1981).

Jacobson, Gary C. *Money in Congressional Elections*. New Haven: Yale University Press, 1980.

Jacobson, Gary C. *The Politics of Congressional Elections*. Boston: Little, Brown, 1983.

Jones, Charles O. *The United States Congress: People, Place, and Policy*. Homewood, Ill.: Dorsey Press, 1982, Chs. 3–5.

Maisel, Louis Sandy. *From Obscurity to Oblivion: Running in the Congressional Primary*. Knoxville: University of Tennessee Press, 1982.

Mann, Thomas E. and Norman J. Ornstein, eds. *The American Elections of 1982*. Washington, D.C.: American Enterprise Institute, 1983.

Mann, Thomas E. *Unsafe at any Margin: Interpreting Congressional Elections*. Washington, D.C.: American Enterprise Institute, 1978.

5

The New Federalism and State Elections

Daniel J. Elazar

Separate Electoral Cycles and Their Impact

While the November 6 election was the biggest election of the quadrennial national electoral cycle for most Americans, it had relatively less direct impact on state electoral politics than any other presidential election in the history of the American federal system. Paradoxically, this is because of the renewed strength of the states as polities, which is, in itself, partially the result of the first Reagan administration. Three points are crucial in understanding why this is so.

First, there is the increased separation of election for major state offices from federal elections. On November 6, only 13 governorships were contested. The elections for the remaining 37 were held in other than presidential years so as to give the gubernatorial races greater separate visibility and to insulate them from the swings and pressures of presidential politics. What is true for the governors is true for most of the other constitutional officers elected in each state. Only the state legislatures and, most particularly, the lower houses with their two-year terms are now subject to the winds of presidential elections.

Second, while the Reagan Administration elevated the effort to renew the strength of the states into the national agenda, President Reagan was merely following a trend begun earlier at about the time of Watergate. It was then that the combination of the world oil crisis, the immobilization of the presidency, and the American retreat from Vietnam led to a great weakening of the federal government and a concomitant shifting of the burden of domestic policy-making in several crucial areas to the states.

Third, the crucial element in this assessment is *not* that the states have less involvement with the federal government, as the Reagan Administration has suggested is its goal, but that within an inevitably intermeshed system the states today are better able and more willing to function as polities, not merely as administrative arms of the federal government.

One of the consequences of the postwar state constitutional reform movement initiated in 1944, with the rewriting of the New Jersey constitution, and which concluded in the early 1970's, was a deliberate effort on the part of constitutional reformers to separate state and national electoral politics to the greatest possible degree. Since one of their other goals was the elimination of the number and frequency of elections and the number of elected officials, had they been fully successful and convinced the various constitutional conventions to accept four-year terms for state legislators, they would have achieved well-nigh complete separation in three quarters of the states. As it is, by introducing four-year gubernatorial terms in 46 states and holding gubernatorial elections in presidential off years in 37, they achieved much of what they were striving for. Their argument was that a truly effective state politics required separation from national electoral issues and presidential coattails so that state voters could focus on state issues when electing state officials.

The separations which their reforms brought about were greater than those which existed even in the "salad days" of the states as polities in the nineteenth century when the federal government was much smaller, the environment much more conducive to the isolation of state from national affairs, and local loyalties were presumably greater, precisely because in those days terms of office for officials were shorter. Even where there was elections in odd years, the same officials had to run for reelection in presidential years.

The results of these changes on state politics have yet to be properly studied. Perhaps it is even too soon to draw strong conclusions. The results of the 1984 elections reflect the way in which presidential elections are no longer decisive in state and local affairs. All told there were only modest shifts in political control in state institutions. Republicans had a net gain of one governorship and one state legislature. Democrats now control 28 state legislatures and Republicans 11. The other 11 are divided.

The Gubernatorial Elections

Prior to the November 6 elections, the Republicans controlled 15 governorships and the Democrats 35. Of those, only 13, or approximately one quarter, were contested in 1984. The Republicans won 8 and the Democrats 5, for a net Republican gain of 1. Four of the 13 victories, 2 Republicans and 2 Democrats, were incumbents who won reelection, but 2 Republican incumbents were defeated in North Dakota and Washington. Of the 7 newly elected governors, 6 were Republicans, including Republican victors in such normally Democratic states as Missouri, North Carolina, and West Virginia. On the other hand, the one new Democratic face surfaced in Vermont, a state which rarely elects Democrats to the state's highest office. Thus the Republican party took four state houses from the Democrats, benefitting from the retirement of popular Democratic governors in North Carolina, Rhode Island, Utah, and West Virginia, and the Democrats took three from the GOP.

Coincidentally or not, Democratic gains were to be found across the northern tier of states, while Republican gains were without exception along the Eastern Seaboard. Indeed, the 16 GOP governorships are concentrated by and large in cultural border areas, where two or even all three of the major political subcultures of the United States come together.*

In Vermont, Lieutenant Governor Madeleine M. Kunin was the first woman to be elected governor of that state and one of the two women governors currently in office (the other is Martha Layne Collins of Kentucky). Governor Kunin won election in her second attempt, in a very close race against Attorney General John J. Easton. She barely cleared the 50 percent mark needed in Vermont to keep the election out of the state legislature. Swiss-born and Jewish, as well as Democratic, her election represents a real departure for that conservative state.

The results in Vermont reflect the demographic changes which are taking place in that state, which has become a haven for environmentalists and back-to-nature types on the liberal end of the spectrum who have flocked into the state and are beginning to be felt in its electoral politics. On one

*See p. 136, American Political Subcultures.

hand, these new Vermonters reinforce the state's commitment to remain something of a backwater when it comes to industrialization, economic development, and other kinds of change; on the other, they also tend to vote Democratic. Kunin benefited from her more personal-style grass roots campaign against Easton's highly media-oriented one, although both touched the tight moralistic chords in Vermont.

In Utah, the retirement of Democrat Scott Matheson opened the door for Republican victory by the speaker of the state's house, Norman H. Bangerter. Matheson was an extraordinarily popular governor. His popularity regularly exceeded 70 percent throughout his three terms in office. He retired for personal reasons. Bangerter won election over Democrat Wayne Owens, a member of the U.S. Congress whose principal campaign issue was Utah's movement toward becoming a one-party state dominated by the GOP. Bangerter became the state's first Republican governor in 20 years. The new governor of Utah will be more conservative than his predecessor on social issues, but since both candidates and the rating incumbent are fully within Utah's highly moralistic and sober political culture, his election does not mark any departure from Utah's general political style.

An example of a very different political culture was to be found in the West Virginia results. Voters in that state returned Republican former governor Arch A. Moore to the statehouse for an unprecedented third term despite the shadow of a 1975 federal indictment and subsequent acquittal on extortion charges. In West Virginia, where the freewheeling combination of an individualistic-cum-traditionalistic political culture with populistic style allows politicians a great deal of latitude in such matters, Moore's actions were not deemed to disqualify him for the governorship.

In Washington, GOP Governor John Spellman could not seem to get his administration into gear and was seen by the voters as floundering at a time when Washington was undergoing great economic difficulties. Hence he was defeated by Pierce County Executive Booth Gardner, a Democrat and heir to the Weyerhaeuser timber fortune. Gardner won 53 percent of the vote by presenting an image of the wealthy businessman in politics usually reserved for Republicans, one which led Governor Spellman to victory four years before. No Washington governor has been reelected since 1972. Washington's political cultural style calls for efficient, businesslike government, something easier to promise than to deliver, giving advantage to challengers who can present the right kind of image, as was the case in the last three contests.

The other incumbent governor to lose was Allen Olson of North Dakota, also a Republican, who was unexpectedly beaten by Democratic state representative George Sinner. Olson had taken the state house from the Democrats in 1980, after 20 years of Democratic control. Sinner, a wealthy beet farmer, had not even been expected to get his party's nomination. He beat out former governor Arthur Link at the Democratic party convention and went on to challenge Olson as a distinct underdog. Sinner ran an aggressive campaign against a lackluster opponent, emphasizing the need to complete the Gamson Diversion water project and screening television ads that showed a farmer pitching manure as a reflection on Olson's campaign rhetoric. Sinner won with 56 percent of the vote, 22 percentage points ahead of the Democratic presidential ticket. His lusty campaign was very much in the North Dakota moralistic populist style.

The Republicans upset the Democrats in Rhode Island when Edward DiPrete, the mayor of Cranston, beat Anthony J. Solomon, the state treasurer. Democrats have controlled the Rhode Island governorship for 45 of the past 52 years, and DiPrete is the first Republican to be elected since John Chafee, who finished his last term in 1969. The key issues in the race revolved around the state's economic difficulties and the long period of Democratic party domination.

North Carolina elected the second Republican governor in that state in the twentieth century when six-term U.S. Representative James G. Martin defeated the state's attorney general, Rufus Edmisten. Martin, an ex-chemistry professor, soft-spoken and restrained in his manner, had to build a statewide coalition while keeping sufficient distance between himself and outspoken ultraconservative GOP Senator Jesse Helms, whose race for reelection dominated public attention in the state. Martin presented himself to the voters as a complete conservative and strong supporter of President Reagan. In the end he received 54 percent of the vote. Martin's principled, moderately conservative, moralistic approach was in the classic mold of North Carolina politics.

Less eventful races included Democrat Bill Clinton's victory in Arkansas, where he won a third two-year term against Republican contractor Woody Freeman. Clinton won his first gubernatorial race in 1978 but was defeated in 1980, in part because of overconfidence. He did win in 1982 after carefully mending his fences in a civil society that combines traditionalism, individualism, and populism in a sometimes elusive synthesis.

Montana's Democratic Governor Ted Schwinden coasted to a second term with 70 percent of the vote over State Senator Pat Goodover. Schwinden had compiled a record of fiscal conservatism and sound management of the state's coal extraction fund that won him substantial support from normally Republican voters. Montana's moralistic political culture usually finds expression at the polls through the election of liberal moralistic candidates to the U.S. Congress and conservative moralistic ones to state office. This often means that the GOP has an edge in the state races, but Schwinden could out-conservative the best of them.

Indiana's Robert D. Orr, on the other hand, almost lost his race to Democratic State Senator W. Wayne Townsend. Townsend's accusations that Orr had misrepresented the state's fiscal situation and had consequently sought an unexpected tax incentive but continued patronage politics as usual succeeded in reducing the governor's comfortable lead in the last month of the campaign. Orr finally won by 52 to 48 percent. The issues were classic ones in Indiana politics. The state's mainstream individualistic political culture retains a certain "old-fashioned" emphasis on little government, low taxes, and patronage politics.

New Hampshire's Governor John Sununu had no difficulty winning 67 percent of the vote for a second two-year term against his Democratic rival, Chris Spirou, state house minority leader. In Delaware, outgoing Republican Governor Pierre S. duPont IV was successful in passing the Republican nomination on to his protégé, Lieutenant Governor Michael N. Castle, who easily defeated the Democratic challenger, William T. Quillen, with 55 percent of the vote. Quillen had been a justice of the state supreme court and had resigned to pursue the governorship.

In Missouri, conservative Republican Attorney General John Ashcroft defeated Democratic Lieutenant Governor Kenneth J. Rothman with 57 percent of the vote. Ashcroft, a 42-year-old gospel-singing lawyer, succeeded GOP incumbent Christopher S. "Kit" Bond to become the youngest governor elected in 1984. Ashcroft appeared to be a traditionalistic populist much suited to Missouri's political culture and style.

1985 Occupants of the Nation's Statehouses

Here is a list of the governors and governors-elect of the 50 states, and the years in which each office is next up for election. The names of governors elected in 1984 are *italicized*. Asterisks (*) denote incumbents reelected.

Alabama—George C. Wallace (D) 1986
Alaska—Bill Sheffield (D) 1986
Arizona—Bruce Babbitt (D) 1986
Arkansas—*Bill Clinton (D) 1986**
California—George Deukmejian (R) 1986
Colorado—Richard D. Lamm (D) 1986
Connecticut—William A. O'Neill (D) 1986
Delaware—*Michael N. Castle (R) 1988*
Florida—Robert Graham (D) 1986
Georgia—Joe Frank Harris (D) 1986
Hawaii—George Ariyoshi (D) 1986
Idaho—John V. Evans (D) 1986
Illinois—James R. Thompson (R) 1986
Indiana—*Robert D. Orr (R) 1988**
Iowa—Terry Branstad (R) 1986
Kansas—John Carlin (D) 1986
Kentucky—Martha Layne Collins (D) 1987
Louisiana—Edwin W. Edwards (D) 1987
Maine—Joseph E. Brennan (D) 1986
Maryland—Harry R. Hughes (D) 1986
Massachusetts—Michael S. Dukakis (D) 1986
Michigan—James J. Blanchard (D) 1986
Minnesota—Rudy Perpich (D) 1986
Mississippi—Bill Allain (D) 1987
Missouri—*John Ashcroft (R) 1988*
Montana—*Ted Schwinden (D) 1988**
Nebraska—Bob Kerrey (D) 1986
Nevada—Richard H. Bryan (D) 1986
New Hampshire—*John H. Sununu (R) 1986**
New Jersey—Thomas H. Kean (R) 1985
New Mexico—Toney Anaya (D) 1986
New York—Mario M. Cuomo (D) 1986
North Carolina—*James G. Martin (R) 1988*
North Dakota—*George Sinner (D) 1988*

Ohio—Richard F. Celeste (D) 1986
Oklahoma—George Nigh (D) 1986
Oregon—Victor G. Atiyeh (R) 1986
Pennsylvania—Richard L. Thornburgh (R) 1986
Rhode Island—*Edward DiPrete (R) 1986*
South Carolina—Richard W. Riley (D) 1986
South Dakota—William J. Janklow (R) 1986
Tennessee—Lamar Alexander (R) 1986
Texas—Mark White (D) 1986
Utah—*Norman H. Bangerter (R) 1988*
Vermont—*Madeleine M. Kunin (D) 1986*
Virginia—Charles S. Robb (D) 1985
Washington—*Booth Gardner (D) 1988*
West Virginia—*Arch A. Moore Jr. (R) 1988*
Wisconsin—Anthony S. Earl (D) 1986
Wyoming—Ed Herschler (D) 1986

Governors for 1985

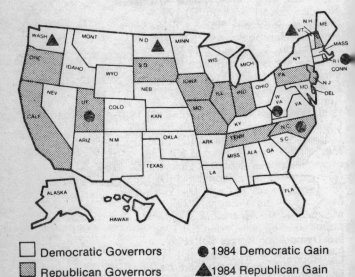

☐ Democratic Governors   ● 1984 Democratic Gain

▨ Republican Governors   ▲ 1984 Republican Gain

Map 1

The Legislative Election Results

The only dramatic change in the 1984 state legislative elections was the GOP victory in both houses of the Connecticut Legislature. The Republicans gained control of the lower houses in Delaware, Minnesota, Nevada, and North Dakota and the senates in New Mexico and Ohio. Democrats, on the other hand, gained control of the Alaska house and Vermont senate. In the aggregate, the GOP gained nearly 300 seats across the country, including significant gains in the South. Republican control of state legislatures is concentrated in the Great Plains-Rocky Mountain heartland while Democratic-controlled legislatures are concentrated in the still-solid (in this respect) South and the Pacific Coast. New England is divided while the states in the rest of the Northeast-Midwest

Party Control of State Legislatures after 1984 Elections

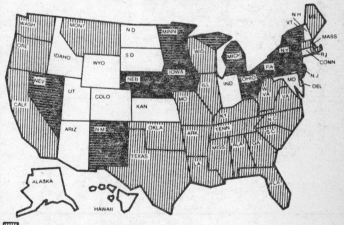

|||| Democrats Control Both Houses

☐ Republicans Control Both Houses

■ Each Party Controls One House

▓ Non-partisan Unicameral

Map 2

Party Control in the States

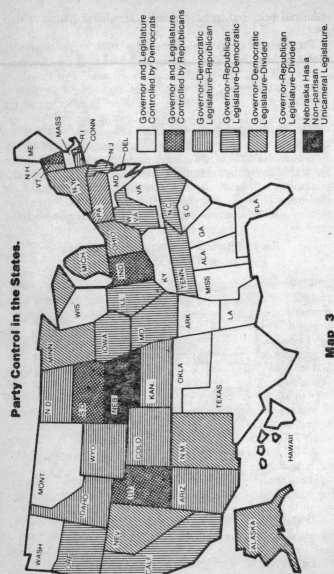

Legend:
- Governor and Legislature Controlled by Democrats
- Governor and Legislature Controlled by Republicans
- Governor-Democratic Legislature-Republican
- Governor-Republican Legislature-Democratic
- Governor-Democratic Legislature-Divided
- Governor-Republican Legislature-Divided
- Nebraska Has a Non-partisan Unicameral Legislature.

Map 3

industrial belt tend to have divided legislative bodies. (Map 2.)

The composite picture of party control in the states is shown in Map 3.

Initiatives and Referenda

A growing feature of American elections in recent years is the use of the devices of direct democracy to directly involve the voters in legislative and constitutional choices through the initiative and referendum. The year 1984 was no exception to this trend, one which takes advantage of every possible election—federal, state, or local. More than 200 propositions were to be found on state and local ballots on November 6. Unlike some previous years, however, there were no clear nationwide trends in these state and local exercises of direct democracy.

While the citizens of the several states were not eager to endorse additional tax limitations, they did exercise their powers of constitutional choice on what is normally called the conservative side of various issues. Thus in Colorado the voters chose to stop state payments for abortions and in Washington to place funding restrictions on such payments. Maine voters decisively defeated a proposed equal rights amendment to the state constitution. Since the existing state laws in Maine sufficiently protect women's rights, it was hard to make a case for the constitutional amendment, and Maine voters responded accordingly. Oregon voters, equally decisively, approved a proposition indicating that the death penalty would not violate the state constitution, and another that made some types of murder capital crimes.

The liberal-conservative division has taken some interesting turns lately. Arkansas and Colorado voters rejected proposals to establish casino gambling in Hot Springs and Pueblo, while California, Missouri, Oregon, and West Virginia voted to establish state lotteries, by now accepted means of "painless" revenue-raising in the states. In the privacy of their voting booths, Utah's presumably staid voters defeated a proposal to ban sexually explicit television programing by 60 percent to 40 percent.

Tax limitation measures defeated included one in Michigan which would have limited property taxes and required voter approval of any future increases. In California, the home of Proposition 13, another proposal which would have closed loopholes that have since been found in the original measure was defeated, as was a proposal in Nevada that would have required virtually all state and local tax increases to be approved by a two-thirds majority of the legislature and a majority of the electorate. Idaho voters rejected a proposal to abolish sales taxes on food.

In one of the most complicated efforts to use the referendum ever tried, Arizona voters were presented with five different proposals, each offering alternate ways to control health costs. The voters, perhaps out of confusion, rejected them all.

Environmental issues drew a predictable response. Voters in the state of Washington passed a proposition urging Congress to overturn a treaty which entitled the Indians living in that state to half of the state's salmon and steelhead trout catch. Voters in South Dakota supported limits on nuclear wastes dumping, while those in Nebraska voted to overturn a state supreme court ruling, thereby lowering property taxes on farmland. Oregon voted by a relatively narrow margin to establish a Citizens Utility Board to give citizens power to control utility rates.

American Political Subcultures

The influence of political culture in electoral politics is not always recognized. American political culture is a synthesis of three major political subcultures that jointly inhabit the country, existing side by side or even overlapping. All three are of nationwide proportions, having spread, in the course of time, from coast to coast. At the same time, each subculture is strongly tied to specific sections of the country, reflecting the streams and currents of migration that have carried people of different origins and backgrounds across the continent in more or less orderly patterns.

Considering the central characteristics that govern each

subculture and their respective centers of emphasis, the three political cultures may be called *individualistic*, *moralistic*, and *traditionalistic*. Each of the three reflects its own particular synthesis of the marketplace and the commonwealth.

The *individualistic political culture* emphasizes the conception of the democratic order as a marketplace. In its view, government is instituted for strictly utilitarian reasons, to handle those functions demanded by the people it is created to serve. A government need not have any direct concern with questions of the "good society" except insofar as it may be used to advance some common conception of the good society formulated outside the political arena just as it serves other functions. Since the individualistic political culture emphasizes the centrality of private concerns, it places a premium on limiting community intervention—whether governmental or nongovernmental—into private activities to the minimum necessary to keep the marketplace in proper working order. In general, government action is to be restricted to those areas, primarily in the economic realm, which encourage private initiative and widespread access to the marketplace.

The *moralistic political culture* emphasizes the commonwealth conception as the basis for democratic government. Politics, to the moralistic political culture, is considered one of the great activities of man in his search for the good society—a struggle for power, it is true, but also an effort to exercise power for the betterment of the commonwealth. Consequently, in the moralistic political culture, both the general public and the politicians conceive of politics as a public activity centered on some notion of the public good and properly devoted to the advancement of the public interest. Good government, then, is measured by the degree to which it promotes the public good and in terms of the honesty, selflessness, and commitment to the public welfare of those who govern.

The *traditionalistic political culture* is rooted in an ambivalent attitude toward the marketplace coupled with a paternalistic and elitist conception of the commonwealth. It reflects an older, precommercial attitude that accepts a substantially hierarchical society as part of the ordered nature of things, authorizing and expecting those at the top of the social structure to take a special and dominant role in government. Like its moralistic counterpart, the traditionalistic political culture accepts government as an actor with a positive role in the community, but it tries to limit that role to securing the continued maintenance of the existing social order. To do so, it functions to confine real political power to a relatively small and self-perpetuating group drawn from an established elite who often inherit their "right" to govern through family ties or social position. Accordingly, social and family ties are paramount in a traditionalistic political culture, even more than personal ties are important in the individualistic where, after all is said and done, a person's first responsibility is to himself. At the same time, those who do not have a definite role to play in politics are not expected to be even minimally active as citizens. In many cases, they are not even expected to vote. Like the individualistic political culture, those active in politics are expected to benefit personally from their activity, though not necessarily by direct pecuniary gain.

States, Parties, and Voter Turnout

While the general rules regarding voter turnout continue to be valid regarding the United States as a whole—namely, that whites tend to vote more than Blacks, people with higher incomes tend to vote more than people with lower incomes, and the very young and very old are less likely to vote than those in between—political culture still has a very strong influence on voter turnout state by state, which is where voting counts in presidential as in other elections. As in the past, states dominated by the moralistic political culture continued to have the highest turnouts, those dominated by the traditionalistic political culture continued to have the lowest, and those by the individualistic fell somewhere in between. This meant that the belt of northern states from the Great Lakes to the Great Basin remained the bastions of the high turnout, joined by one or two of the New England states, while the Southern states continued to have lower than average turnouts.

Two other factors to be considered in looking at the role of the states in the recent election are the changing character of party organization in the United States, and the concomitantly changing character of presidential politics. This is not the place to go into the history of the decline of American political parties over the past generation. It is sufficient to note that reform movements were able to gain control of the party apparatus and, through court decisions, alter the legal framework within which political parties functioned, making them less subject to state regulation and more subject to national party forums. As a result, the American party system was transformed from one of two nationwide confederations of state parties, in which many of the state parties were strong entities, commanding the loyalty of voters and based upon political organizations that could ensure state party control over the political process within state boundaries, to two federations with stronger national party organizations and far weaker state party components.

As state parties grew weaker, they were less able to control the electoral processes within their boundaries, leading to a strengthening of individual candidates at the expense of the party as an entity. Perhaps properly, it was only in those states where party organizations were open and democratic that the organizations have survived in any meaningful way. Where party machines or cliques controlled electoral politics, they were substantially weakened, and open primaries became the rule. So, for example, the Minnesota Democratic-Farmer-Labor party, which from its founding had developed a party organization anchored in broad-based participation from the ward caucus through the state convention, remained a strong party organization relative to its expectations, while the Democratic party in Pennsylvania, which had relied upon a political machine, fell into disarray. In most states, however, a third variant prevailed, like that in California, where earlier state reforms had so weakened state party organizations that neither type survived and control over the electoral processes passed to public relations firms.

By and large, this transformation strengthened the hands of the national party organizations in federal elections but did little to alter state party procedures in state contests. The one exception was the Republican National Committee's program of intervention in the selection of candidates for state as well as federal office as part of the GOP's rebuilding process. The RNC offered campaign services to state and local party organizations. If a state party invited the National Committee to provide those services, it had to acquiesce to an RNC role in candidate selection. In fact, only a relatively limited number of state elections were influenced by those interventions. The national Democratic party, which developed far more elaborate rules for its national institutions involving the minutiae of delegate selection and allocation, paid relatively little attention to state party processes, probably less than the Republicans.

Because of the changing character of presidential politics, as running for president became a full-time job for at least three or four years between elections, it became much more difficult for sitting officeholders to compete for the nomination, since the time it took to campaign would expose them to charges that they were neglecting their present duties. This was even more true in the case of governors than in the case of U.S. senators. While the latter could fudge the issue a bit by moving in and out of Washington and remaining only partially in view as 1 visible among 100, every governor was uniquely visible in his state, and, moreover, charged with a set of responsibilities that could not be put off or avoided without attracting negative attention. As a result, only ex-governors now compete in the presidential race, further separating state and national politics.

The increased reliance on the primary system as a means of selecting presidential nominees, especially when coupled with the decline of state party organizations, has even reduced the role of governors in the nominating process. The old days in which a state party organization would nominate its governors as a favorite son at a state party convention, thereby giving the state party room for maneuver at the national convention up to the last minute, are gone. Nowadays, when people vote in a presidential primary, they vote for serious nominees.

Finally, the introduction of federal financing of presidential campaigns has strengthened the autonomy of individual candidates vis-à-vis all party organization, national as well as state, and has encouraged the development of temporary organizations surrounding each candidate with the concomitant weakening of the permanent party structures. This, too, diminishes the role of state elected officials in party organizations in the presidential nominating process, since candidates need not rely upon them to turn out the vote in the primaries or even the general election in the way they once did. It is true that candidates do seek endorsements of the leading political figures in each state as part of their overall strategy and, where possible, seek such benefits as remain from the support of state party organizations. But these are no longer crucial elements in their campaign, and the ability to mobilize volunteers becomes far more vital than a commitment from a state political organization. While all of this may weaken the role of the states in national politics, it does offer state political leaders an opportunity to develop a serious state politics. This may be one of the antidotes to the governmental centralization which has been a feature of the American federal system throughout the twentieth century and most particularly since the days of the Great Society. If so, this may prove to be another element in the rebirth of the states as polities in the federal system.

The Role of the States as Polities in the Federal System

In recent years there has been a tendency on the part of many, including many decision-makers, to view the states principally as the "middle level" in the federal system. Following the hierarchical principles of contemporary management doctrine, the states are seen as cogs in a pyramidlike machine.

"New federalists" seek to have Washington give them increased administrative tasks. "Urbanists" seek to minimize the states' role in favor of that of the central cities. "Decentralists" want to strengthen the states' management capabilities, while "centralists" want to transform the state governments into shells exercising only those functions which cannot be housed elsewhere. Even friends and leaders of the states have come to accept this definition of state roles uncritically, squaring as it does with the commonly accepted managerial view of contemporary government.

This view is a misperception of the states' true role in the federal system. As such, it has had and will continue to have important consequences in shaping the states' present and future role.

1. *The states as polities*. The true role of the states in the federal system is to function as polities, not as middle managers. The United States, in the words of *The Federalist,* is a compound republic, partly national and partly federal. That is to say, the U.S. consists of a national polity with the whole country for its arena and served by the general government (the nineteenth-century phrase carries much meaning) plus the several state polities, each with its state for an arena and served by its own government. In the words of *The Federalist No. 39:*

> Among a people consolidated into one nation, . . . supremacy is completely vested in the national legislature. Among communities united for particular purposes, it is vested partly in the general and partly in the municipal legislatures. In the former case, all local authorities are subordinate to the supreme; and may be controlled, directed, or abolished by it at pleasure. In the latter, the local or municipal authorities form distinct and independent portions of the supremacy, no more subject, within their respective spheres, to the general authority, than the general authority is subject to them, within its own sphere. In this relation, then, the proposed government cannot be deemed a *national* one; since its jurisdiction extends to certain enumerated objects only, and leaves to the several States a residuary and inviolable sovereignty over all other objects.

The governments of both elements that together compound the republic are complete or essentially complete.

2. *The states as polities are designed to play a political role in the largest sense of the term*. This means that the states' principal tasks are to govern—to make and implement policies within their spheres of competence, not simply administer programs developed outside of their jurisdiction—and to govern the conduct of politics for the republic as a whole. These roles are constitutionally correct and historically accurate. The states are recognized as polities in the federal constitution. When they were at the height of their power, they were actively governing even though they may have done much less administering of programs than they do today. Moreover, until recently, their role in governing the conduct of politics was unchallenged from any quarter.

James Wilson, the Pennsylvanian who was the strongest advocate of a strong national government at the constitutional convention, put it this way in the debate over the ratification of the Constitution: "[There is a] kind of liberty which . . . I shall distinguish by the appellation of *federal liberty*. . . . When a confederate republic is instituted, the communities, of which it is composed, surrender to it a part of their *political* independence. . . . The states should resign to the national government, that part, and that part, only, of their *political liberty*, which, placed in that government, which produce more good to the whole, than if it had remained in the several states. While they resign this part of their political liberty, they retain the *free and generous exercise* of all their other facilities, as states, so far as it is compatible with the welfare of the general and superintending confederacy."

3. *The states' important administrative responsibilities should not suggest that their primary function is managerial.* Quite properly, as the velocity of government has grown, so, too, have the administrative functions of the states increased. This is especially visible in intergovernmental programs, for obvious reasons. Given the current American tendency to think in managerial terms, this has led to a subtle reconceptualization of the states' role, suggesting that it is one of "middle management," functioning within policy parameters set by the federal government with some state discretion in setting the policy parameters for their local subdivisions. (One consequence of this is to encourage federal bypassing of the states wherever Congress or a federal agency wants to set policy parameters for local governments directly.) Thus states are expected to administer, not govern and, indeed, are even chastized if they attempt to act as autonomous governors.

4. *The American system is not a management hierarchy but a matrix of arenas, each designed to be politically responsive to its citizens.* In this respect, federalism is like democracy, which, as George F. Will quoted G.K. Chesterton, the British essayist, as saying:

> "Democracy is not like writing poetry or playing the church organ, because these things we do not wish a man to do at all unless he does them well. Democracy is, on the contrary, a thing analogous to writing one's own love letter or blowing one's own nose. These things we want a man to

do for himself, even if he does them badly." (George F. Will, *Washington Post* 28 July, 1977)

The federal system is not a power pyramid organized on the basis of the federal government on top, the states in the middle, and local governments on the bottom (and, by implication, the people under them all). Rather, it is a matrix of arenas with the federal government framing the whole, the states serving smaller arenas within that whole, and local governments yet smaller ones. While there is a size difference, there are no "higher" or "lower" arenas. Each arena is as important for its purpose as any other. The hierarchical model not only reinforces the notion of the states as middle management but also creates the illusion that policy-making and coordination are best undertaken at the top where things all come together. Under this model, at best, powers are decentralized from higher to lower levels. The matrix model, on the other hand, suggests the reality we all know, namely the constitutionally mandated noncentralized diffusion of powers among the various arenas.

5. *Historically, the states' position in the matrix has been maintained through their political role*. The states were powerful because their governments saw their function as one of governing, not simply administering. Much of that governing was done by legislative policy-making in which the actual tasks of program administration were placed in the hands of the localities. Many of the tasks involved federal-state relations but in a way that recognized the states' proper role.

The states were additionally powerful because the conduct of electoral politics was their preserve. The parties were organized within their boundaries and barely had a national dimension, and the patronage system gave the state and local party leaders control over most federal officials within their jurisdictions. As Morton Grodzins pointed out two decades ago, there is an intimate relationship between the degree of diffusion of power in the party system and federalism.

6. *More recently, there has been a trend away from noncentralization to the view that the federal government should mandate state administrative tasks*. This has taken two forms: congressional legislation establishing programs that the states must implement as if the states were creatures of the federal government, and federal executive or judicial mandating of

conditions which the states and their localities must meet in implementing their own programs. Both of these are reflections of the new view of the federal system as a decentralized pyramid rather than a noncentralized matrix. Two factors have made this possible: a change in constitutional understanding brought about by the courts and the universities, and a decline in traditional party politics with its reliance on state and local organization. It is a tribute to the strength of federalism in the United States and the states in the federal system that, in most cases, noncentralized modes of policy-making and administration still prevail.

7. *The present situation is a kind of standoff; hierarchical assumptions prevail in theory, while older forms of noncentralized government still dominate in practice.*

The Elections and Reagan's New Federalism: The Balance Sheet

After nearly four years of the Reagan Administration, the condition of American federalism is best characterized as ambiguous. This, in itself, represents a great advance for noncentralized government over the situation that had prevailed for the previous fifteen years, during which time the trend was rather unambiguously centralizing. The various "New Federalisms" of the preceding administrations at most sought to replace *noncentralization,* (the constitutional diffusion of power among federal and state, or federal, state, and local centers in such a way that the relationships among them were those of true partnership) with *decentralization* (whereby central government would decide what the states and localities should or should not be doing), even as it relied upon the latter to carry out most federal programs.

The present ambiguity is based upon two trends. On one hand, President Reagan, from the very first moment of his first election campaign, began to reshape American attitudes toward the federal government and the states in particular. The President enunciated a very traditional dual federalist view of the American system, but by enunciating it forcefully, he forced even committed centralists to respond in federalist terms and to justify their extraordinary reliance on federal intervention in those terms. With his flair for communication, President Reagan brought federalism into the headlines, something in a way unequaled by any president in this century.

The Reagan Administration, by its decisive actions in so many fields, has demonstrated how it still is possible to take hold of the reins of government in the United States and begin to reverse presumably irreversible trends—to defy the conventional wisdom that nothing can be done to arrest and reverse the at least 70-year-long thrust toward greater government permeation of society. Yet fulfillment of President Reagan's promise to strengthen the states within that system and thereby strengthen the system as a whole has not been an easy task. In principle, it should be—simply to have the federal government return or turn over certain functions to the states, free certain revenue sources to accompany them, and reduce federal regulatory interventions into state affairs and the process of state governance.

Unfortunately, that is far easier said than done, as successive administrations since the Nixon presidency have discovered. There are several reasons why this is so:

1. Even when there is general agreement in principle, there is great disagreement around the country and even in the administration as to what shall be turned over to the states. This administration is no more immune to this problem than any other. Indeed, its people have suggested new federal interventions almost as frequently as they have federal withdrawals.

2. The states are not necessarily willing to accept added responsibilities. As we have seen at recent governors' conferences, they often have to be forced to be free.

3. There is a reliance on simple notions of striving to separate federal and state functions as a basis for making policy, rather than gaining an understanding of the possibilities of strengthening the states by restoring classic patterns of intergovernmental cooperation. Much of the problem relates to a misunderstanding of the principles of federalism and how they shaped the American political system in better days.

While the Reagan Administration failed to secure the adoption of the most visible portions of its New Federalism program—shifting federal government priorities, reorganizing existing grant programs, and reducing federal domestic expenditures as a proportion of the total federal budget—it did succeed in introducing new attitudes among state and local officials and their constituents. State and local officials learned that it was no longer possible to turn to Washington for solutions to most of their problems, and therefore it was necessary to rely upon state and local efforts and initiatives. All this was accompanied by a shift in the orientation of the federal departments and regulatory agencies in favor of loosening or reducing federal regulation of state and local activities and oversight of intergovernmental programs.

On the other hand, the Reagan Administration did not succeed in restoring anything approximating dual federalism, even in the limited areas in which it made proposals. Quite to the contrary, the general sense that cooperative federalism was the only kind of federalism possible was much strengthened from both directions—that is to say, among those who would have hoped for more federal activity and those who hoped for less.

Worse than that, whenever an issue came forward in which an increased federal role was perceived by the administration to be beneficial to its interests, it acted in what has by now become the usual way of opting for the expansion of federal powers. Two examples of this will suffice: *one*, the federal act allowing double bottom-trucks on most federally aided highways thereby preempting and superseding state standards, and *two*, the enactment of a requirement that states raise the minimum drinking age to 21 or lose a percentage of their federal highway funds. The first was in response to pressures from the trucking industry, an influential force among Reagan backers, and the second was a response to popular pressure, or what seemed to be popular pressure as presented by the media, to do something about drunk driving among teenagers. Since the political payoff was to be found in federal action, the Reagan Administration rose above principle in both cases, as it did in others.

A New Direction

Still, all told, the Reagan Administration has pointed the United States in a new direction. In doing so, it has not generated that new direction out of its own energy so much as it has galvanized and focused a shift that began to be evident even earlier. The idea that new models of intergovernmental, interorganizational, and public/private activity are needed has attracted increasing attention across the entire political spectrum, from Robert Reich's *America's Next Frontier* to Ted Kolderie's look at alternate ways of delivering public services, and from conservative advocates of old-fashioned states' rights to environmentalists interested in the greening of America. Even ten years earlier, similar ideas, whatever their intellectual value, ran against the realities of American civil society.

By the early 1980's, certain shifts in those realities were having their effect. During the postwar generation there was an environmental basis for the centralization which occurred. The nation's economic system became increasingly centralized as locally owned firms were purchased by national (and multinational) corporations. The civil rights revolution led to substantial federal intervention in the educational system. Even organized religion underwent centralization as the various denominations developed strong "national offices" with extensive bureaucracies. The country's communications system, which so influences the public, led the pack toward an almost exclusive focus on Washington as the single center of political power.

More recently, there have been changes in the first three society shifts, and there may be signs of some changes in the fourth as well. While the trend toward further integration of the national economy has not abated—witness the movement to nationwide interstate banking—America's new economic concerns focus on industrial redevelopment and improving foreign markets. Both are spheres in which the states have played and are likely to continue to play a prominent role. Those who are concerned about an American industrial policy are increasingly discovering that they must be concerned with American federalism in their efforts to develop such a policy.

With regard to the educational system, the federal role in everything but civil rights matters had been declining for well over a decade, and since the Reagan Administration, federal intervention in civil rights matters has also diminished. Moreover, criticism of the results of the American educational system, a criticism which has emerged over the past several years, has led to greater involvement of those seeking change in local school affairs and, more particularly, greater state involvement in setting minimum educational requirements and achievement standards. What seems to be emerging is a combination of an increased variety of educational options locally, often on a nonterritorial basis. Both public and private schools offer a greater variety of approaches to education designed to meet the differing needs of different children, coupled with state standard-setting which is designed to set certain basic requirements for all who pass through the elementary and secondary educational networks in the various states.

Noncentralization has come back to the religious sphere with even greater effect. The tendency to transfer power to the national offices of the various denominations, so prominent in the postwar period, had already been stopped by the early 1970's. Since then, the national offices have retreated even further, and the great national seminaries have lost much of their influence. The revival of fundamentalism, which tends to be highly localistic or, failing that, based upon individual evangelists with their own regional or national followings, has increased noncentralization in the religious sphere. As fundamentalists have become involved in politics, they have brought some of that noncentralization with them. Even when they seek national solutions, by and large their national political activity has been devoted to repealing federal policies which interfered with what earlier had been considered issues in the domain of the states, such as abortion policy and school prayer.

Communications is the sphere in which there has been the least amount of change. Political news, especially in the electronic media, still seems to be heavily national in orientation, flowing from Washington and concentrating on the White House. In this respect, the media, following the line of least resistance, have lagged behind the overall trends in American society. In doing so, they have lost the confidence of the American people. Public television, on the other hand, has offered a good model for noncentralized mass communications, with major local stations responsible for programing that is then spread nationwide but remains the product of the original stations. Cable television offers the promise of more public affairs programs that do not originate in Washington or New York, even if as yet their promise has not been fulfilled.

What is characteristic of the new noncentralization is that it does not represent a retreat from nationalization to an older-style territorial democracy but a movement to a new stage which combines territorially based and nonterritorially based actors in a multidimensional matrix. Technological change has made much of the old centralization obsolete, or is rapidly doing so, but the new technology is certainly not restoring the simpler territorial democracy of a more rural age. American civil society is becoming more multidimensional than ever before, having to accommodate people who have embraced different life-styles rubbing shoulders with one another in an urbanized environment, as well as people in different stages of economic growth, with different educational aspirations, religious commitments, and social group expressions.

At first the federal system sought to accommodate this new diversity by ignoring the older territorial divisions, taking the states and localities as administrative vehicles to manage the government activities designed to respond to the new complexities. This has turned out to be an oversimple response, just as those who sought to turn back the clock and reverse in more than modest ways the expansion of the federal government turned out to have offered an inadequate response. For if the system has become too complex simply to turn things back to the states, it has also become too complex simply to rely upon the federal government. There are too many forces in a country of nearly 240 million people spread over three and a half million square miles. States, localities, and sections offer points of identification and expression which have a real vitality in their own right and offer opportunities to deal with a multidimensional society.

It is easy enough to see how this is true in the case of California and Texas. By now it has come to be generally recognized that a state like Minnesota also offers a distinctive way of life, which the institutions of the state foster and maintain. In the last decade, even the people of a state like New York, whose citizens had, in the previous generation or two, virtually abandoned any sense of state identity, have discovered how much their state has a personality, policies, and programs which serve the special needs of New Yorkers.

The Importance of the States

The argument of those who claim that the states are outmoded as polities—that at best they should serve as middle managers, and even then only when they can compete with rivals for that responsibility—usually involves any or all of the following points:

1. The United States is a single nation which has become more highly integrated nationwide over the past two centuries; hence the states are obsolete as embodiments of political aspirations, social character, or cultural distinctiveness.

2. The states are incapable of functioning as polities, having neither sufficient will nor resources to do so.

3. Even so-called improvements in state government have only been as a result of federal pressures, particularly U.S. Supreme Court decisions.

4. Even if the states would and could function as polities, the country is better off with a strong, centralized federal government which will function to promote equality and minimize the impact of local prejudices and passions.

Let us look at each of these in turn:

1. It is precisely because of the nationalization of so many sectors of American life that the states are important. At the very least, they must be strengthened as brakes on the present headlong hurtling of the United States toward a mass society whose ideas are shaped by one-way communication, usually via television, rather than by human interaction in real political and social arenas of the kind which most states can and do provide. The states are vital forces for overcoming alienation, particularly on the part of the politically articulate and active who set the tone for the civil society as a whole.

2. Given what we know about the critical mass needed today to undertake the functions of government and the problems of excess mass when it comes to properly fulfilling those func-

tions, the states turn out to be in an ideal position to become even more important than at any time since before the Civil War. Virtually all states today have attained the critical mass in population and resources necessary to fulfill the functions of domestic governance to the extent desired by their own citizens, whether with regard to those functions which should be provided for every American by virtue of the national consensus, or those which particular segments of the American population, organized in their respective states, wish to provide.

It is important to distinguish between the two. For example, there is an American consensus regarding a certain level of equality when it comes to voting. There is no similar consensus between Vermonters and Californians with regard to the level of public services required for individual comfort. In the latter case Americans should be free to choose whether they want the Vermont or the California model, and there are no better instruments than the states through which to make that choice.

This is not to suggest that the states are perfect instruments; no instrument is or can be perfect. But they are very good political instruments because they are fully articulated polities with decision-making capabilities and proper resource bases. At the same time, the federal government has reached excess mass and can no longer function efficiently to fulfill most of the domestic functions in which it has gotten involved over the past two generations. Most Americans perceive that, which is one reason they elected President Reagan in the first place.

It is important not to underestimate the degree to which each state is a separately articulated polity, with its own history within the framework of American history, its particular sociocultural patterns within the framework of American society and culture, its own laws and traditions within the framework of American law and tradition. While only those involved in state affairs may be aware of these dimensions of statehood, most Americans would become aware of them were they suddenly to disappear. We merely take them for granted because they are not perceived to be in jeopardy. Like so many other very important influences on human affairs, it is not their visibility which is important but their impact.

3. As the Advisory Commission on Intergovernmental Rela-

tions and other public bodies have documented fully, state reform efforts have been massive and principally self-generated. It is true that key U.S. Supreme Court decisions have had an effect on the transformation of certain aspects of state government and on the states as polities, but not always a good or useful one.

U.S. court decisions may have interfered more than they helped in many ways, principally because the states have their own tradition of reform going back to the colonial period, which reached something of a peak in the generation following World War II. Today virtually all states have reached a stage of "modernization" (each relative to its own circumstances) in no significant way inferior to that of the federal government, by virtually every conventional measure. There is no reason to believe that the states could not do whatever they chose to do. Indeed, virtually any one of them could function better as an independent nation than most of the members of the United Nations.

4. There is no question that a federal role is necessary to advance aspects of equality and overcome certain local parochialisms and passions. That is why the United States is a federal system and not a congeries of fifty independent states, or even a confederacy of the kind we had between 1775 and 1789. No one is arguing for replacing the federal system with either. But to say that is not to suggest that centralization is the answer. A proper federal backstopping role, at times pursued actively and at times more passively, will achieve the desired goal without creating a situation in which system overload in Washington is the best possible result, with the worst being deprivation of liberty and the right of self-government for all but a few Americans. That is what federalism is all about, and that is why the states have such an important role to play within that federal system.

President Reagan began his second term by presenting a budget that indicates his intention to press forward his initiative to further reduce the federal role in domestic affairs. Thus, he remains committed to increasing the role of the states but on the basis of "dual federalism" At the same time, his Administration is pressing ahead with its initiative to open the doors to interstate banking, in contradiction to his stand on social issues. In this contradiction, we see the reemergence of a classic nineteenth-century laissez-faire view of the federal system as well as the economy.

There is every sign that Congress, responding to its many constituencies, including most state and local elected officials, will reject many, if not most, of the President's recommendations in this respect, preferring the ''cooperative federalism'' approach as in the past. So the issue is joined. What is encouraging is that both sides start from perspectives conducive to strengthening a more authentic American federalism.

References and Further Reading

Books

Hawkins, Robert B. *American Federalism: Toward a New Partnership for the Republic*. San Francisco: Institute for Contemporary Studies, 1982.

Elazar, Daniel J. *American Federalism: A View from the States*, 3rd ed. New York: Harper and Row, 1984.

Nathan, Richard P. and Fred C. Doolittle. *The Consequence of Cuts: The Effects of the Reagan Domestic Program on State and Local Governments*. Princeton: Princeton University Press, 1983.

Schechter, Stephen L. ed. ''The State of American Federalism 1983.'' *Publius*, Vol. 14, No. 3 (Summer 1984).

Journals

Congressional Quarterly Weekly, especially the November 10, 1984 issue.

National Journal, especially Vol. 10, No. 4, November 10, 1984.

Publius: The Journal of Federalism.

State Government News

6

Economic Issues and Reaganomics

Stephen L. McDonald

President Reagan had several things going for him in his reelection campaign. He was personally popular, and his "stand tall" international policy renewed a sense of pride in America. More importantly, perhaps, the country was at peace as the election took place, and the economy had largely recovered from the recession of 1981–82. This last—a return to prosperity, with more promised for the future—was critical. History suggests that Reagan probably could not have won reelection without it.

It is a commonplace observation that good and improving economic conditions favor the incumbent in presidential races. Less well appreciated is the apparent fact that it is the economic record in the last year preceding the election that matters. In the spring of 1984 Robert J. Gordon analyzed the incumbent vote share for all elections since 1920.[1] He regressed the incumbent vote share on three major variables: the ratio of real output to trend in the fourth quarter of the election year, the growth rate of real output in the four years of the incumbent's term, and the growth rate of real output in the single year ending with the election quarter. Of the three explanatory variables, only the last was statistically significant, and it was highly so. Using the regression equation and the Reagan Administration's official forecast of real growth in 1984, Gordon predicted a victory for Reagan by almost the same margin as that of 1980. (Note that this prediction was published in the spring of 1984.)

To illustrate the principle in the last two elections, the average annual rate of growth of real GNP* during Carter's first three years was 4.4 percent; in the last year of his term, it was −0.3 percent. In the first three years of Reagan's first

---

*See glossary at end of chapter for explanation of terms marked with an asterisk.

term, the annual rate of growth of real GNP averaged 1.4 percent; in the last year of the term, it was 4.9 percent.[2] When one looks at a chart of the unemployment rate under Carter and Reagan, the trace appears thus: Unemployment averaged lower under Carter (6.5 percent) than under Reagan (first term, 8.6 percent), but unemployment *rose* 1.3 percentage points in Carter's final year and *fell* 2.0 percentage points in Reagan's reelection year.[3] Apparently the voter does ask, "What have you done for me *lately,* Mr. Candidate?" Less facetiously put, either the voter has a short memory or he/she tends to project recent experience into the future.

Some Key Economic Statistics, 1976–84

To put the economic factors in the election of 1984 into perspective, it is useful to review some key economic statistics. Data for the Carter period are provided for purposes of comparison, but only on an annual basis. Quarterly data are provided for the Reagan first term.

Table 6–1 contains the basic data for both periods. The first column gives nominal (undeflated) GNP*, which rose from $1,718 billion in 1976 to $3,747 billion in the fourth quarter of 1984. The tendency to rise from period to period was consistent, except for the flat record from the third quarter of 1981 to the fourth quarter of 1982, a period of recession in real economic activity. Much of the period-to-period rise in nominal GNP reflects inflation. As Column 2 shows, the GNP deflator*, our most comprehensive price index, rose from 132.3 (1972 = 100) in 1976 to 226.2 in the fourth quarter of 1984. As we shall see below, the rate of inflation accelerated from 1976 through 1981 and decelerated from 1981 to 1984. When nominal GNP is deflated with the index in Column 2, the result is real or constant-dollar (1972 dollars) GNP, shown in Column 3. Real GNP rose from $1,298 billion in 1976 to $1,657 billion in the fourth quarter of 1984. The rise was irregular, however, reflecting a slight recession in 1980 and a longer and deeper one in 1981–82. Since it is normal for the labor force, employment, and productivity to grow from year to year, a slight recession in real GNP implies a sharp increase in unemployment. Thus, as the fourth column shows, unemployment rose significantly in 1980 and again in 1981–82; it fell during 1976–79 and 1982–84. The rate of unemployment was about the same in 1984 as when Reagan took office in 1981 (7.6 percent), having averaged above that (8.6 percent) for the term as a whole.

· The final column in Table 6–1 is perhaps the most interesting one. It shows real per capita disposable personal income from 1976 to 1984. ("Disposable" means after deduction of personal income taxes.) In 1972 dollars, the figure rose from $4,158 in 1976 to $4,965 in the third quarter of 1984. Again, the recessions left their mark. This measure of income declined in 1980 and again in 1981–82. It rose sharply in 1976–79 and 1982–84. The timing was unfavorable to Carter's reelection and favorable to Reagan's.

Table 6–2 shows *rates of change* in the economic measures reported in Table 6–1. The rate of growth of nominal GNP (Column 1) averaged about 12 percent per year in the more prosperous years since 1976–79, 1980–81, and 1983–84. It was lower, of course, in the recession years, 1980 and 1981–82. Inflation, as measured by the rate of growth of the GNP deflator, was variable, rising from 5.8 percent, 1976–77, to 9.4 percent, 1980–81; then falling to 3.8 percent in 1984. Real GNP (Column 3) grew at highly fluctuating rates, ranging from 5.5 percent, 1976–77, to −0.3 percent, 1979–80, and −1.9 percent, 1981–82, then up to 5.4 percent in 1984. Real per capita disposable personal income grew at relatively rapid rates from 1976 to 1978, somewhat slower rates from 1982 to 1984, and at negative rates in 1979–80 and 1981–82.

The behavior of inflation (Column 2) deserves further comment. Inflation accelerated under Carter and decelerated under Reagan. The latter undoubtedly benefited in both elections, 1980 and 1984, from these facts. Most people seem to feel that inflation is harmful to them, and Reagan could claim with some justification that his policies had brought down the rate of price increase in his first term. Gordon did not include the rate of inflation in his regression analysis, since it did not appear to be important in other research on economic determinants of election results.[4] This omission may have been a mistake. In any case, if the inflation rate had any independent effect, it was favorable to Reagan's reelection. The extent to

Table 6-1

Some Key Economic Statistics, 1976-1984

Year	Nominal GNP (billion $)	GNP deflator (1972 = 100)	Real GNP (billion 1972 $)	Unemployment rate (percent)	Real per cap. disp. personal income (1972 $)
1976	1,718	132.3	1,298	7.7	4,158
1977	1,918	140.1	1,370	7.1	4,280
1978	2,164	150.4	1,439	6.1	4,441
1979	2,418	163.4	1,479	5.8	4,512
1980	2,632	178.4	1,475	7.1	4,487
1981	2,954	195.1	1,514	7.6	4,587
1982	3,073	206.9	1,485	9.7	4,567
1983	3,309	215.6	1,535	9.6	4,671
1981 – 1	2,876	189.8	1,514	7.3	4,548
– 2	2,918	192.6	1,512	7.4	4,530
– 3	3,009	196.9	1,522	7.6	4,593
– 4	3,028	201.2	1,501	8.4	4,572

Period					
1982 — 1	3,026	204.0	1,484	8.8	4,548
— 2	3,061	206.8	1,481	9.4	4,546
— 3	3,080	208.5	1,477	10.0	4,548
— 4	3,110	210.3	1,479	10.6	4,578
1983 — 1	3,174	212.9	1,491	10.4	4,591
— 2	3,267	214.2	1,525	10.1	4,619
— 3	3,347	215.9	1,550	9.4	4,694
— 4	3,432	218.2	1,573	8.5	4,776
1984 — 1	3,553	220.6	1,611	7.9	4,865
— 2	3,648	222.3	1,641	7.5	4,930
— 3	3,695	224.6	1,645	7.5	4,965
— 4	3,747	226.2	1,657	7.3	n.a.

SOURCE: *Economic Report of the President, 1984; Business Conditions Digest*, December, 1984.

Table 6–2

Rates of Change in Some Key Economic Statistics, 1976–1984

Year	Nominal GNP	GNP deflator	Real GNP	Unemployment rate	Real per cap. disp. personal inc.
		(Rates of change from previous period)			
1977	11.6	5.8	5.5	−7.8	2.9
1978	12.8	7.4	5.0	−14.1	3.8
1979	11.7	8.6	2.8	−4.9	1.6
1980	8.8	9.2	−0.3	22.4	−0.6
1981	12.2	9.4	2.6	7.0	2.2
1982	4.0	6.0	−1.9	27.6	−0.4
1983	7.7	4.2	3.4	−1.0	2.3
1981 – 1*	22.1	10.6	10.0	−2.7	0.8
– 2	6.0	5.9	−0.5	1.4	−1.6
– 3	13.1	9.4	2.8	2.7	5.6
– 4	2.5	9.0	−5.4	10.5	−1.6

1982—1	-0.2	4.6	-4.6	4.8	-2.0
—2	4.7	5.6	-0.8	6.8	0.0
—3	2.5	3.4	-0.9	6.4	0.0
—4	3.9	3.4	0.5	6.0	2.4
1983—1	8.5	5.0	3.3	-1.9	1.2
—2	12.3	2.6	9.4	-2.9	2.4
—3	10.1	3.1	6.8	-6.9	6.4
—4	10.6	4.4	5.9	-9.6	6.8
1984—1	14.9	4.4	10.1	-7.1	7.6
—2	11.1	3.2	7.6	-5.1	5.3
—3	5.2	4.1	1.0	0.0	2.8
—4	5.6	2.8	2.9	-10.8	n.a.

*Quarter-to-quarter change at annual rate
SOURCE: Calculated from Table 6–1.

which Reagan can take credit for moderating inflation will be discussed below.

What Reagan Promised

In the campaign of 1980, candidate Reagan proposed a new economic agenda for the United States. At the heart of his proposals was a three-stage reduction in personal income tax rates, 1981–83, ten percentage points at each annual stage, and a lowering of the top marginal rate from 70 to 50 percent. The effective corporate income tax rate would also be lowered, partly by accelerated depreciation allowances for tax purposes. These reductions were seen as not only reducing the burden of government but as stimulating private saving and investment and thereby accelerating growth. The *second* promise was to reduce the size and role of government, partly through deregulation, partly through reduced waste and fraud, and partly through shrunken (social) programs. This, together with tax reduction, would shift resources from the public to the private sector and give greater scope to private initiative. A *third* proposal (and promise) was to enlarge sharply defense outlays in real terms, thereby enhancing our bargaining power in negotiations with the Soviet Union and reversing a perceived trend toward greater communist power and influence in the Third World. This was not to be an economic program per se, but of course it would have economic effects and run counter to the desire to shift resources from the public to the private sector.

A *fourth* promise was to balance the budget by 1984, partly by reducing the size of government, but mainly by raising the tax base through the economic growth that would follow from the greater private saving and investment stimulated by the proposed tax reduction. *Finally,* there was the promise to bring down the rate of inflation, partly by a more restrictive monetary policy, partly by balancing the budget, and partly by stimulating growth of output. The pieces fit together and reinforce each other; they make an impressive whole; they impressed the American voter in 1980.

In the first four years of the Reagan Administration a part of this program has been achieved, and a part of the results desired have been realized. There has been some failure, however, and some results have been realized for the wrong reasons. Let us examine the record to see what we can learn.

The promise to reduce tax rates was essentially kept. The first stage was delayed three months and reduced to 5 percentage points, but a very large, general reduction of about 23 percentage points in personal tax rates was achieved with the help of many conservative Democrats. There was also a massive cut in the effective corporate tax rate, so much so that some of it was taken back in the Tax Equity and Fiscal Responsibility Act of 1982.[5] Increases in Social Security taxes offset much of the benefit of reduced personal income tax rates, but there can be little doubt that tax reductions stimulated consumption and investment by the winter of 1982–83 and helped to bring about recovery from the recession of 1981–82 (about which more later). Tax reduction did *not* increase the saving rate, however. It is arguable, ironically, that if it had done so, the recession would have been deeper and longer, and Reagan could not have campaigned in 1984 in the glow of economic prosperity.

In the Carter years, 1977–80 inclusive, the personal saving rate was 6.0 percent of personal disposable income. In the fourteen quarters of the Reagan Administration through the second quarter of 1984, the personal saving rate was exactly the same, rounded to the nearest tenth of one percent. The gross private saving rate (personal plus business) as a percentage of gross national product averaged 17.0 percent in the Carter years and 17.4 percent in the first fourteen quarters of the Reagan Administration, a difference that is within the margin of error of estimation. The total gross saving rate (personal, business, and government) was 16.6 percent of gross national product in the Carter years and only 14.4 percent in the Reagan period.[6] In 1983, the last full year for which data are available, gross saving was $436 billion (13.2 percent of GNP) and gross private domestic investment $471 billion (14.2 percent of GNP), leaving $35 billion of net capital supplied by foreigners (1.0 percent of GNP). During the Carter years, inflow of foreign capital to finance American investment averaged $6 billion per year, less than 0.3 percent of GNP.[7]

As for the promise to reduce the size of government, Reagan no doubt tried; but he failed. During the Carter years, federal government expenditures increased from $385 billion to $602 billion, an increase of 56 percent. Under Reagan there was a further increase to $895 billion, or 49 percent. In *real* terms, the growth under Carter was from $292 billion to $338 billion (1972 dollars), 16 percent, while the growth under Reagan was to $401 billion, 19 percent. The faster real growth under Reagan was partly accounted for by real defense expenditures, which rose 7 percent from 1977 to 1980, and 20 percent from 1980 through 1983.[8] As a result of still-growing government expenditures combined with large tax cuts, the national income accounts budget deficit* went from $61 billion in 1980 to an estimated $182 billion in 1984.[9] So Reagan fulfilled his promise to increase defense outlays sharply; but in doing so he failed on the promises to reduce the size of government and to balance the budget.

To a very substantial degree, President Reagan delivered on his final promise to bring down the rate of inflation, which was running at over 10 percent per year (GNP deflator) when he took office. After hitting a level of 9.4 percent in 1981, the rate of price increase fell to 6.0 percent in 1982 and 4.2 percent in 1983. It went even lower in 1984, to 3.8 percent.[10] Not only was the rise in final goods prices moderating in 1983 and 1984, but hourly compensation of labor was rising at only 4.3 percent per year, while productivity was increasing at a 3.1 percent rate. Consequently, unit labor costs rose at an annual rate of only 1.2 percent during 1983 and 1984. This is the lowest rate of increase in labor costs since 1960–65.[11]

The decline in the rate of inflation, 1980–84, traces back largely to two factors: the recession of 1981–82 (which we shall examine more fully later) and the rise in the international exchange rate of the dollar, 1980–84. The recession was associated with a decrease in the real demand for goods, increasing spare capacity in industry, and growing unemployment, all of which tend to reduce inflationary pressures. Unemployment weakens the bargaining power of labor, lowers increases in wages and other compensation, and reduces growth of unit labor costs.[12] The trend toward lower price increases continued in 1983 and 1984, despite recovery from the recession, aided by bumper agricultural crops, lower oil prices set by OPEC, and perhaps most importantly, a strong rise in the exchange value of the dollar. From 1980 through the fourth quarter of 1983, the trade-weighted index* of the international value of the dollar rose 42 percent in real terms.[13] This cheapened American imports, reduced demand for American goods, and further depressed the rate of inflation in this country. The rise in the value of the dollar is believed to be due largely to relatively high interest rates here, leading to capital inflow from abroad and strong demand for the dollar in exchange markets. The high interest rates, in turn, are associated with large and growing budget deficits in the United States. Thus the moderation of inflation during Reagan's first term is connected with two unintended events—a sharp recession and record budget deficits.

Reagan was unable to redeem all his preelection promises, but he delivered on those most pertinent to his reelection. Most important was tax reduction, which stimulated recovery from an inadvertent recession and made possible a rise in real per capita disposable personal income from 1980 to 1984, but particularly in the critical year preceding the 1984 election. Also important was the moderation of inflation. Its association with recession and continued large deficits is too complex for the average voter to see, though it was incidental to weaknesses in the Reagan record. Not unimportant was a perceived increase in the nation's military strength and a renewed pride in America. Probably lost on the typical voter was the fact that under Reagan the gross saving rate declined, which helped recovery from recession but reduced the long-run rate of growth of capacity, productivity, and output. Thus the Reagan program as a whole was undoubtedly viewed as a success by the electorate in 1984.

A major part of the Reagan story in his first term is the recession of 1981–82 and recovery from it. The decline in output and employment was, of course, a negative factor, and at the time it sharply reduced Reagan's popularity rating. But the recovery was brisk after the winter of 1982–83, and it more than compensated for the declines in the recession proper. Indeed, the recovery may have been confused in many minds with the faster growth promised for the long run by Reagan and supply-side advocates of massive tax reduction. Let us examine it more closely.

Recession and Recovery

The recession of 1981–82 was caused by a poorly timed restriction in the rate of growth of the money supply in the United States. In 1979–80 the money supply was increasing at about 10 percent per year. This rate of increase, partly aimed at reversing the short but sharp recession of 1980 (which helped do Carter in), was generally recognized as too high to sustain growth without inflation. With the annual turnover of money (called "velocity" by economists) increasing at 3 percent per year, a noninflationary growth of the money supply would have been about 2 percent per year. Given the rapid inflation of 1979–80, it was a little-noted intent of the new Reagan Administration, in council with the Federal Reserve Board of Governors, to bring about a sharp reduction in the rate of growth of the money supply. A cooperative Federal Reserve System (the "Fed") accordingly reduced that rate of growth to 5.4 percent per year from the second quarter of 1981 through the third quarter of 1982.[14] It was thought that this reduction would slow inflation but not shock the economy into recession, particularly in view of the expansive fiscal policy proposed by the President.

But beginning in January 1981, new Fed regulations permitted banks and other financial institutions to pay interest on negotiable order of withdrawal (NOW) accounts. (As a type of checking account, NOW accounts are included in the statistical definition of the money supply.) This increased the attractiveness of money relative to other financial instruments and therefore increased the amount of money the public wished to hold. An increase in the demand for money to hold lowers the annual turnover (or velocity) of money. In fact, velocity fell by 5.5 percent in 1982 and early 1983, almost exactly offsetting the increase in the money supply. Consequently, total expenditure on output (nominal GNP) rose only from $3,009 billion in the third quarter of 1981 to $3,110 billion in the fourth quarter of 1982.[15]

In other words, the growth of expenditure on output went suddenly from +13 percent per year in 1979–80 to essentially zero percent in 1981–82. But due to contractual obligations and cost-of-living adjustments, combined with a slight decline in productivity, unit labor costs continued to rise, at a rate near 10 percent, in 1981–82. The slowdown in demand growth and the resultant profit squeeze depressed output and sent the economy into steep recession. Real GNP fell by 3 percent from the third quarter of 1981 to the fourth quarter of 1982, while unemployment rose from 7.4 percent to 10.7 percent.[16]

The recession bottomed out in the fourth quarter of 1982, and recovery proceeded briskly through the middle of 1984. The stimulus to recovery was provided by a reversal of restrictive monetary policy and the very expansive fiscal policy represented in Reagan's three-stage tax cut. From the third quarter of 1982 through the second quarter of 1983, the rate of increase in the supply of money was 13.9 percent per year; from the second quarter of 1983 to the second quarter of 1984, the rate of increase was 7.1 percent per year. In the meanwhile, the demand for money having adjusted to the payment of interest on NOW accounts, the velocity of money resumed its upward trend of about 3 percent per year. Nominal GNP (expenditure on output) grew 7.6 percent from 1982 to 1983, and 11.7 percent between the second quarters of 1983 and 1984.

As for fiscal policy, a tax cut of 5 percent occurred in the fall of 1981, and further cuts of 10 percent each occurred in the summers of 1982 and 1983—these personal tax cuts supplemented by steep business tax cuts. The result was a stimulus to retail sales, first, and business investment, second, the latter motivated partly by business tax reduction and partly by improved prospects for final goods sales. Real business investment grew at about 40 percent per year between the fourth quarter of 1982 and the second quarter of 1984. Real GNP grew at an annual rate of 7.1 percent in the same period, and unemployment fell from 10.7 percent to 7.5 percent.[17] As earlier noted, inflation continued to moderate in the recovery despite growing demand and falling excess capacity, due largely to low wage increases, improvement in productivity, and the rise in the international value of the dollar. So the economy looked good on the eve of the 1984 election.

President Reagan took care to shift the blame for the 1981–82 recession, attributing it to the high interest rates (associated with high rates of inflation) inherited from the Carter Administration. Actually, interest rates peaked after the middle of 1981 as the Fed decreased the growth rate of money and the public increased its demand for money to hold. This attempt to shift blame is somewhat ironic, for without the deflationary effects of the recession, the tax cuts undoubtedly would have accelerated inflation, and Reagan could not have delivered on his promise to reduce inflation. If only the last year of an incumbent's record matters to his reelection, the recession per se did not hurt him, while the sharp recovery with moderating inflation surely helped him.

The Problems That Remain

As President Reagan enters his second term, several economic problems remain. These include: persistent and perhaps growing federal budget deficits; relatively high real interest rates; large and growing trade deficits;* possible new recession in 1985; and possible rekindling of inflation if recession is avoided.

Budget deficits

In the year Reagan was first elected, the federal deficit (national income accounts) was $61 billion. It rose slightly to $64 billion in 1981, then soared to $148 billion in 1982 and $179 billion in 1983. The estimate for 1984 is about $170 billion and for later years to 1989, even more. The budget adjusted for the business cycle (to take out the adverse effects of recessions) rose from $58 billion in 1980 to $129 billion in 1983, and is estimated at $170 billion in 1984.[18] It is increasingly doubtful that the deficits can be eliminated through growth. Significant reduction requires either deep cuts in discretionary spending or increases in tax rates, or a combination of both. Reagan has reduced his maneuverability by pledging no tax increase, no decrease in Social Security benefits, and no reduction in the increase in defense outlays; he cannot reduce net interest costs, now estimated at $110 billion per year, without a fall in interest rates. Large deficits are likely to be with us for some time to come.

Why are deficits "bad"? It is not because they are inflationary, unless the Fed routinely monetizes them by buying equivalent amounts of government bonds. This the Fed does not do, and will not do. It is *increases* in the cyclically adjusted budget deficit that expand aggregate demand and possibly produce inflation, and the likely further increases are small. Rather, deficits are bad because they reduce aggregate saving, raise real interest rates, divert funds from private investment, and slow the long-run growth of capacity, productivity, and output. To the extent that deficits are financed by foreign capital, they place a burden on future generations without transmitting to them productive capital goods. The deficits we are running now, and promise to run in future, have these adverse effects.

Consider aggregate saving. Total saving consists of personal saving, business saving (depreciation allowances and retained earnings), and government saving. Deficits are negative saving, of course. Given the propensities of persons and businesses to save, negative saving by government makes total saving smaller. It is true that, say, a personal tax cut increases personal disposable income, a part of which will be saved. But a tax cut reduces government saving by the full amount of the cut, while only a part of the increased disposable income (usually 5-7 percent in the United States) will be saved by persons. So a personal tax cut always reduces aggregate saving. It is true, also, that with slack in the economy a personal tax cut raises sales, employment, and income and therefore raises personal saving. But this principle is of no help when there is no slack in the economy and the problem is long-run growth of capacity. Then, less saving means *less* growth of income.

Less aggregate saving, in turn, causes higher real interest rates. The real interest rate (the nominal rate less the rate of inflation) is determined by the supply and demand for financial capital. The lower is aggregate saving, the lower is supply relative to demand, and the higher is the market-clearing real rate of interest. Put another way, deficits divert financial capital* to the government bond market, leaving a smaller supply to satisfy the private demand for capital. Higher real interest rates discourage productive investment of all kinds, from housing to business plant and equipment, and therefore slow down the growth of capacity and productivity. High real interest rates are especially damaging to new housing construction. With nominal mortgage rates at 13 percent and inflation less than 4 percent per year, the current real rate is 9 percent, which is three times the average real rate since the end of World War II.

Real rates would be even higher if it were not for international capital flows. When rates in the United States rise relative to those abroad, foreign capital flows to the United States moderating the difference. But this means we finance a part of our deficits by borrowing from the rest of the world, creating a debt that will burden future generations who must export more and consume less to service that debt.

Growing trade deficits

A further consequence of high real interest rates is international trade deficits, i.e., excess of imports over exports. As noted, relatively high interest rates in the United States attract foreign capital. This increases the demand for dollars in the foreign exchange market as foreigners convert their currencies into ours. Greater demand for dollars raises the price of the dollar in terms of other currencies. This, in turn, raises the price of American goods to foreigners and lowers the price of foreign goods to Americans, decreasing our exports and increasing our imports. If the inflow of capital is strong enough, large trade deficits may be created. In 1984 the United States' trade deficit (goods and services) is expected to be over $100 billion. In 1981 we had a trade surplus of $11 billion.[19]

Our trade deficits must be financed by reduced assets held abroad or increased foreign assets located in the United States. In 1982 American assets held abroad exceeded foreign assets here by $168 billion.[20] We were a net creditor nation by that amount. But since 1982 our cumulative deficits have virtually wiped out that net creditor status. If we continue to run $100 billion deficits in the next four years, we may become the world's largest debtor nation. Then we shall have to reduce significantly our standard of living just to service that net debt. Our present standard of living will have been partly at the expense of that of future generations. As noted earlier, the high value of the dollar and the excess of imports over exports moderate current inflation. Our children may suffer the opposite as they try to cope with a net debtor status because we refuse to pay our bills currently.

New recession in 1985?

In the fall of 1984, before fourth quarter data became

available, the current recovery appeared to be weakening. In the first quarter of 1984 the annual rate of real growth was 10.1 percent; in the second quarter it was 7.6 percent; and in the third quarter it was 1.0 percent. The index of leading indicators*, which usually foreshadows economic activity by about six months, had peaked in May at 168.5, and after fluctuating with a slight downward trend for five months stood at 166.6 in November. Interest rates declined steadily after June as business loans virtually ceased to grow. New housing starts peaked out in mid-summer. The trade deficit was a growing drag on the economy as we increasingly substituted foreign goods for domestic ones. The Fed had allowed no growth in the quantity of money from June to November. There was pressure on the president and Congress to raise taxes or reduce spending, or both, which would further dampen aggregate demand. All signs pointed to at best a "growth recession" (decline in the rate of growth below trend) and possibly a full-fledged decline in output, either of which would raise unemployment and the economic waste that accompanies it.

The fourth quarter of 1984 brought more encouraging news. The quarter-to-quarter rate of growth of real GNP rebounded to 2.9 percent; compared to the same quarter a year before, the rise was 5.0 percent. The Fed accelerated the growth of money to an annual rate of 12 percent. The continued decline in interest rates was interpreted widely as good news, presaging a revival of new home construction and continued vigor in business investment. The stock market, often a forecaster of business conditions, rose sharply in January of 1985. Talk of recession gave way to forecasts of continued growth, at a modest though sustainable rate of 3–4 percent per year, into 1986. Not all of the clouds, however, have gone away. As noted, any sizable action to reduce the deficit at the Federal level will dampen aggregate demand. There is great uncertainty over whether and how Congress will deal with the Treasury's tax simplification proposal. Real interest rates remain high, and the trade deficit continues to grow. If inflation revives in 1985 (see below) the Fed may be constrained to slow the growth of money once again. A recession late in 1985 is still a distinct possibility.

A recession in 1985 and running into 1986 would have mixed political implications. It would increase unemployment, but lower interest rates and inflation. It would worsen the budget deficit, but improve the trade deficit. It might cost the Republicans seats in the Congress in 1986, but insure the election of a Republican president in 1988 if brisk recovery could be engineered in 1987–88. Such are the "what-ifs" and "maybes" of the business cycle.

Possible rekindling of inflation?

To avoid recession in 1985, it may be necessary to postpone budget balancing and to speed up the growth of money; there is now less room for new cuts in taxes. But to avoid a new recession at this stage of the old cycle, a sufficient increase in the rate of growth of money may lay the foundation for renewed inflation and the political malaise it brings with it. This is another dimension of the economic problem facing the administration and Congress in 1985.

In the short run of a year or two, there is no simple relationship between the rate of growth of money and the rate of inflation; real output is often a variable in the short run. But in the long run, the relationship is clear and unmistakable. If there is sustained growth of money at a rate higher than 2–3 percent per year, inflation follows inevitably and in proportion to the difference. This "rule" assumes a slow but steady rise in velocity, but empirical evidence on the relation of money demand to income growth suggests a continuation of the trend in velocity for the foreseeable future.[21] The general connection between the rate of money growth and the rate of inflation is illustrated in Table 6–3.

Generally, as the rate of increase in money has grown from 1960 to 1983, so has the rate of increase in the GNP deflator. The rule is not precise in recession and recovery years because output departs from its long-run growth path in such years. Also, supply shocks, as in 1973–74, can produce spurts in inflation in the short run independently of the rate of money growth. Furthermore, there appears to be roughly a two-year lag between change in the rate of money growth and change in the rate of inflation. Even with all these qualifications, the long-run association of money growth and inflation is evident in Table 6–3.

In 1982 and 1983 the rates of growth of money have been relatively large as the Fed used expansive policy to promote recovery from the recession. If it must fight the tendency to recession in 1985, it is almost certain that the rate of inflation will rise again.

Table 6–3
Rate of Change of Money vs. Rate of Change of GNP Deflator

Year	Percent change from preceding period Money(M₁)	GNP deflator
1960	0.6	1.6
1961	3.3	0.9
1962	1.8	1.8
1963	3.7	1.5
1964	4.6	1.5
1965	4.8	2.2
1966	2.5	3.2
1967	6.6	3.0
1968	7.7	4.4
1969	3.2	5.1
1970	5.2	5.4
1971	6.6	5.0
1972	9.2	4.2
1973	5.5	5.8
1974	4.4	8.8
1975	4.9	9.3
1976	6.6	5.2
1977	8.1	5.8
1978	8.3	7.4
1979	7.1	8.6
1980	6.5	9.2
1981	6.4	9.4
1982	8.5	6.0
1983	9.0	4.2
1984	5.6	3.8

SOURCE: *Economic Report of the President,* 1984, and Federal Reserve Bank of St. Louis, *U.S. Financial Data,* January 25, 1985.

Looking Ahead

There is widespread agreement that as the Reagan Administration enters its second term, the first order of business is to reduce the structural (noncyclical) budget deficit. As indicated above, several of the problems still facing the nation are associated with the deficit—high real interest rates, faltering home construction, the trade deficit, prospective international debtor status, and, not least, restricted long-term economic growth. Faltering home construction and the trade deficit are a drag on complete recovery from the recession of 1981–82; prospective debtor status and lower economic growth promise limitations on our standard of living in the not-too-remote future. The economic legacy that Reagan will leave us depends heavily on what is done (and how soon) about the deficit.

It is also evident that correction of the deficit problem will involve a struggle between the Administration and the Congress, and among interest groups, over what programs will be cut and what taxes will be raised. Tax increases may be mixed with tax reform, further widening the conflict and confusing the issues. On the outcome may depend the political fortunes of individuals and parties for the rest of this century. In particular, the voter realignment that many see in the last two presidential elections could be solidified or reversed by the results of the coming contest over the deficit and its means of reduction.

Much depends on timing. If the premise of this chapter is correct—that it is the economic record in the year preceding the election that really matters—then a speedy resolution of the deficit issue is probably favorable to the election of a Reagan heir in 1988. A large reduction in the deficit may produce a mild recession in the year following; it will be better for Reagan's successor candidate on the Republican side if that recession comes no later than mid-term so that a brisk recovery can be under way in 1988.

More important to the way history will judge the Reagan Administration, however, is whether he can effectively lead in setting the economy of the country on a steeper long-run growth path. Thus far, the record does not support the belief that tax reduction is the way to increase the saving rate and, through that, the growth rate of real output. What is required is at least a balanced structural budget and preferably a surplus. The latter cannot be had without a tax increase. The long-run benefits of a structural surplus in terms of real growth are great enough to offset many times the temporary embarrassment of a "last resort" abandonment of a campaign promise. History will soon forgive such a statesmanlike retreat from principle.

Put more positively, what is required of the president and the Congress in 1985 is a combined tax increase and expenditure reduction that will balance the structural (cyclically adjusted) budget in 1986 and beyond. To avoid a consequent recession the Fed should increase the rate of growth of money to about 10 percent per year during the transition to a balanced budget, then slow it to a non-inflationary 2–3 percent per year once the budget objective is achieved. The immediate consequences to be expected are a fall in real interest rates (with a higher aggregate saving rate and greater liquidity) and a decline in the exchange value of the dollar (with a reversal of capital inflows from the rest of the world). The longer term consequences would be elimination of the trade deficit and revival of export industries, stimulation of capital formation, including new home construction, and a faster growth of productivity and industrial capacity—in sum, a faster growth of real income and welfare per capita. This would indeed be a legacy upon which to build a realignment of voting patterns for the rest of this century.

A Glossary of Some Technical Terms

Budget deficit. The excess of government expenditures over tax receipts in a given year. The deficit is financed by borrowing. The algebraic sum of all past surpluses and deficits is the total public debt. Three deficit measures are in use. The *national income accounts budget deficit* uses concepts and measurement timing corresponding to the national income accounts; it applies to a calendar year. The *unified budget deficit* applies to the fiscal year and embraces transfer programs (such as Social Security) as well as government purchases of goods and services. By this measure, Reagan's first term increased the national debt by $538 billion. The *structural budget deficit* is the calendar-year deficit which remains after allowing for cyclical fluctuations in receipts and disbursements. It is the structural deficit that jeopardizes long-term growth.

Capital. Financial capital is saved funds available to purchase real capital (plant and equipment, houses, inventory).

Dollar–international exchange rate. The number of units of a foreign currency that exchange in the market for a dollar. The greater that number, the higher is the exchange value of the dollar.

Exchange rate—trade-weighted index. An index of the average exchange rate of the dollar, in which different foreign currencies are weighted in proportion to trade effected with them.

GNP—gross national product. This is the market value of all goods and services produced by the economy in a year. Nominal GNP is total product measured at current prices. Real GNP is total product measured at prices of some base period (currently 1972).

GNP deflator. An index of the weighted average of all prices reflected in nominal GNP. The current base of the index is 1972. Nominal GNP is "deflated" to get real GNP by dividing it by the deflator for a given year.

Leading indicators—index. An index of the average of twelve statistical series that typically reach cyclical peaks and troughs in advance of general economic conditions. The index is often used to help predict turning points in the business cycle.

Trade deficit. The excess of imports of goods and services over exports of goods and services in a given year. Such a deficit is a "drag" on current output, as imports are substituted for domestic goods demand. A deficit implies an increase in debtor status, or decrease in creditor status, in relation to the rest of the world.

Notes for Chapter 6

1. Robert J. Gordon, "The Gordon Update," a supplement newsletter (Spring, 1984) for use with Robert J. Gordon's *Macroeconomics*, 3rd ed. (Boston: Little, Brown and Company, 1983), pp. 4–6.

2. *Economic Report of the President, 1984*, Appendix B, Statistical Tables; and *Business Conditions Digest* (U.S. Dept. of Commerce, August 1984), Statistical Appendix.

3. Loc. cit.

4. Gordon, op. cit. p. 5.

5. John L. Palmer and Isabel V. Sawhill, eds., *The Reagan Record* (Cambridge: Ballinger Publishing Co., 1984), p. 111, fn. 4.

6. *Economic Report of the President, 1984* and *Business Conditions Digest* (August 1984).

7. *Economic Report of the President, 1984*.

8. Federal Reserve Bank of St. Louis, *Monetary Trends* (March 1984); and *Economic Report of the President, 1984*.

9. *Monetary Trends* (March 1984).

10. *Economic Report of the President, 1984; Business Conditions Digest*.

11. Federal Reserve Bank of St. Louis, *National Economic Trends* (October 1984); and *Economic Report of the President, 1984*.

12. *National Economic Trends* (October 1984); Gordon, op. cit. p. 2.

13. *Economic Report of the President, 1984*.

14. *Monetary Trends* (September 1984).

15. *Business Conditions Digest* (August 1984).

16. *National Economic Trends* (September 1984).

17. *Economic Report of the President, 1984; National Economic Trends* (September 1984).

18. *Monetary Trends* (September 1984).

19. *Economic Report of the President, 1984*.

20. Loc. cit.

21. Specifically, the income-elasticity of the demand for money is less than unity, so that the demand for money grows more slowly than income (and velocity rises). The resumption in the trend in velocity following adjustment to the payment of interest on NOW accounts suggests the persistence of the postwar income-elasticity.

References and Further Reading

Economic Report of the President, 1984. Washington: U.S. Government Printing Office, 1984.

Evans, Michael K. *The Truth about Supply-side Economics*. New York: Basic Books, Inc., 1983.

Federal Reserve Bank of St. Louis. *Monetary Trends*. Monthly.

————. *National Economic Trends*. Monthly.

Fink, Richard H., ed. *Supply-side Economics: A Critical Appraisal*. Frederick, Mary.: University Publications of America, 1982.

Gordon, Robert J. *Macroeconomics*. Boston: Little, Brown & Co., 1983.

Palmer, John L. and Isabel V. Sawhill, eds. *The Reagan Record*. Cambridge: Ballinger Publishing Co., 1984.

"The Slowdown: How Bad, How Long?" *Business Week* (December 10, 1984), p. 114.

U.S. Department of Commerce. *Business Conditions Digest*. Monthly.

7

"Standing Tall" as a Foreign Policy: Diplomacy and Security in Reagan's Second Term

Cecil V. Crabb, Jr.

The electoral avalanche that returned Ronald Reagan to the White House for a second term has a number of significant implications for American foreign and national security policy. As is customarily true of national elections in the United States, in 1984 domestic issues were at the forefront of public concern. Unemployment, the mounting federal budget, the high level of taxation, the escalating costs of medical care—these were the issues that preoccupied the electorate and, for the most part, influenced the voting behavior of citizens.

As is normally the case with national elections in the American society also, it is difficult to be certain what Ronald Reagan's popular "mandate" means precisely, especially in its diplomatic aspects. American public opinion on foreign policy questions remains characterized by the existence of numerous anomalies and contradictions; and the people are clearer about what they want officials in Washington to avoid than in what they expect the Reagan Administration to do specifically in dealing with issues like the Middle East, Soviet intervention in Poland, racial strife in southern Africa, or political upheaval in Central America.

The Impact of Diplomatic "Lessons"

Yet Ronald Reagan's reelection had several reasonably clear implications for American foreign policy. *First,* the outcome of the 1984 election signified the American people's rejection of the kind of attitude toward diplomatic and national security questions epitomized by President Jimmy Carter's approach to foreign policy issues down to mid-1979. No doubt the "lessons of Vietnam" will influence official and public thinking about foreign affairs for an indefinite period in the future. But the diplomatic record of the Carter Administration added other lessons which left an indelible impression upon the public consciousness, such as the idea that the United States *has* vital diplomatic and strategic interests abroad that it must sometimes protect with military power, and that both the *reality* and the *appearance* of national military strength are essential in achieving favorable diplomatic results.

Moreover, from Ronald Reagan's success in ridding Grenada of a Marxist-based regime and in protecting American citizens there, the lesson was learned (or more correctly perhaps, relearned) that all decisions to rely upon the armed forces for diplomatic ends are not immoral or futile; nor do they automatically lead to "another Vietnam" for the United States. Realistically or not, the American people had been repulsed by the idea, associated with the Carter Administration earlier, that critical national problems defied solution by *any* president.[1]

A *second* aspect of Ronald Reagan's mandate relates to the dichotomous and paradoxical nature of American public opinion on foreign policy questions.[2] Even more perhaps than is normally the case, analyses of public opinion and other evidence of voter sentiment indicate that American attitudes toward foreign affairs are more dichotomous, inconsistent, and incongruous than in the past. The paradoxical quality of public opinion in the United States will unquestionably be one of the most decisive factors influencing President Reagan's diplomacy in the years ahead.

On the one hand, the election of 1984 made clear that the American people have not abandoned their long-standing aversion to the behavior of the Soviet Union and its proxies in Eastern Europe, the Persian Gulf area, Latin America, and other regions. Since the announcement of the Truman Doctrine in 1947, containment has served as America's strategy toward the Soviet Union; and we may fully expect that it will remain the centerpiece of the Reagan Administration's approach to the U.S.S.R. in the future. Public opinion in the United States does not fundamentally disagree with the view of the Reagan White House that Soviet expansionism and interventionist tendencies abroad still pose the primary threat to American security and to global peace and well-being. While the voters obviously favor substantial reductions in spending by the federal government, the American electorate basically accepted record high expenditures for national defense. Moreover, while some sentiment in Congress favors substantial reductions in American troop strength in the NATO area and in South Korea, no evidence can be cited showing that such moves enjoyed any noteworthy public support.

The American people's lingering distrust of the Kremlin and its proxies is also highlighted by experience with the "nuclear freeze" movement during President Reagan's first term. In brief, even the most ardent advocates of an immediate nuclear freeze were in time compelled to admit that only a *verifiable freeze*—the kind which successive administrations in Washington have called for since the late 1940's—is acceptable to a majority of the American people. (With other administrations before it, President Reagan's foreign policy team has become aware that obtaining Moscow's acceptance of a foolproof inspection and control system is an extraordinarily difficult undertaking.) Even by the mid-1980's, relatively few Americans were willing to entrust the nation's security to Soviet pledges and promises of good conduct, especially when evidence was accumulating that the Kremlin's compliance with *existing* arms control agreements was creating rising anxiety among executive and legislative officials in Washington. As spokesmen for the Democratic party conceded after Ronald Reagan's landslide political victory, the American people demanded middle-of-the-road and prudent solutions to national problems; they expected the President and his advisers to "keep trying" in their search for answers to the disarmament riddle, without succumbing to pitfalls like massive unilateral arms reductions by the United States or one-sided concessions to Moscow at the bargaining table.

The Attempt to Revive Detente

Third, the outcome of the 1984 national election underscored the fact that the American people also favor the idea of

Soviet-American détente. Under President Reagan's direction, they want to see American diplomatic initiatives in pursuit of that goal.[3] President Reagan had a preliminary meeting with Soviet Foreign Minister Andrei Gromyko in late 1984. As in the past, the American people nearly always approve the idea of a new heads-of-state "summit" meeting, even if the results of most such conferences in the postwar era have been as ephemeral as "the spirit of Camp David."[4]

At the same time, no discernible public sentiment exists in the United States for unilateral and wholesale American concessions in order to revive détente. The old motto of the Truman Administration—"negotiating from strength"—defines the American attitude today, as in the early postwar period. Recent signs that Castro's Cuba is interested in improving its relations with the United States, many informed observers are convinced, are directly related to the successful application of American military power in Grenada. Nor is Moscow's renewed interest in a resumption of arms control discussions unrelated to the fact that NATO is in the process of strengthening its strategic arsenal.

Moreover, the Reagan Administration has left no doubt that, in its view, the concept of "linkage" is integral to the American conception of détente. Linkage of course is merely a recent variation on the older and familiar principle of "deeds—not words": if the Soviet hierarchy desires more cooperative and peaceful relations with the United States, then it must demonstrate the fact *by its actons* in such settings as Poland, Afghanistan, and Latin America. Yet members of the Reagan foreign policy team must be equally aware that for many years the concept of linkage has been *rejected* by the Kremlin as a component of détente.[5]

While distrust of communism remains high among the American people, it is no less true that strong public support also exists for renewed efforts to improve the overall climate of Soviet-American relations. The people expect officials in both countries to arrive at tangible agreements limiting the arms race, expanding trade and commercial ties, broadening cultural contacts, and taking other steps which will moderate the Cold War. The concept of progress is the American nation's credo, and most citizens expect that it will be made in resolving foreign, no less than domestic, problems. Moreover (and the precedent was established by President Woodrow Wilson in dealing with imperial Germany during World War I), Americans routinely distinguish between the desires of the Russian people—who are, it is assumed, "just like Americans" in their desire for peace—and the aggressive actions of Soviet rulers. As has been expected of chief executives before him, Ronald Reagan must somehow "get through" to the Russian people in his effort to induce them to alter the Kremlin's aggressive behavior.

Americans demand that their leaders explore new avenues toward détente for another reason: the assumption that—for all their ideological militancy and rigidity—Soviet officials are capable of perceiving reality and of engaging in rational decision-making based upon their assessments of it. According to Marxist ideology, dedicated communists are expected to calculate the "balance of global forces" objectively. On that premise, Moscow can only conclude that an unchecked arms race with the United States poses very serious risks for the Kremlin. For the Soviet Union, unrestrained arms competition between the superpowers will likely lead to one of two results. Either the Soviet nation will be severely strained to preserve a position of arms equality with a more productive American society (and the Soviet lag in advanced computer technology has already become evident); or an unchecked arms race may in time lead to catastrophe for those nations involved in it, not excluding, of course, the Soviet Union itself. It is not unreasonable to suppose, therefore, that in their own interests Soviet leaders can be induced to seek a reduction in international tensions and to enter into at least limited agreements with the United States whose effect will be to mitigate the danger of a nuclear holocaust.[6]

Events in recent years have made it incontestably clear that a foreign policy based upon an assumption of rational decision-making by national leaders (including, of course, American leaders) may be an overly sanguine perspective, always involving a calculated risk. Throughout the world, the "irrational" quotient of political behavior is high—and appears to be increasing with each passing year. But what is the alternative to assuming rational conduct by the Soviet hierarchy, especially when it involves reliance upon nuclear weapons to achieve foreign policy objectives? The contrary assumption—that Soviet officialdom is impervious to rational and humanitarian arguments in favor of arms control and other measures designed to avert a superpower conflict—would perhaps foredoom civilization itself to ultimate extinction in a nuclear conflagration.

During his second term, therefore, Ronald Reagan will simultaneously maintain a high level of American military preparedness—with proposed defense expenditures of $286 billion for 1986—while seeking to convince the Kremlin that communist goals can only be achieved by methods which do not risk a global nuclear conflict. This is not a philosophically neat and totally consistent approach to the challenge of Soviet-American relations. Instead, it is typical of the kind of "pragmatic" frame of mind toward diplomatic issues that more often than not characterized Ronald Reagan's foreign policy during his first term. Left-wing critics have frequently complained that it fails to consider the Soviet point of view sufficiently and does not adequately take account of the Russian society's historic preoccupation with security. Right-wing dissidents denounce this approach because it is a "no-win" policy in the global struggle against communism and it leaves the diplomatic initiative largely to the Kremlin.

Yet regardless of such defects, the Reagan Administration's outlook on Soviet-American relations largely accords with the middle-of-the-road propensities of the American people and their desire for moderate solutions to external problems. As the election results indicated convincingly, Ronald Reagan understands the American mentality on contemporary international issues better than most of his critics. He has received overwhelming public approval to engage in sensible and moderate efforts to resolve outstanding differences with the Soviet Union and other diplomatic adversaries. Conversely, Americans demonstrated beyond question in 1984, as in the past, that extremist solutions to national problems have little public support in the United States.

The Presidency and the Foreign Policy Process

Fourth, on the basis of his impressive political victory, The Great Communicator will possess wide latitude during his second term to engage in diplomatic undertakings without seriously risking public repudiation of his activities in foreign affairs. As the Reagan White House's earlier diplomatic misadventures in Lebanon clearly indicated, the voters are less prone to blame a chief executive who "tries" and fails than one who gives the appearance of being immobilized in the face of adverse developments abroad. In retrospect, the era of pervasive national anxiety about the behavior of the "imperial presidency" may well have ended (such fears may always have been more limited than many critics of recent American foreign policy imagined). Even after the Vietnam War and Watergate, the American people continue to look to the White House for diplomatic leadership and guidance.

For reasons we shall examine at a later stage, relatively few citizens anticipate that Congress will provide the required leadership, especially not in the foreign policy field. Americans, it goes without saying, expect the chief executive and his subordinates to adhere to the Constitution and to engage in diplomatic activities that are consonant with cherished American principles and values. As long as the Reagan White House observes such constraints—and the evidence from Reagan's first term indicates that he understands and will observe them—the President can expect broad public support for his diplomatic undertakings.

Fifth, the second Reagan Administration will almost certainly witness the same underlying *continuity* in American foreign policy which, with relatively minor variations, has characterized the diplomacy of the United States throughout much of the post-World War II period. Despite his often intemperate ideological rhetoric, in reality Ronald Reagan has followed a diplomatic course which has been consonant with the foreign policy behavior of the Truman or Eisenhower, or more recently the Nixon or Carter administrations in dealing with a number of specific global problems.[7]

During the second half of the 1980's, the United States will still seek to contain expansionism by the Soviet Union and other communist nations; it will endeavor to preserve the cohesion of the Western alliance; it will continue to assist in the modernization of the Third World; it will seek to promote the cause of democracy and respect for human rights abroad; it will use its influence to eliminate trade barriers and to expand opportunities for American sales and investments overseas; it will endeavor to resolve the Arab-Israeli conflict; it will encourage the emergence of racial justice in southern Africa and other settings; it will support the creation of effective regional institutions in East Asia and other areas—to mention only some of the leading items which have been high on the American diplomatic agenda for many years.

Stated differently, many of the internal controversies over diplomatic issues are concerned primarily with the *means* for achieving these goals. The fact that most of these have not yet been achieved affords convincing evidence that (as in the case of the Carter Administration's well-publicized commitment to international human rights) earlier administrations have not been conspicuously successful in attaining them. A relatively new challenge—devising an effective American strategy for counteracting international terrorism—will demand expertise, intensive efforts by the President and his advisers, and inordinate patience by the American people.

"Dissonance" and Diplomatic Decision-Making

Even before Ronald Reagan had taken the oath of office a second time, his Administration confronted a problem that plagued its diplomatic efforts during the previous four years and that will require the President's attention during his second term. Perhaps more than any administration since World War II, Ronald Reagan's has been characterized by a high and continuing level of "dissonance" or disunity among his diplomatic advisers; and on some occasions, this phenomenon has imposed serious obstacles to the effectiveness of American diplomatic efforts. Fundamental disagreements between Secretary of State George Shultz and Secretary of Defense Caspar Weinberger at the end of 1984 over a broad range of foreign policy questions indicated that the problem still existed—and, by some criteria, it was perhaps even more serious than when Ronald Reagan entered the White House.[8]

Disunity among executive officials over foreign policy issues can be traced back at least to the era of President Franklin D. Roosevelt, who consistently "bypassed" the State

Department in making key diplomatic decisions and allocated major and minor responsibilities in foreign relations to a growing list of executive agencies. What coordination existed among these efforts (and it was often minimal) was provided by FDR himself! A noteworthy attempt to provide more systematic and continuing coordination among agencies involved in foreign affairs was the creation of the National Security Council in 1947, which was expected to blend diplomatic and defense components into a unified "national security policy." In practice—and the tendency was especially pronounced under the Nixon and Ford administrations—NSC operated as a "rival State Department." Under the forceful leadership of President Nixon's national security adviser, Henry Kissinger, the White House staff clearly overshadowed the State Department in the decision-making process; and Kissinger served as the Administration's chief foreign policy spokesman.[9] Conflicts between the White House staff and the State Department were also endemic under the Carter Administration. Ultimately, Secretary of State Cyrus Vance resigned after his views during the Iranian hostage crisis were disregarded by the President.[10]

Ronald Reagan's first secretary of state, Alexander Haig, experienced several encounters with the rival State Department in the White House; he found his effectiveness so impaired that he resigned his position. According to Haig's interpretation of events, Reagan's White House advisers were determined to "protect" him from viewpoints which were legitimate and which he needed to hear before arriving at major foreign policy decisions. In contrast to the Nixon-Kissinger era, however, in Reagan's case very few of his staff were experienced or well informed in the foreign policy field; and the President's own training and experience in that realm were also extremely limited. In some measure, Haig's own personality contributed to his lack of rapport with Reagan's other advisers.[11] By contrast, his successor, George Shultz, apparently enjoys the President's continued confidence; he keeps Reagan fully informed on significant developments in foreign affairs and is able to gain access to the Oval Office when crucial decisions must be made.

Early in 1985, the White House announced that former Secretary of the Treasury Donald Regan would become the new chief of the White House staff in President Reagan's second administration. Regan left no doubt that he believed in the principle of administrative "hierarchy," and that other White House aides would be expected to report through him to the president. Regan's appointment presaged a significant change from the pattern of White House decision-making during Ronald Reagon's first term. Implicitly, at least, the President's selection of a new chief of the White House staff was an admission that intraexecutive disunity had too often hindered his Administration's efforts in the past, and that more effective coordination among executive officials was needed to meet the diplomatic challenges which lay ahead.

Donald Regan's assignment would not, however, be easy. By the late twentieth century, it had become clear that a high level of intraexecutive discord in dealing with diplomatic issues was an integral feature of the American foreign policy process. One contributing factor was the reality that—in a global environment consisting of more than 160 independent nations, most of which were in the Third World—America's diplomatic course of action was inherently more complicated and productive of disagreement than in the early post-World War II period. How *should* the United States react in the 1980's to expansionist moves by North Vietnam, or to growing political instability in the Philippines, or to worldwide terroristic activities by Libya, or to the prospect of mass starvation throughout Africa, or to the escalating foreign debt owed by a number of Third World nations? Such questions usually elicited highly divergent answers, even from well-informed students of American foreign relations.

Basic policy differences, for example, between Secretary of State Shultz and Secretary of Defense Weinberger in the Reagan Administration could be interpreted as high-level attempts to confront and discover answers to a number of questions which had largely remained unclarified since the end of the Vietnam War. A major one is the issue of when it is *legitimate* for the United States to rely upon armed forces to achieve its foreign policy ends. The ritualistic response—that the United States must avoid "another Vietnam"—provides little useful guidance for policymakers, since both American diplomatic interests and circumstances in the Middle East or Central America and other settings are usually different from those existing earlier in Southeast Asia.[12] Nor can the Reagan Administration's successful prevention of communist control of Grenada be generalized into a response applicable widely to other countries confronting a communist takeover.

From a different perspective, "legalistic" solutions to the problem of American interventionism abroad—such as those attempted in the War Powers Resolution of 1973—furnish little helpful guidance when the White House confronts challenges to American security overseas.[13] On the basis of recent experience with the resolution, it is clear that in the last analysis Congress will (however reluctantly) nearly always *accept* the president's determination that American troops must be employed to protect the nation's diplomatic and security interests. The War Powers Resolution, for example, has had minimum relevance for such episodes as the attempt by the Carter Administration to rescue American hostages in Iran and the Reagan Administration's intervention in Lebanon and Grenada. During Reagan's first term, few legislators were intrepid enough to challenge The Great Communicator in a test of public support of his reliance upon the armed forces abroad; and on the basis of the outcome of the 1984 election, they are likely to be even less inclined to do so during his second term.

Chronic disunity exists within the executive branch on foreign policy issues for another reason. During the post-World War II period, external policy questions have become increasingly "domesticized": today, there is hardly a federal agency which does not have some major or minor responsibilities in the foreign policy field. In a crisis-ridden world, the involvement of the Defense Department in foreign relations has expanded steadily; the huge size of the Pentagon's budget virtually guarantees this result. (Yet during Reagan's first term, Secretary of Defense Weinberger was sometimes prone to forget that military force is—or should be—the *instrument* of foreign policy, to achieve objectives ultimately decided upon by the nation's highest civilian officials. This conception presupposes that the White House *has* reasonably clear and consistent objectives abroad—a precondition which appeared to be lacking in the Reagan Administration's diplomacy in Lebanon.)

One by one since World War II, a growing list of executive agencies has acquired major and minor responsibilities in the foreign policy field. For almost two centuries, the Commerce Department has sought to expand American trade and investment opportunities abroad. Today, the Treasury Department is concerned about international monetary and currency questions. The Department of Labor reflects the viewpoints of millions of American workers, a substantial number of whom are genuinely concerned about the effect of imports upon their economic well-being. The Agriculture Department is closely attuned to the attitudes and needs of the nation's farmers, whose prosperity is often heavily dependent upon selling commodities in foreign markets. Even the Interior Department has an official interest in "foreign policy" questions like water use and reclamation projects with Mexico.

Meanwhile, the agency which is nominally charged with administering the nation's foreign policy—the Department of State—has experienced a steady erosion of its influence and prestige since World War II. For some forty years, the department has witnessed continuing encroachments upon its historic domain by other bureaucracies in Washington. The dominant position played by Henry Kissinger in the foreign policy process during the Nixon Administration symbolized this tendency. While no other national security adviser has subsequently exercised Kissinger's influence, it would not be unwarranted to conclude that by the mid-1980's the State Department had suffered a *permanent* decline in its once paramount influence in the foreign policy field.[14]

In some measure, the disunity existing within President Reagan's official family on foreign policy issues reflects the ambivalence in the American public mind we have identified earlier. Judging by their indicated political preference in the November election, the American people want the president to "stand tall" in dealing with foreign affairs, while at the same time avoiding "another Vietnam." They approve an extraordinarily high level of defense spending—but they also want the federal deficit to be substantially reduced (not excluding the Defense Department budget). They want the United States and its allies to preserve access to the Persian Gulf area—but they are wary about American military involvement in Lebanon and other locales in the Middle East. While the Reagan Administration is expected to remember the Vietnam War experience, it is also clear that the American people want the White House to take a firm stand against communist encroachments in the Western Hemisphere.

Every chief executive has his own distinctive "administrative style," and Ronald Reagan is no exception. With little formal preparation for his role as the nation's diplomat-in-chief, Reagan has been heavily dependent upon his advisers during his first term. After four years' experience, his own knowledge of foreign affairs has no doubt improved, and in his next term the President should be able to exert his own influence more forcefully in arriving at diplomatic decisions. Moreover, as the chief executive, Reagan likes to keep his diplomatic options "open" for a prolonged period, giving his aides ample opportunity to debate and discuss controversial issues fully before a decision is reached. This mode of decision-making perhaps inevitably fosters and encourages the kind of dissonance within the executive branch which has become a hallmark of Reagan's diplomacy.[15]

If mechanisms like the National Security Council, interdepartmental committees, and other devices have done little since World War II to create more unified executive efforts in the foreign policy realm, only one other possibility offers hope of providing at least a partial solution to the problem. This is *firm and unequivocal presidential leadership* in dealing with diplomatic issues. This means that after he takes the oath of office a second time, Ronald Reagan will need to assume more direct responsibility for "static suppression" within the executive branch. In an earlier (and admittedly less complex) era, President Harry Truman left no doubt who was "in charge" of American foreign policy—and this realization went far toward making his administration one of the most internally unified in American diplomatic history. Not coincidentally, the Truman Administration also had one of the best records of diplomatic *accomplishment* of any in recent American experience. For reasons which we have identified, today the most even a forceful president can do, perhaps, is to reduce the noise level within the foreign policy establishment, without eliminating such disunity entirely. But unless Ronald Reagan takes this step, in his second term he is likely to find his diplomatic efforts seriously impaired.

An "Assertive" Congress and Reagan's Diplomacy

During Ronald Reagan's next four years in the White House, he will of course be required to cooperate with Congress in order to gain legislative approval of, and funds needed to finance, many of his diplomatic undertakings. On the basis of the election results in November, that could prove in some respects a more difficult challenge than during his first term. Reagan's Republican majority declined in the Senate, which will consist of 53 Republicans and 47 Democrats. Although the GOP gained fourteen seats in the House of Representatives, that body will consist of 182 Republicans and 253 Democrats.

The Reagan White House will confront a Congress in which two potent, but contrary, forces will shape its foreign policy role. One of these—evident since the end of the Vietnam War—is the determination of the legislative branch to achieve a position of full "partnership" with the executive in the conduct of foreign relations.[16] Recent events indicate that there has been some diminution in this tendency vis-à-vis the mid-1970's. Even a number of experienced legislators, for example, now concede that constraints imposed upon the president's authority by the War Powers Resolution have not operated as intended. Ironically, such legislation has in some respects *strengthened* the position of the president in foreign relations. In any case, it would be difficult to identify any significant impact such legislation has had upon the diplomacy of the first Reagan Administration.

Nevertheless, during Reagan's first term legislative attitudes toward foreign affairs unquestionably did influence his diplomatic moves. For example, the decision by the White House to evacuate American forces from Lebanon was taken against a background of ongoing disaffection on Capitol Hill with Reagan's diplomacy in that strife-torn country. Repeated pressure by executive officials upon the government of El Salvador to respect human rights and to implement democratic reforms also stemmed in part from congressional insistence upon such steps. Moreover, executive officials are unquestionably aware of legislative opposition to direct American military involvement in behalf of the *contras* and other forces seeking to overthrow the Sandinista regime in Nicaragua.

The impetus toward congressional assertiveness in foreign affairs will no doubt continue in the years ahead. Members of the House and Senate can be counted upon to bring pressure to bear upon the Reagan Administration to oppose South Africa's policy of *apartheid*; to insist upon respect for human rights and democratic freedoms by governments like Chile, the Philippines, South Korea, Pakistan, and other regimes which have close relations with the United States; to urge the White House to use its influence in behalf of the rights of the Polish people; and to abandon or scale down certain proposed new weapons projects (like the MX missile system).

More generally, it can be confidently predicted that Congress will demand that President Reagan and his advisers engage in more meaningful consultations with legislators *before* they assume major commitments abroad. Legislators will insist that Reagan translate his professed desire for "bipartisanship" in foreign affairs into genuine efforts to involve the House and Senate at an early stage in policy formulation, including keeping legislators informed of significant changes in the external environment which affect the nation's diplomatic obligations. Such sentiments, it is important to emphasize, are not identified merely with Democratic members of the House and Senate. Late in 1984, for example, Senator Barry Goldwater (R-Ariz.) emerged as a leading advocate of reduced defense spending by calling for the elimination of the MX missile project.[17]

If Congress can be counted upon to assert its diplomatic prerogatives forcefully in the future, other currents on Capitol Hill and throughout the nation may well limit and counteract this impulse. According to some criteria, President Ronald Reagan may be in an even stronger position in dealing with Congress after 1984 than was the case during his first term. In the *first* place, the election results indicated a high degree of overall public satisfaction with the Reagan Administration's foreign and domestic policies. As we have noted earlier, extremist positions in foreign affairs—like calls for a unilateral American nuclear freeze, or for the withdrawal of America's military presence from Central America—received no significant public support. The same point can be made of course about right-wing demands, such as the idea that the United States abandon the quest for improved relations with

Moscow or that Washington greatly intensify its efforts to overthrow the Sandinista regime in Nicaragua.

In the *second* place, experience since the Vietnam War has demonstrated that the desire of Congress to play a more influential role in diplomatic decision-making is not matched by its *capacity* to do so effectively. That capacity may be even more limited in the contemporary period than during the 1970's or earlier eras. In the view of many experienced legislators and informed students of the legislative process, Congress has increasingly become a "leaderless" institution which finds it more difficult every year to formulate coherent national policies in both internal and external affairs.

Party discipline is almost nonexistent on Capitol Hill. The old seniority principle has been widely and effectively challenged by junior members of the House and Senate, who are no longer disposed to defer to the accumulated wisdom of their seniors. While the size of legislative staffs has escalated, the principal result appears to have been a steady expansion in the number of legislative committees, subcommittees, and staff members who seek "a piece of the action" in foreign affairs.

Today, nearly every committee of the House and Senate claims jurisdiction over some aspect of foreign policy, resulting in a considerable erosion in the authority and prestige of the Senate Foreign Relations and House Foreign Affairs committees. (As the nation approaches the fortieth anniversary of the landmark Greek-Turkish Aid Program of 1947, followed by the Marshall Plan a year later, it seems questionable whether such bipartisan undertakings could be enacted expeditiously by substantial majorities in Congress today!)[18]

In their approach to diplomatic issues, members of the House of Representatives are in fact engaged in a two-fold struggle: to enhance the influence of Congress vis-à-vis the White House in foreign policy decision-making; and to elevate the House to a position of equality with the Senate in dealing with foreign policy questions. Thus far, the Senate has exhibited considerable reluctance to relinquish the dominant role which the Constitution and precedents for almost two centuries have assigned to it in the diplomatic field.

The record of Congress in recent years in putting the legislative house in order—and after that, in *following* its own revised procedures—is not impressive. Legislative committees and subcommittees continue to proliferate, and effective coordination among their activities remains minimal. According to a number of legislators themselves, the performance of Congress in addressing critical national issues has declined in recent years and shows no sign of being improved.[19]

In the *third* place, in its effort to contest the dominant position of the chief executive in the foreign policy process, during Ronald Reagan's second administration Congress will face other serious obstacles. Committees, subcommittees, and individual legislators on Capital Hill may disagree with various aspects of the Reagan Administration's diplomacy toward the Soviet Union, toward the Middle East, toward South Africa, and in other settings. Yet in the final analysis, as the performance of Congress from 1981 to 1984 demonstrated time and again, legislators will be reluctant *to assume the responsibility* for a major American diplomatic defeat, especially one which jeopardizes the national security of the United States. (Many of Reagan's legislative critics are old enough to remember how for many years the Democratic party was burdened with the politically damaging charge that it had "lost China" to communism.) On several occasions, President Reagan has said that if Congress does severely inhibit his diplomatic freedom of action in regions like the Middle East or Central America, he will publicly place the blame on the House and Senate for any resulting diplomatic reverse. In different terms, to date the President's critics have been unable to formulate attractive alternatives to his diplomatic undertakings, which promote the nation's interests abroad, while engendering widespread public support.

In the *fourth* place—and this may be the most potent constraint upon a forceful role by Congress in foreign affairs—the national legislature continues to rank below the president in the confidence exhibited by the American people toward them. As has been true at least since the New Deal, the American public almost invariably looks to the White House for solutions to pressing internal and external problems; routinely, the people expect the president "to do something" which solves (or at least alleviates) the problem. As The Great Communicator, Ronald Reagan will likely experience no difficulty in using this long-standing behavior pattern to his advantage. Most especially in foreign affairs, Americans expect forceful executive leadership and—as the political demise of Jimmy Carter indicated—they are harsh in their judgments about an incumbent administration which does not provide it.

For many years, studies have shown that Congress enjoys distressingly low esteem in the eyes of the American people—and its performance in the recent past has not improved the record. Even when Presidential popularity is at a low level, it nearly always exceeds the rating which citizens give to Congress as a national institution. Stated differently, most Americans still prefer to place their confidence in *a single individual*—the nation's chief executive—to provide needed guidance in responding to a complex external environment rather than in a collection of 535 legislators who find it increasingly difficult to make Congress into an effective law-making body.[20]

Unilateralism and American Diplomacy

One final challenge facing the Reagan White House in the years ahead remains to be mentioned. It was highlighted by the Reagan Administration's action, late in January 1985, in refusing to accept the jurisdiction of the World Court over the question of political upheaval and foreign intervention in Central America. As a legal matter, the Reagan Administration's position was unquestionably *correct:* no sovereign nation can be compelled against its will to submit a dispute to the World Court or to accept its rulings. Washington also had grounds for doubting whether its case would be heard fairly and objectively by the international judicial tribunal.

As a symbolic matter, however, the World Court episode called attention graphically to a long-standing characteristic of American diplomacy which colors its approach to global problems from Latin America to East Asia. This behavior trait did not originate with the Reagan Administration. One of the earliest and most influential pronouncements in American diplomatic history—the Monroe Doctrine (1823)—was a classic illustration of this tendency. And the tradition has been perpetuated by the Truman, Eisenhower, Carter, and other doctrines of American foreign policy in the post-World War II era.

This is the tendency of the United States to arrive at *unilateral diplomatic decisions* which its allies and friends abroad are expected to support enthusiastically. Unilateral decision-making—or what was called during the long isolationist era, the concept of "the free hand"—has been an element in the American approach to foreign relations for some two centuries.[21]

Diplomatic unilateralism in Washington is a common denominator of several concrete problems demanding the attention of the president and his foreign policy advisers. For a number of years, for example, NATO has been in a state of greater or lesser "disarray." While the reasons for the phenomenon are complex—and the attitudes and activities of the European allies no doubt at times contribute to it—a major cause has been the tendency of every administration from Harry Truman's to Ronald Reagan's to formulate diplomatic decisions unilaterally. Implicitly, the principal contribution expected from the NATO allies is to *support* decisions made by officials in Washington. European officials, for example, recall that during the climactic Cuban missile crisis of 1962, the Kennedy Administration sent emissaries to other governments to *inform them* how Washington proposed to respond to the installation of Soviet missiles in Cuba.

By contrast, it was no coincidence that one of the most conspicuously successful American diplomatic ventures since World War II—the Marshall Plan, launched in 1948 for the reconstruction of war-devastated Europe—was a *cooperative enterprise* between the United States and European participants. At all stages, the plan involved close and continuing policy collaboration on both sides of the Atlantic; and this fact was crucial in accounting for the Marshall Plan's successful implementation.

It may be contended, of course, that this was a unique case and that conditions were especially favorable for a collaborative European-American effort to achieve the Marshall Plan's goals. Undeniably, the sense of common purpose and agreement upon means to attain the goal which marked the experience of the Marshall Plan cannot always be duplicated in other settings. (In the Persian Gulf area, for example, considerable disagreement exists among the nations involved in protecting its security concerning the nature and gravity of the threat or threats to the region. In Central America, many foreign governments and observers are convinced that interventionism by the United States is a primary cause of regional violence and instability.)

Nevertheless, opportunities exist, and should be expanded, for broadening the base of American foreign policy to gain regional and international support for the diplomatic activities of the United States. The determination of the Reagan Administration to "stand tall" in foreign affairs does not necessarily mean that it must *stand alone* diplomatically.

In efforts to preserve the security of the Persian Gulf region; in new attempts to resolve the Arab-Israeli conflict; in negotiations with the Soviet Union on strategic and conventional arms control; in the quest to revive and redefine détente; in Washington's determination to contain communism and encourage democracy in Central America—toward these and other specific problems, American officials need to enlist the support, ideas, and contributions of other nations. If the Reagan team can do so successfully, the probability that the United States will achieve its foreign policy objectives will be improved. And the long-range prospects for global peace and stability will be significantly enhanced.

Notes for Chapter 7

1. See the analysis of Ronald Reagan's electoral victory in *Newsweek*, 104 ("Election Extra," November-December, 1984), pp. 35–37. The evidence of public opinion polls showed convincingly that Democratic efforts to depict the Reagan Administration's diplomacy as "dangerous" and provocative diplomatically failed to convince a majority of the American people. See the poll data cited in *The New York Times* (September 19, 1984), dispatch by David E. Rosenbaum. Preelection polling found that 44 percent of those interviewed believed that Reagan was better able to keep the nation out of war versus 39 percent who believed Walter Mondale was better able to do so

2. A detailed discussion of the diplomatic goals of President Reagan during his second term may be found in *U.S. News and World Report*, 97 (November 19, 1984), pp. 22–24

3. See, for example, the views of an unnamed Democratic

party official, as quoted in *U.S. News and World Report*, 97 (November 19, 1984), p. 38. Yet some 67 percent of a sample of the voters—and 90 percent of those who voted for Ronald Reagan—also said they expected him to make a good faith effort to arrive at a new arms control agreement with the Soviet Union. See *The New York Times* (November 19, 1984), dispatch by Adam Clymer. After the election, a Gallup Poll found that 78 percent of the American people favored an immediate and verifiable nuclear freeze between the two superpowers. See the Baton Rouge *Sunday Advocate* (November 18, 1984).

4. Dichotomies and contradictions in the American public mind about foreign affairs are emphasized in the analysis by T. D. Allman in *The New York Times* (November 9, 1984). This observer believed that by the period of the November election, the American people widely shared the two-fold idea of preserving national military strength in the face of the Soviet threat, while concurrently seeking to achieve Soviet-American arms reduction. See also the analysis of American public opinion in *The New York Times* (October 20, 1984), dispatch by David E. Rosenbaum.

5. During his earlier campaign in 1980, Ronald Reagan had stated several times that no improvement in Soviet-American relations was possible without significant changes in Moscow's international behavior. On numerous occasions during his tenure as secretary of state, Alexander Haig had communicated this idea directly to Soviet officials. See Alexander Haig, *Caveat: Realism, Reagan, and Foreign Policy* (New York: Macmillan and Co., 1984), pp. 31, 105–110, 219–221, 231–232, 242–247.

6. According to several reports, Soviet officials doubted the sincerity of the Reagan Administration in its professed desire for a new strategic arms control agreement between the superpowers. At the same time, Soviet officials had several strong incentives to resume arms control negotiations with the United States. See *The New York Times* (December 14, 1984), dispatch by Leslie H. Gelb; the commentary by Fred W. Neal in ibid. (December 20, 1984); by Paul Warnke in ibid. (December 2, 1984); and the discussion in *Newsweek*, 104 (December 3, 1984), pp. 26–28.

7. A recent study emphasizing the basic continuity of post-World War II American foreign policy is I.M. Destler, Leslie H. Gelb, and Anthony Lake, *Our Own Worst Enemy: The Unmaking of American Foreign Policy* (New York: Simon and Schuster, 1984).

8. The recurrent problem of intraexecutive conflict in the

foreign policy field is examined in greater detail in Cecil V. Crabb, Jr., and Kevin V. Mulcahy, *The President and the Administration of Foreign Policy: the Problem of "One Secretary of State at a Time"* (Baton Rouge, La.: Louisiana State University Press, forthcoming).

9. Henry Kissinger's dominant role in the American foreign policy process during the early 1970's is highlighted in his memoirs, *White House Years* (Boston: Little, Brown and Co., 1979) and *Years of Upheaval* (Boston: Little, Brown and Co., 1982).

10. Endemic conflicts among President Jimmy Carter's foreign policy aides are described more fully in Cyrus Vance's memoirs, *Hard Choices: Critical Years in America's Foreign Policy* (New York: Simon and Schuster, 1983).

11. Alexander Haig's difficulties in trying to carry out his responsibilities as secretary of state are described in greater detail in his *Caveat: Realism, Reagan, and Foreign Policy,* op. cit.

12. By the end of 1984, according to several reports, fundamental policy differences existed between Secretary of State George Shultz and Secretary of Defense Casper Weinberger with regard to several diplomatic issues confronting the Reagan Administration. These included: the strategy the White House should follow in arms control discussions with the Kremlin (and, specifically, whether certain proposed new military projects, like the "stealth" bomber and the MX missile, should be used as "bargaining chips" in these talks); America's reliance upon armed forces to achieve its foreign policy goals; the most effective American response to growing international terrorism, and other questions. See the discussions of intraexecutive conflict within the Reagan Administration in *The New York Times* (December 7, 1984), dispatch by William J. Broad; (December 9, 1984), dispatch by Hedrick Smith; and (December 12, 1984), dispatch by James Reston.

13. A detailed analysis of the War Powers Resolution of 1973 may be found in Pat M. Holt, *The War Powers Resolution: the Role of Congress in U.S. Armed Intervention* (Washington, D.C.: American Enterprise Institute, 1978). Commentary on the resolution's effectiveness after 1973 is available in Cecil V. Crabb, Jr., and Pat Holt, *Invitation to Struggle: Congress, the President and Foreign Policy,* 2nd ed. (Washington, D.C.: Congressional Quarterly Press, 1984), pp. 143–152, 158.

14. The decline of the State Department as the agency effectively "in charge" of American foreign relations under the president's direction is a basic theme of Crabb and Mulcahy, *The*

President and the Administration of Foreign Policy, op.cit. See also I.M. Destler, *Presidents, Bureaucrats and Foreign Policy: the Politics of Organizational Reform* (Princeton, N.J.: Princeton University Press, 1972).

15. During his first term, President Reagan often gave the impression of being "detached" from—and sometimes, uninterested in—the decision-making process. Normally, he permitted full and prolonged discussion among his advisers before arriving at decisions. Reagan has been reluctant to suppress the policy dissonance existing within his official family, even after it had become widely publicized and raised pervasive questions at home and abroad about whether his administration even *had* a foreign policy. Some evidence existed, however, that by the beginning of his second term, the President had begun to realize the seriousness of the problem and was prepared to use the influence of his office to "moderate" such overt disagreements as those between secretaries Shultz and Weinberger. Yet doing so would also impose new demands upon the President's time and energies. See *The New York Times* (December 11, 1984), dispatch by Hedrick Smith.

16. Congressional assertiveness in the foreign policy field, especially since the Vietnam War, is the main focus of Crabb and Holt, *Invitation to Struggle,* op. cit. See also Louis Fisher, *Politics of Shared Powers: Congress and the Executive* (Washington, D.C.: Congressional Quarterly Press, 1981); and Thomas Franck and Edward Weisband, *Foreign Policy By Congress* (New York: Oxford University Press, 1979).

17. As the incoming chairman of the Senate Armed Services Committee, Senator Barry Goldwater (R-Ariz.) announced his skepticism about the MX missile project. See *The New York Times* (December 17, 1984), dispatch by Bill Keller.

18. Forces and tendencies impairing the institutional effectiveness of Congress are examined in greater detail in Crabb and Holt, *Invitation to Struggle,* op.cit. pp. 217–259. See also Phillip Brenner, *The Limits and Possibilities of Congress* (New York: St. Martin's Press, 1983); and Steven S. Smith and Christopher J. Deering, *Committees in Congress* (Washington, D.C.: Congressional Quarterly Press, 1984).

19. For complaints about the performance of Congress—frequently by legislators themselves—see "What Congress Really Thinks of Itself," *U.S. News and World Report,* 92 (March 15, 1982), pp. 22–24; Martin Tolchin, "Howard Baker: Trying to Tame an Unruly Senate," *The New York Times Magazine* (March

28, 1982); J. William Fulbright, "The Legislator as Educator," *Foreign Affairs*, 57 (Spring, 1979), pp. 719–733.

20. Public attitudes toward Congress are analyzed more fully in Crabb and Holt, *Invitation to Struggle*, op. cit. pp. 239–241. In recent years, public opinion polls have shown that popular "approval" of congressional performance tends to range from 19 to 38 percent—nearly always lower than the rating which the American people give to the performance of the incumbent president. *Ibid.* p. 240.

21. The American tradition of diplomatic unilateralism is discussed more fully in Cecil V. Crabb, Jr., *The Doctrines of American Foreign Policy: Their Meaning, Role, and Future* (Baton Rouge, La.: Louisiana State University Press, 1982).

References and Further Reading

Barrett, Laurence I. *Gambling with History: Reagan in the White House*. Garden City, N.Y.: Doubleday and Co., 1983.

Baugh, William H. *The Politics of Nuclear Balance*. New York: Longman, 1984.

Brown, Harold. *Thinking About National Security*. Boulder, Colo.: Westview Press, 1983.

Brown, Seyom. *The Faces of Power: Constancy and Change in United States Foreign Policy from Truman to Reagan*. New York: Columbia University Press, 1983.

Coker, Christopher. *U. S. Military Power in the 1980s*. Salem, Mass.: Salem House, 1983.

Crabb, Cecil V., Jr., and Kevin V. Mulcahy. *The President and the Administration of Foreign Policy: the Problem of "One Secretary of State at a Time."* Baton Rouge, La.: Louisiana State University Press, (forthcoming).

Dellek, Robert. *The American Style of Foreign Policy*. New York: Alfred A. Knopf, 1983.

George, Alexander L. *Managing U. S.-Soviet Rivalry: Problems of Crisis Prevention*. Boulder, Colo.: Westview Press, 1983.

Hoxie, R. Gordon, ed. *The Presidency and National Security Policy*. New York: Center for the Study of the Presidency, 1984.

Leiken, Robert S., ed. *Central America: Anatomy of a Conflict*. New York: Pergamon Press, 1984.

Schwartz, David N. *NATO's Nuclear Dilemmas*. Washington, D.C.: Brookings Institution, 1983.

Steel, Jonathan. *Soviet Power: the Kremlin's Foreign Policy—Brezhnev to Andropov*. New York: Simon and Schuster, 1983.

Stern, Paula. *Water's Edge: Domestic Politics and the Making of American Foreign Policy*. Westport, Conn.: Greenwood Press, 1979.

Talbott, Strobe. *The Russians and Reagan*. New York: Random House, 1984.

U.S. Defense Policy, 3rd ed. Washington, D.C.: Congressional Quarterly, 1983.

Weisberger, Bernard A. *Cold War, Cold Peace: the United States and Russia Since 1945*. New York: American Heritage, 1984.

8

The 1984 Election and the Future of American Politics

Walter Dean Burnham

Some years ago, the authors of that pioneering voting study *The American Voter* proposed a typology of presidential elections. Broadly speaking, there are three types in this scheme: *maintaining* elections, which are dominated coalitionally and structurally by the status quo of that era; *deviating* elections, in which powerful short-term forces produce victories for the minority party or huge landslides for the majority party, but after which things return pretty much to "normal"; and *realigning* elections, where major changes occur in voting coalitions and public policy, and the changes prove later to be durable. Ever since the 1980 election, talk of realignment has been in the air, and not without reason. Some very big changes in public policy occurred in 1980's aftermath, and Ronald Reagan is the most sharply ideologically defined president of modern times.

Nevertheless, 1984 seems much better understood as a maintaining election—an election perpetuating the status quo of the era in which it is situated—than any other variety. As everyone knows, its chief results were the landslide reelection of Ronald Reagan over his Democratic challenger Walter Mondale, and the failure of that personal landslide to be translated into major Republican gains in Congress or at the state political level. All these levels of electoral politics will require some examination. But it seems necessary first to give at least some outline of what this current status quo is, and hence why 1984 seems best regarded as an election falling in the *middle* of a political era rather than beginning or terminating one.

This status quo has several levels. In 1980, public revulsion against the accumulated pains and failures of the Carter Administration led to the first defeat of a previously elected incumbent president since Herbert Hoover's loss to Franklin

Roosevelt in 1932. Ronald Reagan and his conservative allies came to power with a right-wing ideological program, a good deal of which they were able to carry out. This program was essentially a call for stopping the previous rot which had gripped the economy, the empire, the political system, and the culture, a rot which first became manifest not long after John F. Kennedy's assassination in 1963. It amounted not only to a repudiation of the interest-group liberal synthesis that had developed across the preceding 20 years, but a 180-degree turn in public policy. For reasons we shall explore below, the American electorate resoundingly confirmed this changed order—at least insofar as it is embodied in the person of Ronald Reagan—by sweepingly reelecting him.

The repudiation of 1980 seemed to extend a long way beyond rejection of Jimmy Carter. As we all recall, Republicans picked up 12 Senate seats (and control of that body, for the first time since the 1952 election) and 34 seats in the House. And it had been on this basis that the policy "counterrevolution" of 1981 was forged. Much of this ground was lost in the House in 1982, at the trough of the worst recession since 1938, but even there Republican losses were rather less than economic conditions might have indicated, and their Senate campaigns succeeded brilliantly in maintaining the post-1980 partisan balance. In the wake of 1980, there were some legitimate reasons for thinking that a general conservative realignment might be in the works, and on balance the results of the 1982 election left that question open.

As we shall see in some detail, 1984 represented something of an acid test on this dimension. After all, when popular incumbent presidents run for reelection under conditions of relative peace and prosperity, elaborate explanations for their success are hardly necessary. And still more is this the case when, as with Ronald Reagan, the incumbent's exceptional personal qualities as a manipulator of the American symbolic code are joined to the apparent success of his policies in mastering a protracted crisis in the nation's public affairs. But personal majorities are one thing, stable policy majorities quite another. In general, the 1984 election morphologically "fits" most closely with the 1956 and 1972 elections, and far more closely with either than with 1980. The present essay is essentially devoted to exploring this apparent fit and its broader implications for American politics.

If we view the arena of American electoral politics in historical perspective, we can say that the contemporary status quo extends back to some point in the mid-to-late 1960's. In his recent study *The Permanent Campaign*, Sidney Blumenthal has advanced the argument that a critical realignment in fact occurred at about the point—1968—where many analysts had been expecting it.[2] They were, however, looking for realignment in the wrong place. For crucial to this one, and the "sixth electoral era" which he argues followed from it, was a development that was the exact opposite of all previous events of this type. Instead of being channeled through—and thus revitalizing—the political parties, this realignment involved the conclusive marginal displacement of these parties by "the permanent campaign." This is an electoral politics whose activities and motivations at the elite level are structured by the mass media, individual candidates, and their staffs of pollsters, media consultants, and image manipulators. Inevitably, "party decomposition" is the norm in such an era. Volatility over time increases in the nature and identity of voting coalitions, and quite diverse coalitions develop from one level of election to another even at the same time. Congressional elections in this era thus become increasingly disaggregated: partisan swing in seats is continuously damped down, and the electoral advantages of incumbents become ever more overwhelming. As image predominates, the motivations of politicians to conduct serious issue debates, not to say ideological campaigns, disappear. The older linkages between rulers and ruled become ever hazier, ever more problematic. A structural crisis of rule, the "governability crisis" so actively discussed in the 1970's, is also permanently embedded in the politics of the "permanent campaign."[3]

It was this part of the modern status quo which the 1984 election results seem to have dramatically confirmed. This is an important reason for giving a close look to the election as a whole, rather than confining ourselves to the presidential race only. We will first examine presidential nomination politics on the Democratic side, and then move to demographic and attitudinal features of the Reagan-Mondale contest. Thereafter, our focus will shift to the "other" 1984 elections, primarily for the House of Representatives, and then we will attempt to draw conclusions and implications from our tour of this immensely complex event we call a national election.

The Nomination Campaign

The Republicans, of course, had no such campaign. President Reagan and Vice President Bush were renominated by acclamation at the party's Dallas convention—together, for the first time in American political history. No challenge at all had emerged during the primary season extending from February to June. The display of unity was truly monumental, and as is usually the case when this occurs, the party's candidate was very well positioned for the general election campaign.

The Democrats, of course, were an entirely different story. This party can well be regarded as a "party of representation" or a "party of access" for many peripheral groups of Americans whose leverage on the political process is otherwise limited. This, however, has hardly been an advantage when its candidate appeals to the electorate in a general election. The McGovern-Fraser Commission reforms of 1971–72 were adopted to restore the legitimacy of the process after the riotous Chicago convention of 1968. The numerous critics of these reforms have insisted that they paved the way for the nomination of George McGovern and for the rise and fall of Jimmy Carter, candidates who could scarcely have been nominated under the "peer-review" rules of the older order. In 1984, indeed, reflecting the party's extraordinary preoccupation with its rules and their revision, a whole corps of "superdelegates" composed of congressional and other party leaders were added to the delegates chosen in the states. Interestingly, the number of states choosing delegates in connection with some sort of popular primary vote also dropped from its all-time high of 34 in 1980 to 28 in 1984. In the end, this hardly helped. When a party lacks a coherent general-interest theme, fragmentation is likely to ensue in any case, and more or less regardless of rules tinkering. So it was, yet again, in 1984.

It is worthy of note that, in the four elections since the first

process under the new rules went into effect in 1972, there
has only been one essentially two-candidate contest, 1980;
and only one occasion, the same year, in which the Democratic nominee won an absolute majority of the presidential
primary vote. But this *was* 1980, after all. Jimmy Carter was
the incumbent seeking renomination and reelection; and the
fact that he was kept to 51.2 percent by Edward Kennedy's
determined challenge spelled not party unity but Carter's
ouster in November. By contrast, no other nominee (McGovern in 1972 at 25.3 percent, Carter in 1976 at 38.8 percent, or
Mondale in 1984 at 38.2 percent) won as much as 50 percent
of the primary vote.

In this respect, what happened to Walter F. Mondale en
route to his nomination is particularly striking. In the sharpest
contrast to the situation in 1972 and 1976, Mondale was from
beginning to end the candidate of choice among the party's
"peer-review" leaders as well as of organized labor, the
teachers, the National Organization for Women, and other
core interests close to this party elite. This was made clear
from very early on. Toward the end of 1983, much conventional wisdom had it that Mondale would move through the
primaries in a kind of "coronation" procession en route to
overwhelming approval at San Francisco. But by a number of
criteria, this was a strange choice on whom to concentrate. In
the contemporary electoral era, presidential politics is—certainly
for worse rather than better, but inexorably in any case—
ruled by the conventions and operations of the "permanent
campaign." The first rule of such a campaign is that the
candidate be reasonably telegenic and reasonably comfortable
with the electronic media. As Mondale himself commented
following his loss to Reagan, he is neither.

Beyond that, there is another iron and quite obvious rule of
politics. If you want to win an election, never, never nominate the vice president of a repudiated administration. Unless
we except the special case of the Southern Democratic bolt-
ers' choice of John C. Breckinridge in 1860, the first time
this rule ever came into play empirically was in 1968, when
Hubert Humphrey was nominated and lost to a candidate with
striking weaknesses and liabilities, Richard Nixon. That Jimmy
Carter's administration was repudiated, and in some quite
deep sense, was a chief lesson of the 1980 election. This
lesson was visible to professional students of elections and to

the man in the street alike. Yet there have been not a few activists associated with this ex-majority party who seem to have thought that the electorate made a mistake in 1980, that the situation was retrievable when one considered the class warfare being conducted by Ronald Reagan and his allies. Nothing could be further from the truth, as the event proved. Little that one could imagine expresses so clearly than such sentiments and this choice that the Democratic party's leadership utterly lacked any serious social analysis which could explain its political world effectively.

The big "permanent campaign" surprise which erupted in 1984 was the candidacy of Senator Gary Hart of Colorado (and, connected with this and his own image problems, the rapid eclipse of Senator John Glenn's candidacy). As Pat Caddell observed in a privately circulated memo in late 1983, the Democratic party threatened to fracture along a fundamental fault line.[4] The Hart candidacy was to make the threat a reality. In a real sense, though very transmuted in terms of explicit issues, this is the fault line which has separated "New Politics" liberals from the old New Deal core groups and leadership within the party ever since 1968. The New Politics groups are clearly growing demographically as the American social structure continues to evolve radically away from the classic 1940 model. In all sorts of respects, much of the Hart electorate as it came to be defined during the campaign season, forms a kind of bridge between the "Old Politics" Democrats and the Republicans. In a personalized "permanent campaign" setting, candidates, of course, get their votes from many quarters. But typical Hart voters are relatively well-off, younger than Mondale voters, and better educated.

What keeps them from being Republicans? Quite a few of them finally did vote for Reagan in the end—according to *The New York Times-CBS News* exit poll in November, 34 percent of them, compared with 65 percent who remained with Mondale.[5] Within the Democratic ranks, then, this is a significant "swing" group, notably less anchored to the party's nominee than their counterparts in the old New Deal group. Yet what keeps them from being Republicans outright almost certainly is the network of issues of vital interest to middle-class "new liberals," socioreligious issues. In the wake of Mondale's heavy defeat in November and his retirement from politics, it is already clear that a chief intramural issue for Democrats in the wilderness years ahead will be that of finding some effective way of bridging over that "fundamental fault line" which Caddell and many other have identified. This inevitably means finding some candidate who can do this. It will hardly be an easy task.

The Hart onslaught came as a stunning blow to the Mondale forces from the very first primary (New Hampshire, February 28) onwards. Thereafter, the Hart challenge was "contained" in late March and early April as major old-industrial states (Illinois, New York, Pennsylvania) came to the rescue. In the final time periods, the aggregate situation boiled down to a dead heat between the two. Instead of a "coronation parade," at the end Mondale eked out a 38.2–36.5 percent lead over Hart among all primary voters. The time flow is revealed below. (Table 8–1.)

But, as this table duly documents, there was a third force at work too: the candidacy of the Reverend Jesse Jackson. The coalition Jackson sought to forge was a cross-racial "rainbow" coalition of forces which, in any but an American context, would form the nucleus of a socialist movement. In the end, support for Jackson's candidacy was largely confined to Blacks (who were eventually to constitute nearly one fifth of Mondale's support in November, and who constituted about one percent—one hundredth—of Reagan's 1984 coalition), and Jackson himself created an explosive backlash among another core Democratic group, Jewish Americans. Nevertheless, it can hardly be sufficiently stressed that Jesse Jackson represents something quite new in mainstream American politics—something that seems in all probability to reflect an irreversible change with imponderable consequences for the future.

Whatever else seems to have happened in 1984, Jackson emerged from his campaign as the first nationally acknowledged leader of American Blacks since the death of Martin Luther King sixteen years previously. But Jackson's goals and politics reflect a quantum change from those of the civil rights revolution of two decades ago. Cues to this change can be found in the extraordinary salience of foreign policy to Jackson personally and to his campaign as a whole. These foreign policy concerns, which have included embracing Yasir Arafat and securing the release of a Black American pilot

Table 8–1

Democratic primaries, 1984: The Flow of the Campaign

Time Period		Total Vote	Mondale	Percentages: Hart	Jackson	Other
Hart upsurge	2/28–3/13	3,124,220	30.4	35.1	13.4	21.2
Mondale comeback	3/20–4/10	5,560,279	43.6	34.4	19.0	4.0
Home stretch	5/1–5/22	4,954,615	36.8	37.2	21.2	4.9
Super-Tuesday	6/5–6/11*	4,036,293	39.8	39.6	18.4	2.2
Totals**		17,675,407	38.2	36.5	18.5	6.9

* 6/11: North Dakota only
** Excludes Puerto Rico

from Syrian custody, reflect a commitment which is in more or less radical opposition to much American foreign policy in general, and foreign policy under Ronald Reagan in particular. They rest on the conviction that there is a seamless web connecting Black struggle in the United States and Third World struggles of "colored" peoples everywhere—and not just in South Africa, where the tensions and injustices are at an extreme point. The implicit assumption is that there is such a thing as (white) American imperialism, and Jackson is determined to oppose it as part of the same thing which weighs on Blacks at home.

In many ways, American Blacks (and other minorities, such as many Hispanics) are inevitably placed in a kind of bridge or halfway position between a dominant, largely prosperous white America and the often miserable and exploited populations of the Third World. One doubts that this is a matter of preference. It arises, rather, from the domestic and international dynamics of the world capitalist economy and— more particularly—from the fact that Blacks have been among the chief losers from the rise of conservatism among the white middle classes in the United States itself. The Jackson campaign, interacting with Reagan's domestic and foreign policies, has thus substantially *radicalized* attitudes among its followers, and one suspects particularly among Black professional and intellectual elites.

One may suggest a certain analogy, farfetched as it may seem at first blush. The development and radicalization of political consciousness among the Catholic majority in Ireland was the dominant theme in that subjected country's politics from Emancipation in 1829 to the Easter Rising against British rule in 1916. The pivotal figure in this process was Charles Stewart Parnell. In temperament and social background, it would be very hard to find two more different political leaders than Jesse Jackson and Parnell. Yet it seems evident that, if American electoral law was founded on proportional representation, Blacks would have long since organized their own "national" political party. Naturally, they do not have the same possibilities for territorial autonomy that the Catholic Irish had. But it strikes this observer that the functional positions of the two populations in a larger, dominant and "white" political and social system may not be so very different after all. In this sense, we may speculate that

Jesse Jackson is, as it were, the Charles Stewart Parnell of the contemporary Black "revolution" in this country. The implications would be profound indeed if this were even roughly close to the mark—not least for the political future of the Democratic party. In any event, the Jackson candidacy must be regarded as one of the most significant of all the many things that happened in 1984.

Reagan versus Mondale: The Presidential Election

1. *Turnout.* There was never an election in modern times where the issue of turnout and voting abstention was more actively discussed or more the subject of extensive organizational effort than in 1984. For, if one analyzes the location of the "party of nonvoters" in American society and then looks at the demographics of choice among those who do vote, it is clear that Reagan's landslide victory with our contemporary mini-electorate was a foregone conclusion. So much so that, toward the end of the campaign, a leading spokesperson in the Democratic National Committee observed that Mondale could not win with the existing electorate. In the nomination campaign, Jesse Jackson and his allies had been deeply involved in organizing so that Black registration would increase greatly from its usually poor levels. On the other side, the Reverend Jerry Falwell of the Moral Majority and other conservative spokesmen undertook major registration drives among conservative white Christians, especially in the South. This competitive race between polar opposites did spark a perceptible increase in registration as a share of the potential electorate. This went up from 71.6 percent in 1980 to 73.0 percent in 1984.

In view of all this activity, and the slight "aging" of the electorate since 1980, total presidential turnout might have been expected to go up by an equivalent amount. It did not. While the Center for the Study of the American Electorate reports a turnout increase of about 0.3 percent and we so far lack the official return statement of all votes including those for minor party candidates, it seems quite doubtful that it rose at all. The reason, of course, is that the denominator grows quite rapidly across a four-year period: from 159.2 million adult citizens theoretically eligible to vote for president in 1980 to 168.3 million in 1984, a gain of 9.1 million or 5.7 percent. The total presidential vote in 1980 was 86.5 million (54.3 percent of citizen adults, or 75.9 percent of those registered). The virtually complete two-party totals as reported shortly after the election in 1984 showed a total of 90.36 million, or a turnout of 53.7 percent; adding another million for minor party candidates and final two-party tallies would bring the 1984 participation rate to 55.3 percent, identical with that of 1980 and only 74.3 percent of 1984 registered voters. This leaves a "party of nonvoters" of some 77 million Americans, some 24 million more than voted for Reagan.

Barring final and complete returns, commentary on the 1984 participation pattern will necessarily be both limited and tentative. It appears that it went up somewhat in the Middle Atlantic states and most of the South, and sporadically elsewhere. Declines appear to have been particularly concentrated west of the Mississippi, though they appear considerable in some East North Central and New England states as well. The largest increases were in the heavily Black District of Columbia and in heavily conservative-Christian North Carolina. The largest decreases were concentrated in the Mountain States, which have shown particularly strong tendencies toward Republican realignment over the past generation. In Colorado, for example—where full returns are available as of this writing—the 1984 turnout was 53.4 percent of the potential electorate, down 4.4 percent from 1980, and the lowest presidential election participation level since the state's admission to the union in 1876.

The extent to which the 1984 turnout increased but little nationally, despite this frenetic registration activity, can best be appreciated by examining the flow of participation in presidential elections over the past quarter-century. It has long been a truism of voting research that turnout as a percentage of registered voters has always tended to be far higher than turnout as a fraction of the potential citizen electorate. Yet *both* registration and turnout have fallen as a share of this electorate since 1960; and 1984 showed much the largest share of registered nonvoters in this entire period.

Table 8–2 presents the basic information.[6] We can summarize it by saying two things. *First,* registrants reached the highest share of the potential electorate since 1972, though somewhat below 1960 levels; while voting turnout scarcely budged from its modern 1980 low, rising only 0.7 percent to 55.0 percent of adult citizens. *Second,* if we take 1960 as the base, by 1984 3.6 percent of registrants had been lost, as had 12.7 percent of those registrants actually voting, and 15.9 percent of adult citizens actually voting, i.e., in the active electorate. Reagan's landslide, while impressive by most standards, still gave him but 32.3 percent of the potential electorate, compared of course with Mondale's 22.3 percent. While substantial, this fraction of the potential electorate stands below those won by Eisenhower in both of his elections, Nixon in 1960 (and of course 1972), Kennedy in 1960, and Johnson in 1964.

Thus, while it remains true that three quarters, more or less, of the adult citizenry are registered, the abstention rate *among registrants* rose very substantially in 1984. This was, of course inevitable, granted the fact that a 3.3 percent increase in registration was translated into only a 0.7 percent increase in actual voting turnout. It remains worthy of note that President Reagan's 32.3 percent of the potential electorate stood about 8 percentage points below the total of the French potential electorate which Valery Giscard d'Estaing received in that country's 1981 presidential election when he *lost* to François Mitterrand.

Little more needs to be added on this score, except to reiterate that the extreme class skew in American participation, which was strikingly visible and lavishly documented in the published 1980 data, remained virtually unchanged in 1984.[7] As before, the core of the "party of nonvoters" is disproportionately made up of the blue-collar working class (both white and minority), Blacks, Hispanics, and adults in the youngest age cohorts: people who in this society and its politics are peripheralized or marginalized. As before, the core of the active electorate is white, middle class, and middle-aged. These are in the main just the elements of American society to whose cultural values and interests—both economic and geopolitical—Reagan speaks so eloquently. As I have had occasion to point out more than once in the past, the growth of this "party of nonvoters" over the past genera-

Table 8–2

Registration and Voting as Shares of the Potential Electorate, 1960–84

Year	Total Citizen Adult Population (in millions)	Total Est. Registered	Total Vote Cast	Percentages: Regis. of PE	Percentages: Voting of PE	Voting of Regis.	Registered of Non-Voting
1960	105.3	82.5	68.8	78.3	65.4	83.4	37.4
1964	111.6	87.0	70.6	78.0	63.3	81.2	37.6
1968	117.4	90.0	73.2	76.7	62.4	81.3	38.0
1972	136.3	103.0	77.7	75.6	57.0	75.5	43.2
1976	147.7	106.5	81.6	72.1	55.2	76.6	37.7
1980	159.2	115.0	86.5	72.2	54.3	75.2	39.2
1984	168.3	127.0	92.6	75.5	55.0	72.8	45.5

tion reflects, at least as fully as does Reagan's gains among "middle Americans" who do vote, the long-term disintegration of the Democratic coalition which was originally forged during the New Deal.[8] 1984 changes nothing in all this; it just underscores and ratifies it. The full magnitude of the two-way movement out of that coalition into nonvoting on one hand and support for Ronald Reagan on the other will probably come out very clearly when microanalysis is done. The data to do that are not yet available for 1984, but the general pattern is clear enough. (Table 8–3.)

2. *The Active Electorate.* Round up the usual suspects: that, in the main, is how they voted. *The New York Times-CBS News* poll provides an admirably detailed picture of the electorate and its demographics.[9] If we rank-order the leading support groups for both candidates, a very sharply defined picture emerges. Essentially, like turnout, it suggests a study in contrast between the "core" and "periphery" of American society. This contrast is no longer territorially defined, as in earlier eras of our history, but sociologically and economically. (Tables 8–4 and 8–5.)

The figures largely speak for themselves. The complete array of 61 categories in this poll would include some elements—notably occupation and education levels—not included above; but this simply underscores the general collective portrait. Apart from the partisan variable, Reagan's strength

Table 8–3

United States: Percentages of the Potential Electorate Voting, Nonvoting and by Party, Presidential Elections, 1960–1984

Year	Voting	Percentage of Potential Electorate Nonvoting	Democratic Vote	Republican Vote	Other Vote
1960	65.4	34.6	32.5	32.4	0.5
1964	63.3	36.7	39.0	24.5	0.1
1968	62.3	37.7	26.6	27.1	8.6
1972	57.0	43.0	21.4	34.6	1.0
1976	55.2	44.8	27.6	26.5	1.1
1980	54.3	45.7	22.3	27.6	4.5
1984	55.0	45.0	22.3	32.3	0.4

* Estimated

Table 8—4

Twelve Top Reagan Support Groups, 1984

Category	% of Electorate	Reagan	Mondale	Reagan Lead
Republicans	35	92	7	85
1980 Reagan voters	50	88	11	77
Conservatives	35	81	18	63
White born-again Christians	15	80	20	60
Married men, family income $50,000 & over*	..	74	25	49
White Protestants	51	73	26	47
Southern whites	25	72	28	44
Persons family inc. $50,000+	13	68	31	37
Persons family inc. $35,000-49,999	18	67	32	35
Midwestern whites	25	67	32	35
Male independent identifiers	13	67	31	36
Married men	32	65	34	31

is concentrated among people most completely rooted in the "have" segments of the American social structure, and those who—like born-again Christians and white Protestants more generally—are most linked to traditional white social mores. These are whites who are comparatively very well-off financially, Protestant, married, and especially concentrated in the South and Midwest. The Mondale citadels are populated, apart from partisan or 1980 voting categories, among Blacks, Jews, Hispanics, labor, the poor, the single, and the unemployed: marginalized and "have-not" groups. To these should clearly be added another group which is "peripheralized" in Ronald Reagan's America: faculty and students in liberal arts colleges and some state universities (e.g., the universities of Massachusetts, Wisconsin, Iowa, and California [Davis]), where aggregate returns for their localities suggest an average Mondale percentage of 59, a lead of 18 over President Reagan.[10]

This "core-periphery" polarization is highlighted further in

Table 8–5
Twelve Top Mondale Support Groups, 1984

Category	% of Electorate	Mondale	Reagan	Mondale Lead
Blacks	10	90	9	81
1980 Carter voters	31	80	19	61
Democrats (all)	38	73	26	47
Liberals	17	70	29	41
White Democrats	27	68	31	37
Unemployed	3	68	31	37
1980 Anderson voters	5	67	29	38
Jews	3	66	32	34
Hispanics	3	65	33	32
Single men, inc. under $12,500*	..	62	35	27
Union households	26	53	45	8
All, fam, inc. under $12,500	15	53	46	7

*New York Times, December 16, 1984, p. 40

a follow-up report which appeared in *The New York Times* on December 16, 1984.[11] The much-discussed "gender gap," so visible in 1980, partly disappeared in 1984. Despite the presence of Geraldine Ferraro on the Democratic ticket, women swung more strongly to Reagan between 1980 and 1984 than men did. What really looms large in 1984 is the differential between people of both sexes who are married (reported as 67 percent of the 1984 electorate) and those who are single (28 percent). Taken as a whole, Reagan won 63 percent of the married vote compared with 52 percent of the single vote, a differential of 11 points. (The gap between men and women in 1984 closed to 4.5 percent, compared with 8.5 percent in 1980.) In retrospect, this differential makes considerable sense. The contribution to it made by homosexual preferences among some singles is apparently small. Much more central is the fact that many singles are strikingly more vulnerable both socially and economically than are married people. Many of them stand some considerable distance from the Norman Rockwell-style traditionalist family images projected by the Reagan campaign's political advertising, and many of them need the material resources which government programs have provided.

While some significant exceptions can be made to the generalization, on the whole the top and the bottom of the social structure—and liberal-academic communities—did not show very many radical changes between 1980 and 1984. In the case of the Blacks, there was little enough room for swing since as a whole they had split 88–12 for Carter in 1980. But very little movement was visible as well among a wide variety of other groups toward the "top" and the "bottom" alike. Swings to +2 percent or less included, for example, Republicans, all people with a college degree or higher educational attainment, members of union households, people with professional or managerial occupations, black Democrats, Hispanics, and individuals with incomes of $50,000 and above. Reagan's gains were concentrated among Middle Americans, his losses among a remarkably motley collection of voting groups. The contrast is presented below in terms of 1980–1984 two-party swing. (Table 8–6.)

The most noteworthy shifts, perhaps, involve the clearly antagonistic swings involving white born-again Christians on one hand and Jewish voters on the other. This reflects the substantial role played in the Reagan campaign by conservative evangelicals. In the end they gave Reagan 80 percent of their vote; Jewish voters gave him only 33 percent, the latter thus returning to their traditional position as a vital core group in the Democratic coalition. Apart from these, the key groups decisively more Republican in 1984 than 1980 were the youngest age cohort, people of at best low-middle income, white Southerners, and—despite Geraldine Ferraro—women. There was also something of a consolidation of white Protestants around Reagan compared with 1980: not only the 14 percent swing toward him among white born-again Christians, but a swing of 5 points among less evangelically oriented Protestants, yielding a division among the latter of 72–28 in the 1984 presidential vote.

Table 8–6
Percentage Swing, 1980–1984*

Top Pro-Reagan		Bottom Pro-Reagan	
White born-again Christian	14	Some college educated	0
Females, 18–29	11	Easterners	0
All, 18–29	10	Liberals	0
Income, $12,500–24,999	10	Males, 45–59	0
Females, 60 & over	10	Liberal academic areas	0
Females, high school grad.	8	Union households	-1
Females, total	7	Westerners	-1
All, 60 & over	7	Independents	-1
All, high school grad.	7	Professional-Managerial	-1
All, white females	7	Female, 30–44	-1
Male, 18–29	7	Male, college grad.	-1
All whites	6	Hispanics	-2
Midwesterners	6	All, 30–44	-2
Conservatives	6	Income, $50,000+	-2
Females, 45–59	6	Democrats	-2
Males, high school grad.	6	White Democrats	-2
		Males, some college	-2
		Blacks	-3
		Males, 30–44	-3
		Unemployed	-12
		Jews	-13

*Recalculated on a two-party basis for both elections.

Attitudes and "Ideology"

Back in the summer of 1984, Richard Reeves had predicted in *The New York Times* that this would be an ideological election. In the end, it was anything but that on any manifest level. This was so in large part because both campaigns went out of their way to avoid any such confrontation. Reagan's campaign was a classic replication of that well-known incumbents' ploy in economically good and socially quiet election years: "You've never had it so good." Mondale's campaign, on the other hand, swerved from traditional Republican themes—closing the budget deficit, for example—to appeals to the interests of the core groups in the Democratic coalition, to stresses on the unfairness of what was going on under Reagan. In his comments just after his defeat, the candidate admitted candidly that he had never really developed a coherent theme. Without such a theme, ideological confrontation is hardly possible. The Reagan campaign's choice of themes that stressed the voting electorate's economic and psychological well-being was logical enough under the circumstances. The failure of the Democrats to mount a coherent challenge is deeply embedded in the conditions and contradictions that led to Reagan's election in the first place. Had the groups and activists within and around the party resolved those contradictions, someone other than Walter Mondale would of necessity have become the nominee.

The related questions of ideology, polarization, and political realignment in 1984 do not lend themselves to any easy resolution. Whatever may have been the case at some time in the past, the quite consistent message of contemporary survey research has been that the American electorate today is in the main not motivated by ideological considerations. There seems already to be enough data from the 1984 election to give credence to that view—which, as we have said, would in any case be reasonable enough granted the nature of the two campaign appeals. Presidential elections in the age of "the permanent campaign" are largely decided by candidate image, secondarily by the broad issues of the day, and—very much in last place, as a rule—by partisan or ideological considerations.[12] This is hardly to say that the election event lacks structured dimensions or that—as the media so tiresomely argued during the campaign—Ronald Reagan has some quite unique personal magic that overwhelms everything else. What generally is at stake, as such scholars as V. O. Key, Jr., and Morris Fiorina have demonstrated, is that the element of *retrospective judgment of performance* is of prime importance in determining the outcomes of elections generally, and presidential races in particular.[13] Ultimately, it is precisely for this reason that Edward Tufte's two-variable model (presidential popularity and economic growth in the election year) "works" as well as it does, and as it splendidly did in 1984.[14]

When we turn to the attitudinal data reported in the November 6 *Los Angeles Times* poll, reworking and ranking the responses by each candidate's share of the vote in each response category, the attitude structure of the election becomes readily apparent. (Table 8–7.)

Reagan's personal ascendancy stands out in bold relief, both in positive and negative terms. Of the 27 percent of this sample who selected as their reason for voting that "he has strong qualities of leadership," fully 86 percent chose Reagan, and only 14 percent were in Mondale's favor. Put another way, 62 percent of Reagan's voters—compared with 22 percent of Mondale's—gave as their reason either that he was a strong leader or that he was more capable than the other candidate. Conversely, Reagan's largest negative rating (apart from his age) was that "he's not fair to everyone," while Mondale's negative references centered on his perceived weakness (or lack of competence for the job), and there was a surprisingly large bulge of respondents who expressed a generalized lack of trust in Mondale.

One is inclined to suspect a connection between the 38 percent of Reagan's 1980 voters who chose him because "it's time for a change," and the 40 percent of his 1984 voters who chose him because "he has strong qualities of leadership." Certainly, explicit ideology—limited enough in 1980, when 11 percent voted for him as a "real conservative" —played a minor role in 1984 when, according to *The New York Times* account, this had dropped to 3 percent of Reagan's supporters.[15] When one focuses on the personal component of the election, it bears all the earmarks of generalized retrospective judgment: support of an incumbent president in times of relative peace and relative prosperity. It is also worth noting that three-quarters of the group of respondents in the *Los Angeles Times* poll who expressed no issue content at all voted for Ronald Reagan. This too is exactly what one would expect from the "I like Ike" model of the American electorate developed a generation ago by the authors of *The American Voter*.[16]

Yet it might be premature to conclude that nothing has been going on at the level of the mass electorate. It seems to be becoming generally more Republican and more conservative, with a 1980–1984 increase from 30 to 35 percent in both categories. Moreover, the youngest age cohort (18–24-year-olds) went for Reagan by 60 to 39 percent in 1984, contrasted with a 47–42 percent Carter margin in 1980. Needless to say, the youngest age cohorts are both the least participant and the

Table 8-7
Attitudes Toward Candidates and Issues

I. One's Own Choice: Why Did You Vote for Him?

Response	% of Total	% of Vote in Category Mondale	Reagan
He will stand up to Russians	3	12	88
He has strong qualities of leadership	27	14	86
He is more capable	18	33	67
He has a better vice president	4	40	60
He has a clearer vision of the future	15	52	48
He's my party's candidate	7	65	35
He cares about people like me	19	68	32
He impressed me in the debates	7	73	27

II. The Opposition: What Do You Like Least about Him?

	% of Total	% of Negative Comments Mondale	Reagan
He's wishy-washy	14	82	18
He's too tied to the past	7	77	23
He can't handle the job	17	75	25
I don't really trust him	24	69	31
He has too many ties to special interests	15	60	40

	% of Total	% of Vote in Category	
		Mondale	Reagan
He's not fair to everyone	18	17	83
He's too old	5	12	88

III. The Most Important Issues: Pro-Reagan to Pro-Mondale
(Respondents could check 2 boxes)

	% of Total	% of Vote in Category	
		Mondale	Reagan
Inflation	17	16	84
Taxes	17	20	80
No issue content	12	25	75
Government spending	22	31	69
Foreign relations	19	33	67
Farm problems	4	47	53
Budget deficit	19	51	49
Unemployment	14	57	43
Nuclear arms control	18	67	33
Environmental protection	4	73	27
Civil rights	12	74	26

SOURCE: Los Angeles Times Exit Poll, November 6, 1984.

most politically volatile, for fairly obvious reasons. Still, the 1980–1984 two-party swing among this entrant group (not necessarily the same people, of course) was 14 percent, placing it at the very top of identifiable group movements. The Democrats might well be alarmed at the prospect that they may be losing their future as they contemplate this and a parallel datum: 39 percent of first-time voters professed Republican party identification, compared with 34 percent identifying themselves as Democrats.

The issue profiles in the *Los Angeles Times* survey seem also to be telling us a coherent, structured story. Among voters for both candidates who selected issues, fully 84 percent of those concerned with inflation voted for Reagan, and almost as many—80 percent—of those expressing concern with taxes. Issues whose choosers gave a majority to Mondale were unemployment, nuclear arms control, environmental protection, and civil rights. These are of course issues central to the core of the modern Democratic party and its collection of "out-groups." In the budget battles which will be shaping up very shortly, a major Reagan asset is surely the—to be sure, often generalized—support which he has within his core coalition for keeping inflation low, not raising taxes, and reducing or at least freezing government spending.

We may briefly note the distribution of candidate support among those who chose inflation and unemployment as major issues. By now, the polar trade-offs between unemployment and inflation are well known to the scholarly literature as essentially a "left-right," class-linked issue set. As Hibbs and others have pointed out, people who suffer or fear unemployment most are concentrated in the working classes, while those who are more concerned by inflation tend to be in middle- or upper-class brackets.[17] The latter, of course, need rather rarely fear being thrown out of work; but they are concerned about the erosion of their nominal incomes and investments.[18]

Thus, it is hardly surprising that the inflation-concerned group gave nearly five out of six of their votes to a man whose policies brought the inflation rate down from the double digits of 1980 and 1981 to the 4 percent of 1984. It might at first blush be rather more surprising that Mondale won only 57 percent of the votes of those who were concerned with unemployment. When the appropriate professional work is done on relating these issue concerns with the personalism of choice in a candidate-dominated election, the strength of Reagan's personal image and the weakness of Mondale's will probably be found to account for much of the difference. For in the United States there really is no organized left, which is why Hibbs was able to observe that this political system is markedly more tolerant of unemployment and intolerant of inflation than are its West European counterparts. In such a setting, the active electorate is much more middle class in its composition than is the adult population as a whole. And, as the entire setting and results of the 1984 election demonstrated, the conservative right is much more unified than are the forces which are on the left or center of this political spectrum.

This discussion of attitudes would not be entirely complete without some discussion of so-called "social issues," i.e., those associated with the so-called "religious right."[19] Evidence available at this time of writing is relatively scanty. There is little doubt that Ronald Reagan was the vastly preferred candidate of white Protestants as a whole, and especially (as we have seen) of white born-again Christians. *The New York Times-CBS News* survey indicates that fully 19 percent of respondents selected "traditional values" (not mentioned in the *Los Angeles Times* poll counterpart) as a major reason for their presidential choice (each respondent was allowed two choices). This ranked fourth, following "experience" (27 percent); and it appears that about 70 percent of those responding with this category voted for Reagan. "Traditional values," however, can cover a wide variety of things in the American-value pantheon—from the Norman Rockwell nuclear family to free enterprise, limited government, or other elements.

In general, the Reverend Jerry Falwell of the Moral Majority has produced a consistently negative impression in public-opinion surveys ever since he appeared on the national political scene. This is duly confirmed in the *Los Angeles Times* survey, showing indeed more negative than positive sentiments even among Reagan voters. On the other hand, of the respondents who did have a positive opinion of the Reverend Falwell (16 percent of the total), 86 percent voted for Ronald Reagan, compared with 43 percent among those with a negative opinion of him (46 percent of the sample). The intense energy and dedication found among Moral Majority people, many other born-again Christians, and such denominations as the Mormons may well give them a positive electoral and political importance to the Reagan cause out of all proportion to their actual numbers. The political significance of intense minorities is a well-known fact of life in pluralist systems.

By the same token, it is noteworthy that only 23 percent of this poll's respondents supported a constitutional amendment to prohibit abortion (only 32 percent of Reagan's supporters did so, compared with 12 percent of Mondale's). On the other hand, among all who expressed support for this proposal, 21 percent voted for Mondale and 79 percent voted for Reagan, a deviation of 20 percentage points from the national average. Moreover, in Colorado this November the voters were presented with a referendum calling for the elimination of all state funds to pay for abortions. More people, 23,046, actually voted on this question than voted for president, and the proposal narrowly won by a vote of 627,067 to 616,815. It is quite characteristic, perhaps, that when the percentage voting yes for this question is regressed on Reagan's percentage of the two-party presidential vote, the correlation coefficient is only a very feeble .123, thus "explaining" only 1.5 percent of the variance in Reagan's vote across the state's 63 counties.

It is of course very hard to see how such limited support for an antiabortion amendment as survey data displays could be parlayed into the actual adoption of one. For this would require a concurrence of two thirds of both houses of Congress and three fourths of the states. But about that, two things can be said. First, there is always the historical precedent of nationwide Prohibition to consider, an event unthinkable at any time prior to 1917. Secondly, there are deeply felt moral issues that will simply not go away, and this seems to be one of them. The abortion issue energizes one more passionate minority which, once probably evenly divided between the parties if not as a rule Democratic, turned up in Ronald Reagan's conservative coalition by a margin of four to one. Led by committed members of the Roman Catholic hierarchy and many evangelical Protestant leaders, the antiabortion movement shows some promise of remaining a longterm barricade in the path of Democratic presidential candidates.

In general, it seems clear that the religious dimension in

the 1984 campaign was much less salient than the state of the economy, the images of the candidates, and, perhaps, the international issues as well. Yet the contribution of the religious right and its allies to the 1984 campaign was patent and at times—as with the confrontation between Roman Catholic Archbishop John O'Connor of New York and Democratic vice presidential candidate Geraldine Ferraro—quite spectacular. These forces represent a major and powerful buttress of the American politico-economic right, even though there are many conservatives on secular issues who are anything but comfortable with Moral Majority spokesmen. It is worth remembering, for example, that if born-again white Christians and Jews swung equally strongly but in opposite directions, there are five times as many of the former in the American electorate as of the latter. It may happen, as it has happened before in American history, that the relative salience of such groups will decline as traditionalist revitalization proceeds. In that case, Reagan's very success as revitalizer will in this respect come to be seen as a self-liquidating enterprise. In the meantime, most of the passion, organizing talent, and other resources on these questions are concentrated on one side, and their sectoral importance to the Reaganite political synthesis should not, therefore, be lightly dismissed.

The Other 1984 Elections and the "Mandate" Issue

Ronald Reagan's presidential victory over Walter Mondale, while not the largest landslide in our recent history, was notable for its remarkable sweep across white America, from Maine to California and from Michigan to Alabama. Thus, one of the records achieved in 1984 was that it showed the smallest cross-state (i.e., regional) variance in the presidential vote in more than a century.[20] Even as late as the New Deal period, the existence of the solid Democratic South had meant a high degree of regional variations in outcomes. By 1984, the overwhelming impression, which aggregate statistical data analysis confirms, is one of striking uniformity of result across the whole country. As good a way as any of underscoring this point is to recall that Reagan missed by only a couple of thousand votes (in Minnesota) of achieving an electoral vote sweep of all the states. The final Mondale margin over Reagan in the former's home state was 3,761 votes out of more than 2 million cast; thus a net switch of 1,881 votes (1/2 + 1 of the margin) would have carried the state for Reagan. At the presidential level, surely, American politics has now become fully "nationalized."

Democratic politicians can only regard the electoral situation at this level with gloom, if not desperation; for there is now very little doubt that the country has become "normally" Republican in presidential elections. Yet Republicans have considerable reason for concern at other levels of electoral politics. They too were disappointed with the election's outcome. Despite the breadth of Reagan's personal victory over Mondale, Democrats lost only 14 or 15 seats in the congressional elections,[21] and actually made a net gain of two Senate seats. At the state level—vitally important politically for congressional reapportionments if nothing else—Republicans made rather substantial gains in state legislature outcomes. But elsewhere (i.e., gubernatorial and other state-office elections) there was virtually no evidence at all that a presidential election was going on at the same time and in the same polling booths.

If there is no substitute for victory at the presidential level, there is also no substitute in policy terms for partisan victory at these other levels of election in our complex layer-cake constitutional structure. Instead of this, we find that 1984 broke yet another record. The number and percentage of states with split partisan control (Republican governor, Democratic legislature or vice versa, or any combination thereof) has now reached its highest point since the creation of the Republican party in the 1850's—27 states out of 49 (excluding Nebraska with its nonpartisan legislature), or 55.1 percent of the total. Of the other 22, 18 showed solid Democratic "control" across all branches of state government, compared with only 4 equally solid Republican states.[22]

The lack of major Republican gains in the House elections— few anticipated striking shifts among the 33 Senate seats up for election—came as a major disappointment for that party's strategists. To be sure, everyone had long become aware that congressional elections had evolved along their own peculiar path since the 1950's. More than a decade ago, David Mayhew pointed out that "marginal seats"—those closely competitive between the two parties—were a vanishing breed.[23] My own essay on the 1976 election devoted considerable attention to the contemporary shape of congressional elections, stressing the statistical near invulnerability of incumbents and the radical structural differences between majority coalitions in presidential and congressional electorates.[24] Morris Fiorina, Mayhew, the present author, and many others have linked this dramatic structural change to the rise of interest-group liberal politics and the increasingly successful manipulation of electoral environments by incumbents, political operatives, and others in the age of the "permanent campaign."[25] In a nutshell, the system becomes more efficiently "wired" every year, and partisanship as such becomes less and less relevant to the wiring process.

But the advent of programmatic conservative politics under Ronald Reagan was supposed to have changed all this. Indeed, one important reason for stressing the magnitude of the Republican *partisan* failure to make a breakthrough in these elections is that such a very serious partisan effort was made by Republicans in 1984. President Reagan and Vice President Bush devoted considerable energies in the closing days of the campaign to the virtues of voting not just for Reagan but for Republicans. This was in the sharpest possible contrast with the situation in 1972, when Richard Nixon and the Committee to Re-elect the President virtually ignored the Republican party and its other candidates. By the same token, the relationships between the President's personal campaign organization and the Republican National and Congressional Campaign Committees were models of teamwork and cooperation compared with 1972. In 1980, Ronald Reagan's lead over Jimmy Carter, in two-party terms, was 10.6 percent. Yet this was associated with a Republican gain in the House of 34 seats, enough to produce the famous conservative tax- and budget-cutting majorities of 1981. In 1982, at the trough of the worst recession since 1938, the Republicans lost 26 seats—and it was only through some luck and very effective campaign management on their part that the loss was not a good deal larger. In 1984, Ronald Reagan's margin over Walter Mondale was 18.2 percent, or nearly twice as large as it had been over Carter in 1980. Assuming some general partisan

realignment process at work, what was more logical than to
assume that the Democrats would lose back those 26 seats
they won in 1982, and very likely more besides?

But in the end the actual Republican gain seems to have
been 14 or 15, leaving an apparent House balance of 253
Democrats to 182 Republicans, with one race undecided.
Conservative explanations for this have varied. Richard
Viguerie, the master of conservative mailing-list operations in
politics, expressed irritation with the Reagan campaign's stress
on the "America is back" theme, with its overtones of
satisfaction and the overcoming of a long-standing crisis in
America's public affairs. For if the message of satisfaction
and well-being is preferred to one stressing ideological rigor,
then why stop at voting for the incumbent president? Why not
vote for *all* incumbents regardless of party? And in truth,
something very close to this is what happened in both the
House and Senate races, in both cases to an historically
unprecedented degree. *The Wall Street Journal,* for its part,
pointed to returns apparently showing a dead heat in the
national congressional vote and criticized the gap between
this total and the 71-seat Democratic majority as proof of the
iniquities of gerrymandering and other political artifacts. The
purpose of the essay, of course, was to stress Reagan's *policy*
mandate (not just his personal one) and to discount Democratic arguments to the contrary.

This compilation, of course, apparently excluded the millions of votes cast in congressional races where no major-
party opposition candidate was running. There were 53 such
seats on the Democratic side and 12 on the Republican, for a
total of 65, or 15 percent of the House total—pretty much
falling within a normal range. Excluding all these would yield
a total of 199 Democrats to 171 Republicans, which looks
somewhat more reasonable. But the basic fact of the matter is
that Democrats generally fared far better, and Republicans far
worse, than their respective presidential candidates. A simple
table suggests something of the differential.

On the average, Democratic candidates ran rather better
than nine percentage points ahead of Mondale. Only once in
the 23 elections since 1896 was the gap even larger (in 1972,
of course), and only one other election—1956—showed one
of the same order of magnitude. All three, of course, are
contemporary "candidate-oriented" elections, and all involved

Table 8—8
1984: Mean Percentages Democratic by Major Offices
(2-party vote)

Office category	Pres.	Gov.	US Sen.	USHR	Gap
13 states, gubernatorial elections	38.6	49.2			10.6
32 states, Senate elections	38.4		46.4		8.0
Non-Southern states, congressional el.	39.1			48.5	9.4

situations where Republican incumbents were overwhelmingly reelected to the presidency. Yet to repeat, 1956 was a classic nonideological election, while Nixon ran not with but away from his party in 1972.

Moreover, in many crucial races this year, the gap was far larger than these aggregates suggest. For example, the median margin by which incumbent Senate Democrats ran ahead of Mondale was 21.9 percentage points, while Republican incumbents ran a median of 4.5 percent ahead of Reagan. With Ronald Reagan winning more than 70 percent of Nebraska's presidential vote, incumbent Democratic Senator J. J. Exon needed to run 23.6 percent ahead of Mondale in order to win a narrow reelection victory over Republican challenger Nancy Hoch. And in New Jersey there were near equivalent landslides for Reagan and for incumbent Democratic Senator Bill Bradley. The latter ran 25.1 percent ahead of his presidential running mate (Mondale) and carried every one of the state's 21 counties! Nor are such true orgies of split-ticket voting hard to duplicate in some House races as well. Democratic Representative Dan Glickman of the 4th Kansas (Wichita), for instance, won 74.5 percent of the two-party vote in his bid for reelection, while the same constituency's electorate gave Mondale 35.9 percent, a spread of 38.6 percent. In North Dakota, finally, its lone and very popular Democratic Representative, Byron Dorgan, secured 78.5 percent of the state's vote in his reelection bid, while Mondale could muster only 34.3 percent—a spread of fully 44.2 percent of the vote!

The traditional model of realignment presupposes reasonably effective *partisan* channeling of the vote. Republican strategy in 1984 was partly predicated on the idea that such channeling—stiffened, of course, by the right advertising and media appeals—was feasible in 1984. One of the most significant results of this election was its conclusive demonstration that this was not the case. One may well ask, if not in 1984, then when, if ever?

There are various relatively straightforward ways of measuring the extent of this partisan decomposition; its substantive implications will be discussed more fully toward the end of this essay. Let us return to the categories of states reported in the last table. These are the 13 states in which gubernatorial elections were held in 1984 simultaneously with the presidential race; the 32 states with Senatorial elections concurrent with the presidential contest; and all states outside the South with the congressional election concurrent with the presidential election.[26] What, state by state, has been the relationship between presidential coalitions and those centering around these other offices since 1896? The stronger the aggregate partisan bonds are, the closer the measure of association (r^2, or the proportion of variance in a dependent variable explained by the independent variable) will approach a "perfect fit" of 1.0. The weaker these bonds are, the closer r^2 will come to zero. Table 8–9 shows the long-term evolution toward this zero point.

Long ago, I pointed out that partisan decomposition—beginning not long after the establishment of the "system of 1896" at the turn of the century, deepening across the lifetime of that "system," reversing during the New Deal era, and then decisively resuming its course in and after the mid-1960's—was a dominant leitmotiv of political change in the United States across the last century.[27] This table well captures these movements, from near perfect partisan channeling in 1896 and 1900 through the downward, upward, and then downward movement in r^2 across this century. The year 1984 shows an uptilt since 1980 in the strength of relationship between the presidential and U.S. House coalitions, but a decline in the Senate relationship. And both in 1980 and in 1984, the variance in the gubernatorial vote "explained" by the presidential vote is so low that we can say that there is no such relationship at all between these two voting coalitions. The upward movement in r^2 involving the presidential and

Table 8–9
Disintegration of Party Coalitions:
r^2 by State, President vs. U.S. Senate, U.S. House, Governor
(% Democratic of two-party vote, 1896–1984)

Year	r^2 = President with: U.S. Senate	U.S. House	Governor
1896		.941	.963
1900		.970	.941
1904		.798	.726
1908		.769	.794
1912		.610	.891
1916	.835	.475	.606
1920	.798	.695	.546
1924	.549	.265	.877
1928	.295	.239	.678
1932	.606	.317	.685
1936	.700	.559	.598
1940	.763	.657	.613
1944	.879	.680	.758
1948	.813	.598	.884
1952	.620	.750	.649
1956	.723	.503	.555
1960	.425	.546	.358
1964	.136	.388	.149
1968	.229	.257	.096
1972	.012	.125	.170
1976	.070	.187	.439
1980	.236	.064	.003
1984	.143	.258	.012

Explanations and definitions.
1. Partisan percentages: Percentage Democratic of two-party vote, 1896–1908, 1916–1920, 1928–1944, 1952–1984; Percentage Democratic of three–party vote, 1912; Percentage Democratic and Progressive of three–party vote, 1924; Percentage Democratic + Progressive + States' Rights Democratic of total vote, 1948.
2. States with uncontested Senate or (for whole state) House elections omitted. For Senate, only elections for full terms are included. (Number of states ranges between 27 and 33.)
3. The base of House elections are the contiguous 48 states less the 11 states of the ex-Confederacy; also less any other state where, statewide, there was no major-party opposition in any election. (Number ranges from 34 to 37.)
4. The bases of gubernatorial elections are those 13 states in which, in 1984, presidential and gubernatorial elections occurred simultaneously. (N in 1896 = 12; thereafter 13.)

House coalitions in 1984 may or may not be a harbinger of something new and more partisan in voting behavior. But with barely a quarter of the House vote "explained" in this way by the presidential vote pattern, we are far removed indeed from the typical situation in the 1936–1960 period, not to mention the truly overwhelming partisanship of the era around the turn of the century. Were we to conclude with Sidney Blumenthal that we moved into a "sixth electoral system," that of the "permanent campaign," around 1968 or 1970, this regression pattern would form considerable support for this argument. Nor would it stand alone by any means.

That very large parts of "the people" simply do not think today in partisan terms has by now become a commonplace of electoral research. So far as congressional elections are concerned, Donald E. Stokes and Warren E. Miller pointed out a generation ago that these were elections of relatively very low visibility. Their analysis concluded that voters know relatively little about their congressional candidates. What little they know is highly favorable to him or her.[28] A *New York Times-CBS News* poll taken during the 1984 campaign suggests that the Miller-Stokes analysis retains its validity. Respondents were asked if they had heard much about a number of candidates, and if so whether their opinion of them was favorable or not. The distribution of opinions among the probable electorate about their congressmen are indicated in Table 8–10.

Table 8–10
Visibility of House Candidates, 1984

Response category concerning	Probable Electorate Total	Party of Respondent's Member of USHR USHR Member*	
		Dem.	Rep.
Heard of, favorable	35	42	48
Heard of, not favorable	6	8	6
Heard of, undecided	9	9	8
Not heard enough	47	39	35
No opinion	3	2	3

*As identified by respondent

Of those who had heard of their representative and had formed a judgment, 85 percent of total respondents, 84 percent of those in Democratic districts and 89 percent of those in Republican districts were favorable to their incumbents.

So far as the partisan side of matters is concerned, a Yankelovich poll taken in September provides some arresting information.[30] This question set was asked of Reagan-Bush voters. When these voters were asked what their main reason was for voting for that ticket, the responses were precisely on target with the themes developed earlier in this essay (Table 8–11).

Table 8–11
Chief Reason for Voting the Reagan-Bush Ticket, 1984

Reason	% of Respondents
Performance in office (has been a good president, is an effective leader)	39
State of the economy	14
Anti-Mondale	14
Other (unspecified)	12
Don't want to change while things are going well	6
Views are closest to my own	5
Foreign policies	3
Party reasons (he's a Republican)	2

This is an almost perfect opinion profile of a candidate-dominated election. If we add quasi-ideological (views closest), specified domestic policy (economy), foreign policy and party reasons together, the total is only one quarter of the electorate. And it should be stressed that in this survey, at any rate, partisanship as a *main* reason for supporting the Reagan-Bush ticket is at almost chemical-trace levels (2 percent of respondents).

This survey then went on to ask respondents whether they felt that their support for the Reagan-Bush ticket made them more likely or less likely to vote for Republican candidates for other offices, or made no difference at all. The relatively huge indifference to party stands out very clearly in the response (Table 8–12).

Table 8–12
Reagan Voters and Republican Candidates, 1984

Response Category— Voting Reagan-Bush makes you:	Percentage of Respondents
More likely to vote for Republicans	29
Less likely to vote for Republicans	4
Makes no difference	65
Not sure	3

Now we turn to the structure of the 1984 congressional elections. This was remarkable in a number of respects. For one thing, the number of incumbents of both parties seeking reelection reached an all-time high: 408 out of 435 seats, or 93.8 percent. By the same token, the number (392) and percentage (96.1 percent) of incumbents winning reelection reached the highest point in 150 years' worth of congressional elections. The overall pattern is of some interest, highlighting as it does a very well known contemporary difference in partisan "mobility" as between incumbent-held and open seats (Table 8–13).

Table 8–13
Winners and Losers, 1984 House Election

Category of Seat	1984 Result by Party			
	Won	Lost	Total	% Lost
Democratic incumbents pre-1982	185	8	193	4.3
Dem. incumbents elected 1982–83	55	4	59	6.8
Open seats, former Democratic incumbent	8	6	14	42.9
Open seats, former Republican incumbent	12	1	13	7.7
Rep. incumbents elected 1982–83	21	0	21	0
Republican incumbents pre-1982	131	3	134	2.2
Total*	412	22	434	5.1
All incumbents	392	15	407	3.7
All open seats	20	7	27	25.9

*1 Undecided (Ind. 8th Democratic incumbent elected 1982)

Thus, before the election, Democratic incumbents constituted 62.0 percent of all incumbents, and afterwards 61.2 percent, a shift of only 0.8 percent. Among open seats, on the other hand, the pre-1984 partisan distribution was 14 Democratic to 13 Republican (51.9 percent Democratic), while it became 9 Democratic to 18 Republican (33.3 percent), a swing of 18.6 percent. These open seats, in the main, constitute almost the last trace of the much greater movement in congressional elections which prevailed in eras when partisanship was far more important than incumbency in determining their outcomes. It gives a faint suggestion of what the Republicans might have accomplished in the House in 1984 if partisanship had retained anything like the importance in voting decisions which it had had as late as 1952.

Thus, the structure of the 1984 election across levels of office dramatically reinforces the view that diverse coalitions flourish in an age of candidate-dominated, media-driven elections. In fact, on a number of dimensions of measurement, the 1984 structure is at or close to the most extreme levels recorded across a century and a half:

—As we have said, both the number and percentage of congressional races contested by incumbents was at an all-time high (408, or 93.8 percent of all seats).

—The number and percentage of these incumbents being reelected also reached their highest points ever (392 and 96.1 percent respectively).

—However one chooses to measure it, in 1984, aggregate congressional election competitiveness reached the lowest point ever recorded. This point is better appreciated by concentrating on the outcomes in Northern and Western states, since across a century and a half the Southern (and, to a lesser degree, the Border) states had a strikingly deviant political history from that of the rest of the country. In 1984, only 34 of the 285 congressional races in the North and West (11.9 percent) were decided within a closely competitive range (45.0–54.9 percent of a two-party vote). This contrasts, for example, with the 37.8 percent achieved in 1948 or the 24.0 percent recorded in 1974, not to mention such "ancient history" elections as 1882, when fully 53.2 percent of all races in these regions were decided within this closely competitive range. Another way of making the same point is to note that in 1984 74.9 percent of all winners in the country's 435 congressional districts won 60 percent or more of the total vote, the highest recorded since the first available observation, the 1824 election. In the North and West, 76.5 percent of seat winners won 60 percent or more of the total vote in their districts. This was not only by far the highest ever recorded (contrast it, for example, with 33.9 percent in 1948, or 41.5 percent in 1960); it represents a sudden jump of 12.2 percent over the 1982 level.

Incumbents, of course, know these facts. The "permanent campaign" takes on particular exigency when the elections come around every two years. Scholars and journalists have spelled out the many devices these incumbents employ to anchor their seats, among the chief of which is developing a nonpartisan image as defender of the constituency's interests as a whole against the claims of all other constituencies and their politicians. Further and detailed information on these points is readily available, e.g., from the pages of *National Journal* or *Congressional Quarterly*.[31]

Incentives promoting the entrenchment of incumbents extend to business elites and other major contributors to political campaigns. The structure of contributions to contemporary congressional election campaigns, with the help of the Federal Election Commission, is becoming better known all the time. Ideologists such as Richard Viguerie, not to mention national party elites, see the election as a whole and seek a general policy mandate from it. Business elites have important class-wide interests in electing Republicans and defeating most non-Southern Democrats. But in practice, there is much reason to suppose that they operate mostly not as a class-wide cartel of firms with ideological aims, but on the level of individual firm interest. This interest calls for *access* to people whose probability of reelection, as we have seen, is around .96. This can and does promote considerable business giving to liberal Democratic representatives, especially if these representatives have committee chairmanships or other posts of exceptional influence over the legislative process. The problem is essentially a straightforward one of public choice. As Mancur Olson long ago pointed out, collective goods are only likely to be provided in group political struggles to the extent that individual interests are also thereby maximized.[32] In modern congressional elections, firm rationality may very often be in basic opposition to class rationality. But if so,

Table 8–14

Campaign Contributions by Incumbency Status: House Races, 1984*

Category of Seat	Number	Total Contributions	% Democrats of $	Mean $ per seat
Unopposed Democrat	53	$10,885,132	100.0	$205,380
Democratic incumbents, contested races	202	68,448,022	73.9	338,852
Open ex-Democrat	13	5,317,584	58.4	409,045
Open ex-Republican	13	6,151,804	39.2	473,216
Republican incumbents, contested races	142	45,135,105	19.9	317,853
Unopposed Republican	12	2,605,420	0	217,118
Totals: Democrat $		75,989,151		
Republican $		62,553,916		
Total:	435	138,543,067	54.8	318,490
All Dem. incumbents & D. open unop.	255	79,333,154	77.5	311,110
All open, contested.	26	11,469,388	48.1	441,130
11 Rep. incumbents	154	47,740,525	18.8	310,003
			% Inc.	
All incumbents:				
Opposed	344	113,583,127	76.4	330,184
Unopposed**	65	13,490,552	100.0	207,547
Total incumbents	409	127,073,679	78.9	310,694

* Reported through September 30, 1984; see USA Today, October 26–28, 1984, p. 6A. All "not reporteds" counted as zero (these are all found in incumbent-held seats with overwhelming incumbent advantage)

** This includes one Democratic case of an open seat won unopposed in the general election (Texas 23rd, A. Bustemente)

Table 8–15

Campaign Contributions by Perceived Closeness of Race: House Races, 1984*

Classification	Number	Total Contributions ($)	% Dem. of $	Mean $ per Seat	Outcome: Dem.	Outcome: Rep.
Unopposed Democrat	53	$10,885,132	100.0	$205,380	53	0
Other safe Democrat	148	35,313,025	89.0	238,602	148	0
Democrat favored	22	10,124,449	63.4	460,202	20	2
Leans Democratic	24	14,118,466	57.6	588,269	20	4
Contested Democrat	194	59,555,940	77.2	306,989	188	16
No clear favorite	23	16,762,601	53.9	728,809	10	13
Leans Republican	19	10,053,610	42.3	529,137	0	19
Republican favored	19	9,221,745	29.7	485,355	1	18
Other safe Republican	115	29,458,619	10.5	256,162	0	115
Unopposed Republican	12	2,605,420	0	217,118	0	12

Contested Republican	153	48,733,974	20.7	318,522	1	152
Totals:	435	138,543,067	54.8	318,490	252	183
All unopposed	65	13,490,552	80.7	207,547	53	12
All safe seats	263	64,771,644	53.3	246,280	148	115
All favoreds	41	19,346,194	47.3	471,858	21	20
All leaning D or R	43	24,172,076	51.2	562,141	20	23
No clear favorite	23	16,762,601	53.9	728,809	10	13

* Classification provided by Congressional Quarterly Special Report, Elections '84, October 13, 1984, plus detaching unopposed from other safe seats for each party.

class rationality is likely often to lose out. This may prove a very important reason indeed for the failure of Republicans and conservative spokesmen like Mr. Viguerie to get what they wanted in 1984. For if ideologists and national party elites see congressional elections as a whole, there is every reason to suppose that incumbents (skilled politicians that they are) and, for that matter, major campaign contributors see them one at a time, district by district and case by case. The Republicans made a mighty effort to "nationalize" the 1984 congressional election, while Democrats did everything they could to particularize it. On this level, at any rate, the result was a clear-cut Democratic victory.

The structure of contributions to the 1984 congressional elections is broadly congruent with this well-known picture, though the data stop with September 30, and the brush with which we paint is a necessarily very broad one. The pattern is presented in a simplified way in tables 8–14 and 8–15—the first showing the relationship between incumbency status and volume of contributions, and the second the relationship between perceived closeness of the race and the volume of giving.[33]

It is well known that, overall, the financial resources available to the Republican cause are vastly greater—perhaps on the order of 9:1—than those on which Democrats can rely.[34] But general propositions do not decide concrete cases. In the *first* place, while the financial edge for contested incumbent Democrats is somewhat less than for contested Republicans, it is still overwhelmingly large. *Secondly,* it remains striking that there are so many seats left uncontested by candidates of one or the other of the major parties, and that the Democratic edge among such seats is 53:12, or (in percentage terms) 82:18. This of course reflects to a large—through recently decreasing—degree the history of Southern congressional politics. It remains worth noting that, in Britain, one must go back to the "khaki election" of 1900 to find so large a share of uncontested parliamentary seats; and in Canada, there is no historical precedent at all. In those countries, no matter how hopeless the contest, virtually all seats are contested by major-party candidates.

A *third* point, revealed in the "perceived closeness" table (Table 8–15), is that the cost of elections naturally climbs very substantially with perceived closeness: on the whole, 3.5

times as much money is spent in elections with no clear favorite as in unopposed elections, and 3.0 times as much in the former category as in elections which, while contested, are regarded as "safe" for one party or the other. A *fourth* point, duly demonstrated in both tables, is that Democratic incumbents and Democrats in "safe Democratic" seats (virtually the same thing) have no trouble raising overwhelmingly large campaign contributions, and they remain quite competitive in this regard even in the "closest" categories (leaning Democrat, no clear favorite, leaning Republican).[35] One could also add a *fifth* and final point. The casual observer may frequently wonder why it is that $13.5 million was given to candidates who had no major-party opposition at all, nearly one tenth of the total money raised. The answer would clearly enough seem to be that contributors were interested in purchasing access, and most of the candidates, at least, were only too happy to receive the money. One always wonders, to be sure, what they do with it when they get it, since in the overwhelming majority of these 65 cases, there was no serious opposition to their election or reelection either in the primary or the general elections.

In the end, then, the Republican effort to gain ground in the House (and Senate) elections with the help of Ronald Reagan's coattails failed. In substantial measure, it failed for the same reasons which partly explain Ronald Reagan's very success; the dynamics of politics dominated by candidate images and professionalized media operations. Moreover, we should consider the extensive discussions of partisan realignment over the preceding four years and the reality of a quite genuine policy realignment beginning in 1981, and consider as well that Reagan and his party devoted unusual efforts and resources to electing Republicans generally in 1984. In that context, the failure must be read as *decisive*, at least for as far ahead as we can see. With a popular and partisan President, cooperation among party and candidate organs, and a landslide at the presidential level, the overall political conjuncture could scarcely be more favorable in the foreseeable future.

Implications and Conclusions

The most conservative and ideological president of this century won a convincing landslide. If only the white population is considered, this was one of the truly great presidential landslides in American political history. At the same time, liberal Democrats did extremely well against the President's partisan running mates in congressional elections, running roughly eight to thirteen points on the average ahead of the Mondale-Ferraro presidential ticket. If one works hard enough, one can find scattered evidence pointing toward a political realignment favoring Republicans. But this evidence, such as it is, seems largely if not almost exclusively confined to the presidential level. Republicans have the serious political problem of attempting to acquire some genuine popularity as Ronald Reagan eventually departs from the political stage. Democrats have the even more serious problem of finding some way—and these days, that inevitably means finding some specific candidate—to overcome their serious deficits of support at the presidential level. As for turnouts, these scarcely budged from their 1980 levels. It is now the case that even in presidential years, fewer than half of the potentially eligible adult citizenry bothers to cast votes in congressional elections.

Back in 1967, Lloyd Free and Hadley Cantril published a study called *The Political Beliefs of Americans*.[36] A leading conclusion of this work was that Americans are divided not along one dimension so far as liberalism/conservatism are concerned, but along two. Most white Americans are more or less ideologically conservative: they are hostile to "big government" and its intrusions in general. But most of them are also more or less liberal on the operational dimension: they may dislike big government, but they like the programs which big government dispenses, which they enjoy, and from which they profit. This attitudinal dichotomy—some, particularly programmatic liberals or conservatives, might call it schizophrenia—is faithfully reflected in our complex constitution and its system of divided powers.

The single big national office, the presidency, is preeminently the chief visible symbol of national identity and national purpose, especially in the context of world politics. The president is chief of state and also leader of such government as we have. This fusion of executive functions has a concrete political importance which has often been rather slighted. It is out of it that the president's unique symbolic role arises. And this is closely linked with the civil-religion component in the American political culture.

A key to success in modern presidential elections is the perceived quality or image of the incumbent's leadership. Success here, of course, is linked to the delivery of results in very concrete areas: the economy primarily, but also a sense of effectiveness in maintaining the country's military strength and international respect. Reagan's success in 1984 rested squarely on this perceived "service delivery," and scarcely less on vivid memories of painful failures in the preceding Carter-Mondale Administration. But in addition to this, Reagan is one of the modern virtuosi of symbol manipulation, and particularly the manipulation of those symbols close to the heart of the American civil religion. The collective environment of the present and recent past has been one of protracted structural crisis, economic stagnation, imperial decay, and perceived erosion in traditional cultural bonds. It is hardly surprising that the message Reagan delivers is that of conservatism in all these areas, of "getting back to basics" and "good old days." As long as results continue to be delivered, the message will have wide appeal indeed—particularly among the youngest Americans.

Congress, on the other hand, is today the institutional center which reflects a continuing, concrete, program-oriented liberalism among the American public. There seems little doubt that little leeway for new and expensive programs will exist in the foreseeable future: the budget deficit and a conservative president will both see to that. On the other hand, a multitude of programs now in being have many defenders in the public more generally and in Congress, especially the House of Representatives. The balance of political forces in both houses—the majority Republicans in the Senate, after all, have 22 seats to defend in 1986—raises very serious doubt that the Reagan revolution can be extended much further. For that matter, it raises some doubt that any decisive resolution of the imbalance between post-1981 tax revenues and growing budget expenditures will be achieved short of a huge crisis and its attendant climate of panic.

These ambivalences were most brilliantly highlighted in the "state of America's future," California. Since 1948, this state has only once (in 1964) been carried by a Democratic presidential nominee. It was also the cradle of the tax revolt under Howard Jarvis's leadership. Ronald Reagan defeated Walter Mondale by just under 1.5 million votes, winning 58.2 percent of the state's two-party vote. Yet while all this was going on, a whole series of conservative initiative propositions went down to defeat. Chief among these were a new Jarvis tax-limit proposition (Proposition 36, losing by 45.3 to 54.7 percent), a proposition taking away the power to reapportion from the Democratic legislature (Proposition 39, failed by 45.1 to 54.9 percent), and a proposition to limit welfare aid to families with dependent children by imposing a "cap" no more than 10 percent higher than the average of payments in the other 49 states (Proposition 41, failed decisively by 37.0 to 63.0 percent). Meanwhile, six state bond issues and two tax-increase measures were adopted, in all but one case by overwhelming margins. Naturally, the Democratic speaker of the house, Willie Brown, was delighted with these results. On the other side, Paul Gann spoke for many conservatives in expressing amazement that the voters had approved every tax increase and rejected every tax and budget cut.[37] Policy "mandates" in such crosscurrent environments are singularly difficult to identify.[38]

If we stand back from the details of this immensely complicated event we call the 1984 election, what patterns can we detect, what observational priorities seem to make sense? How does this event fit into modern American political history. Let us attempt at least to sketch the outline of such a pattern.

The traditional American party system began to break up in certain vital respects across the postwar period. This decay accelerated very sharply from the mid-1960's onward.

In retrospect, the critical realignment that so many people looked for around 1968 actually happened around that date, but in the "wrong" place. Instead of producing an "emergent Republican (or any other) majority," parties themselves were decisively replaced at the margins by the impact of the "permanent campaign," linked inseparably to the mass media and those who knew how to use them effectively in politics. Taken as a whole, the 1984 election pretty clearly falls in the middle of this "sixth electoral system," and is a "maintaining election" within that system's terms of reference.

Inevitably, the replacement of parties by "permanent campaigning" was associated with huge increases in the class bias of voting participation, within the overall discipline of such participation. Equally inevitably, it is associated with the emergence of a major "governability crisis." From very early in our history as a nation, it has regularly happened that whenever party is absent or heavily eroded, the result has been paralysis, deadlock, and "governability crisis."[39] This is because, without the countervailing weight of partisan bonds and channels of political action, the centrifugal constitutional scheme itself becomes a literally unworkable instrument of government. "Permanent campaigning" can and does win elections; indeed it dominates all political calculations and activities. But it cannot and does not provide acceptable substitutes for party, or mechanisms by which politicians in constitutionally separated institutions are forced to be more or less "in the same story" with each other.

The appropriate form of state during the last partisan alignment era, the New Deal, was the *interest-group liberal state* based on government programs and, often, interventions into formerly private realms of social and economic life. This was the warfare-welfare state of yesteryear, and was largely predicated until the mid-1960's on a range of activities for which there was relatively broad public consensus. By contrast, the appropriate form of state during the sixth, or "permanent campaign," electoral era is that of an *interregnum state*.[40] In this state, public policy became increasingly divorced from any clear mass base of support, especially over the intermediate term. Energized minorities proliferated, since targets of opportunity now abounded. As this process unfolded, the capacity of the Democrats in particular to maintain general-purpose appeals and bonding themes deteriorated. This was so because the party is, far more than its opposite number, a coalition of minorities more or less peripheral to the main business of America, which is business.

The first major policy change accompanying the rise of the interregnum state was an intensification and broadening of originally New Dealish interest-group liberalism so extensive as virtually to involve qualitative as well as merely quantitative change. But such policy was made, as it were, like bricks without straw. No stable majority was ever constructed by the creators of the "Great Society" and later programs, nor did they seek to construct such a majority. When the world-political and economic conjuncture underwent a decisive change, and business elite opposition to the interest-group liberal synthesis became consolidated, the legitimacy of this policy structure came under devastating attack.[41] It intensified across the 1970's and down through 1980.

The "Reagan revolution" of the 1980's, at least as contemplated by its activists and intellectuals, represented a near 180-degree turn in policy course. The changes of 1981, by any standard, were the most sweeping and comprehensive in 50 years. But again, such policy change in the past had always been the fruit of partisan realignment producing solid majorities in the electorate, the presidency, and Congress to undergird the policy. The year 1981, like its "Great Society" predecessor, was fundamentally different: it was a *policy* realignment without *electoral* realignment.

At this point, the attentive reader will have noticed that the author believes the Reagan phenomenon to be part of the interregnum state and its crises rather than its resolution. Who can be absolutely sure either way? Only the future, and concrete developments affecting the performance of the economy, the position of the United States geopolitically and in the world economy, and our political elites and institutions can possibly decide the issue. Essentially, the American electorate voted in 1984 for "America is back" and for peace and quiet after years of crisis and failure. In the main, it wants what it has always wanted, which is economic growth, assurance that the American Dream still works and does not require drastic revision, and—more recently—physical security in a world of nuclear threat and nuclear proliferation. The active electorate—far more than the total population, of course—is dominantly middle-class, an electorate of "haves" rather than "have-nots." However dimly, most of its members recognize this fact, as stories of Lebanese civil wars and Ethiopian famines are poured forth on the six o'clock news. Ronald Reagan promises all the desired things, as does the business class which is at the core of his following. His policies are his—and their—monument.

One of the prices to be paid for these policies, of course, is a class polarization which directly and very differentially affects the well-being of Americans. Quite literally, as the most recent household-income and other data have shown, the rich are growing richer and the poor poorer, while—so far at least—the Great Middle is treading water. The Democrats have systematically, one often thinks inevitably, avoided the risks involved in recognizing this fact and putting that recognition into political practice. The Mondale campaigners, in this sense, cooperated from the beginning to end with their Republican opposite numbers to ensure that, whatever else happened, 1984 would not become the "ideological election" which knowledgeable observers had forecast. For that to occur, one suspects, an altogether new party would be required, a party of which—in some, though very far from all, respects—Jesse Jackson would be a prophet. Barring huge crisis, particularly in the economy, it is very difficult to see any such possibility as realistic in the foreseeable future. The key to any such development would seem to lie in the answer to the question whether major sectors of the Great Middle will stop treading water and begin losing ground in a significant way across the years ahead.

It is this prospect which has recently worried the conservative analyst Kevin Phillips.[42] What if, following the bankruptcy of interest-group liberalism, Reagan's conservative revitalization movement also fails to deliver the goods? This may not be so idle a fear, for characteristic of the broadest conditions giving rise to the interregnum state is a kind of escalating entropy, a rise in the general level of disorder in economy, politics, and society. Faced with that kind of vacuum, Phillips fears, the time may be ripe for a real fascist-"populist" movement complete with its Führer figure.

Perhaps. But skepticism intrudes itself. Quite apart from the fact that Hitlers, most fortunately, are singularly rare phenomena in world history, America is not now and is most unlikely to become even remotely similar to Germany in the 1918–33 period. Even "after hegemony," the United States exercises a power in the world which is enormous. Even though its resources and options are declining gradually in world terms, it still retains a remarkable capacity to export its problems and contradictions to the rest of the world, and especially to the semideveloped countries of the so-called Third World.

Secondly, the linkage between economic business cycles and critical realignments over the past century should not be ignored. Prior to 1933, as capitalism passed from its industrial-accumulation to its developed stage, its business cycles were unregulated by the state. Such sharp, deep, and protracted collapses as those of 1873, 1893, and 1929 produced awesome political effects—one mini-realignment and two of the real thing. The whole purpose of the New Deal's policy activity, fleshed out by total American victory in World War II and the global economic hegemony which followed, was to damp down the capitalist business cycle. This was to be accomplished by modest redistribution of income and various mixes of fiscal and monetary policy interventions. The rationale, of course, was duly provided in time by Keynesian economics. The business cycle was in fact damped down, and income loss, when and where it occurred, was largely masked by transfer-payment programs and by inflation.

To be sure, it may be possible that if the Administration and its allies achieve their heart's desire sufficiently to restore an unregulated capitalist environment, they will pave the way at some point for a reasonably spectacular modern-day equivalent of 1873, 1893, and of 1929. But somehow one doubts it, not least because of the large and growing "military Keynesian" component in the budget and the gross national product. Stabilizers, in short, really do stabilize, at least to the extent that sudden and dramatic collapses followed by very long bouts of painful stagnation may have been banished from the scene. And if they have, an important stimulus or "trigger" for partisan realignment in electoral politics may well have been banished as well.

Taken as a whole then, the 1984 election faithfully reflects the ambiguities and crosscurrents of electoral politics with decayed partisan-voter linkages and with "permanent campaigns" in a dominant position. It strikes this observer as unlikely that the Reagan synthesis will succeed in delivering the goods even on its own terms. More probably, we are in for a protracted period of deadlock and drift, yet within a pervasive conservative definition of politics and policy agendas. There is a certain lack of neat and tidy definition in all this; the pudding appears to lack a theme. Moreover, the crisis in the country's political structure has only—and, one suspects, just barely—receded beneath the surface of Ronald Reagan's glittering electoral victory. In the end, what didn't happen in 1984 may prove as important to future historians as what did. What didn't happen in 1984 was a reversal of the trend toward structural disaggregation to which I called attention twenty years ago. The interregnum state, its characteristic political styles and processes, continues to hold center stage. When, how, by whom, and through what means it will be replaced by something else is, at this point, anyone's guess.

Notes for Chapter 8

1. Angus Campbell, Philip E. Converse, Donald E. Stokes, and Warren E. Miller, *The American Voter* (New York: Wiley, 1960), pp. 531–538; and by the same authors, *Elections and the Political Order* (New York: Wiley, 1966), pp. 63–77.

2. Sidney Blumenthal, *The Permanent Campaign* (New York: Simon & Schuster, 1982), especially pp. 17–26, 301–334.

3. For discussions of the contemporary "governability crisis," see Irving Kristol and Nathan Glazer, eds., *The American Commonwealth, 1976* (New York: Basic Books, 1976), and Samuel P. Huntington's essay in Michel Crozier et al., *The Crisis of Democracy* (New York: New York University Press, 1975), pp. 59–118. The reason for suggesting that this crisis is "permanently embedded" in the politics of the "permanent campaign" is broadly structural: the constitutional structure laid down in 1787 seems incapable of working with even minimum adequacy as a frame of government without not only the existence but the centrality of political parties. See footnote 38 below and the related discussion in the text.

4. Patrick H. Caddell, "The State of American Politics," typescript dated October 25, 1983.

5. It is worth noting that the *Los Angeles Times* exit poll of November 6, 1984, asked respondents how they would have voted in a hypothetical race between Ronald Reagan and Senator Gary Hart. Only 6 percent of Mondale's voters indicated that in that case they would have defected to Reagan, compared with the 34 percent of Hart primary voters who actually did so, according to *The New York Times-CBS News* exit poll (*New York Times* (November 8, 1984), p. A19.

6. Information on estimated registration was provided by the Committee for the Study of the American Electorate, *Non-Voter Study '86–'85*, news release dated November 9, 1984, Notes

page 3. The total citizen adult population is based on my own calculations. Note that in 1984, this figure is 5.6 million less than the usually employed voting-age population, or 3.2 percent less, thus excluding that—conservatively estimated but census-based—share of aliens in the total population 18 years of age and over. The vote cast for 1960–1980 is from *America Votes*, Vol. 14 (1980), and my personal estimate for 1984 (the committee's estimate is very close but slightly lower, 92.0 million).

7. See Census Bureau, *Registration and Voting in the 1980 Election*, Series p. 20, for a wealth of detail.

8. See Walter Dean Burnham, *The Current Crisis in American Politics* (New York: Oxford, 1982), pp. 121–203.

9. *The New York Times* (November 8, 1984), p. A19.

10. An extreme case of this is the "Athens of America," Cambridge, Massachusetts, which is dominated by Harvard University and the Massachusetts Institute of Technology. This city gave Mondale 76.5 percent of its vote to 23.5 percent for Reagan, a Mondale lead of 53 percent, and nearly 30 percent more Democratic than Massachusetts as a whole. In another heavily university-oriented Massachusetts town, Amherst (University of Massachusetts, Amherst College), Mondale led Reagan by a margin of 71.2 percent to 28.8 percent.

11. *The New York Times* (December 16, 1984), p. 40.

12. The literature on this is pretty extensive. For a useful recent study see Martin P. Wattenberg, *The Decline of American Political Parties, 1952–1980* (Cambridge: Harvard University Press, 1984); and also, e.g., Samuel Popkin et al., "Comment: What Have You Done For Me Lately? Toward an Investment Theory of Voting," *American Political Science Review*, Vol. 70 (1976), pp. 779–805 (this performs the useful service of calling attention to the unique importance of the presidency—and more generally a constitutional and behavioral structure which makes party a poor predictor of presidential performance) and, for the classic 1950's model, Campbell et al., *The American Voter*, op. cit., passim.

13. V. O. Key, Jr., *The Responsible Electorate* (Cambridge: Harvard University Press, 1966), the first clear statement of the "retrospective voting" argument based on empirical evidence. An important theoretical rationale for this, of course, was first clearly articulated by Anthony Downs, *An Economic Theory of Democracy* (New York: Harper & Row, 1958). For the latest empirical word on the subject, see Morris Fiorina, *Retrospective Voting in American Presidential Elections* (New Haven: Yale University Press, 1981).

14. Edward R. Tufte, *Political Control of the Economy* (Princeton, N.J.: Princeton University Press, 1978), especially pp. 3–64. To make this point a little more concretely, let us present a two-independent-variable multiple regression equation for the 1956–1980 period and apply it "predictively" to 1984 with opinion data for April of that year but not the actual election results. The first variable is growth of per capita disposable income in the election year (1984 estimated at +5.0 percent), and the second, taken from the May 1984 Gallup Report (Report No. 224, p. 15), the percentage of "highly favorable" ratings going to the incumbent (62 percent for Reagan in April 1984, as between Reagan and Mondale only).

The 1956–1980 equation yields a multiple R^2 of .888; and reads $Y = 26.490 + 0.383 \, x_1 + 0.466 \, x_2$. With 1984 x_1 estimated at +5.0 percent (the third-highest presidential year growth rate in per capita disposable income on record), and x_2 at 62 percent, the "prediction" for 1984 turns out to be 57.3 percent of the two-party vote for the incumbent (Reagan), falling 1.8 percent below the actual result. If we assume that Reagan's popularity share of Gallup's "highly favorable" ratings was actually larger by several percentage points in November (say, 65 percent rather than 62 percent) over April, and that the "proper" per capita disposal income growth figure should be +6.9 percent (the actual growth from second quarter 1983 to second quarter 1984), then the model would "predict" a Reagan percentage of 59.4 percent, or 0.3 percent more than he actually received: a tight fit indeed! With 1984 now factored in, the 1956–1984 election set under the original assumptions shows a slight improvement in R^2 (.891) and a similar equation: $Y = 27.087 + 0.578x_1 + 0.450 \, x_2$, though this time with greater weight falling on the economic growth than on the personal-popularity side. Finally, one should note a possibly very significant datum from these AIPO (American Institute of Public Opinion, more familiarly known as the Gallup Poll) records. The percentages of respondents giving "highly favorable" ratings (+4 or +5 on the scale) to *both* presidential candidates looks like this:

Year & Month	Total High-Favorable	Year & Month	Total High-Favorable
1956 July	94	1972 Aug.	63
1960 May	79	1976 May	47
1964 Aug.	76	1980 Aug.	51
1968 May	55	1984 Apr.	47

The figure for 1984 stands in striking contrast to the enthusiasm projected by the Reagan campaign, though one should add not only 29 percent "highly favorable" responses to Reagan and 18 percent to Mondale, but 21 percent to Hart and 11 percent to Jackson to complete the array for all major candidates in 1984.

15. Adam Clymer, "Poll Finds Reagan Failed to Obtain a Policy Mandate," *The New York Times* (November 12, 1984), pp. 1, 30.

16. Angus Campbell, Philip E. Converse, Warren E. Miller, and Donald F. Stokes, *The American Voter* (New York: Wiley, 1960).

17. Douglas A. Hibbs, Jr., "Political Parties and Macroeconomic Outcomes," *American Political Science Review*, Vol. 71. (1977), pp. 1476–1487.

18. Wall Street claims that there are about 42 million investors in the United States today. One would give much to learn the details of that specific group's voting and attitudinal preferences. A recent French survey study discloses that—in that admittedly *very* different political system—gross income levels seem much less significant as predictors than whether or not respondents have investment and property income, and if so how much. See Jacques Capdevielle et al., *France de Gauche, Vote à Droite* (Paris; Presses de la Fondation Nationale des Science Politiques, 1981).

19. Walter Dean Burnham, "The 1980 Earthquake," *The Hidden Election*, eds. Thomas Ferguson and Joel Rogers (New York: Pantheon, 1981), pp. 98–140, and especially at pp. 132–140.

20. For the 48 contiguous states, the mean percentage Democratic vote was 38.9 percent (compared to a raw-total figure of 40.8 percent), the variance around this mean was 32.75, and the standard deviation was 5.72. This variance was slightly less than the ones recorded in 1960 (34.77) and 1976 (36.86). Contrast such figures with those for 1944 (160.25), 1916 (206.63), or 1904 (385.61).

21. As of January 3, 1985, the date of meeting of the Ninety-ninth Congress, 434 congressional races had been decided. The 435th is the 8th Indiana, represented in the Ninety-eighth Congress by Frank McCloskey (D), who had defeated a Republican incumbent in 1982. On the original face of the returns, McCloskey had defeated his Republican challenger, Richard D. McIntyre, by 72 votes out of more than 233,000 cast. Recounts under Indiana's remarkably complex election law gave apparent ground for the state's Republican secretary of state to issue a certificate of election to Mr. McIntyre. The House Administration Commit-

tee may well perform its own recount (this happened once before in modern times, following the 1960 election in the state's 5th district; there, Democrat J. Edward Roush was ultimately declared the winner by a margin of 99 votes). The partial final partisan balance in the House will probably remain undecided for months to come. Tables in this essay reflect this curiosity. For stories, see Steven V. Roberts, "The Indiana Imbroglio," *The New York Times* (January 3, 1985), p. A18, and *Congressional Quarterly Weekly Report* (December 29, 1984), p. 3165.

22. As late as 1940, three quarters of the states held at least some gubernatorial elections at times of presidential races. Over the decades, the tendency among state politicians has been to lengthen gubernatorial terms to four years and schedule these elections in nonpresidential years. This has reduced the number of states continuing to elect governors in years like 1984 to 13, barely one quarter of the total. This of course has much to do with Democratic ascendancy at the state executive level, since 29 Democratic governors were elected between 1981 and 1983 and only 8 Republicans. Still, there was a huge amount of turnover in 1984 among these 13 gubernatorial races. Republicans lost 3 of their 7 seats (N.D., Ver., Wash.), while Democrats lost 4 of their 6 (N.C., R.I., Utah, W. Va.). Thus, 7 out of these 13 seats changed hands, and Republicans picked up only 1 net gain. The preelection balance nationwide was 35 Democratic to 15 Republican governors; afterwards, the balance was 34 to 16.

23. See David R. Mayhew, "Congressional Elections: The Case of the Disappearing Marginals," (paper presented at 1973 meeting of New England Political Science Association).

24. "The 1976 Election: Has the Crisis Been Adjourned?" *American Politics and Public Policy*, eds. Dean Burnham and Martha W. Weinberg (Cambridge, MIT Press, 1978), pp. 1–25.

25. See David R. Mayhew, *Congress: The Electoral Connection* (New Haven: Yale University Press, 1974); Morris Fiorina, *Congress: Keystone of the Washington Establishment* (New Haven: Yale University Press, 1977); Tufte, *Political Control of the Economy, op. cit.* See also Walter Dean Burnham, *The Current Crisis in American Politics, op. cit.*, pp. 166–228, for discussions of various aspects of this problem.

26. This includes only non-Southern states with at least one contested congressional election in each presidential year from 1896 through 1984, with the congressional vote tallied up to produce statewide totals and percentages.

27. Walter Dean Burnham, "The Changing Shape of the

American Political Universe," *American Political Science Review*, Vol. 59 (1965), pp. 7–28.

28. Donald E. Stokes and Warren E. Miller, "Party Government and the Saliency of Congress," *Elections and the Political Order*, Angus Campbell et al., *op. cit.*, pp. 194–211.

29. *New York Times-CBS News* poll, taken September 30–October 4, 1984, released October 6; questions 9 and 9a. "Probable electorate" means the portion of the whole sample of persons interviewed who (in the researchers' judgment) were *likely* to vote in the November election.

30. Yankelovich, Skelly, and White poll, September 1984, Job #5693, questions 15b and 15c. I am indebted to Mr. Thomas Graham for making this and some other surveys cited here available to me.

31. See, "Today's House Freshmen," *e.g.*, *Congressional Quarterly Weekly Report* (December 22, 1984), pp. 3137–3142.

32. Mancur Olson, *The Logic of Collective Action* (New York: Schocken, 1966).

33. The classification here is provided by *Congressional Quarterly's* preelection issue, *Elections '84* (October 13, 1984). In order of ascending competitiveness, each seat is classified as "safe," "favored," "leaning," and "no clear favorite."

34. See Michael Malbin, ed., *Money and Politics in the United States* (Chatham, N.J.: Chatham House, 1984), especially pp. 70–121.

35. This remains the case all the way to the top in the ten most expensive congressional races in the country in 1984. (Okal. 1st, N.Y. 15th, Calif. 38th, Conn. 3rd, Ore. 1st, Tex. 8th, Mary. 2nd, Ark. 2nd, Ariz. 5th, and Va. 8th). Of the six Democratic incumbents holding these seats, three lost to Republican challengers (Calif. 38th, Mary. 2nd, Ariz. 5th), while three were reelected (Okla. 1st, Conn. 3rd, Ore. 1st). All three Republican incumbents in this category were reelected (N.Y. 15th, Tex. 8th, Va. 8th), while the one open seat (Ark. 2nd), vacated by a Republican was picked up by a Democrat. In the aggregate, Democrats raised $6,092,306 and Republicans $5,211,931 in these ten seats, for a mean contribution total per seat of $1,130,424.

It may be noted that the issue here appears to be not whether there is a skew in results favoring one party or another, granted an equivalent amount of cash to spend, but whether the money is raised equally in the first place. A regression analysis of percentages of contribution dollars and votes (Democratic percentage of two-party totals in both cases) indicates an extremely strong relationship between resources and outcomes across 182 selected congressional districts ($r^2 = .858$). Moreover, at the point on the regression line where Democratic contributions equal 50.0 percent of the total, the Democratic share of the two-party is a nearly identical 49.6 percent.

36. Lloyd Free and Hadley Cantril, *The Political Beliefs of Americans* (New Brunswick, N.J.: Rutgers University Press, 1967).

37. *San Diego Union* (November 8, 1984), pp. A10–11.

38. More interesting still—and very characteristic—were the results of a *Los Angeles Times* survey of 1,088 registered California voters, concluded October 15, 1984 (No. 89, questions 83–92). When the conservative propositions were generally mentioned, those respondents aware of them were mostly favorable. But on a follow-up question, when their provisions were explained in detail, the majority turned negative (as did the final election result).

Proposition	General mention			Detailed Explanation	
	Not aware Not sure	Favor- able	Unfavor- able	Favor- able	Unfavor- able
36 (Jarvis tax cut)	49	29	22	39	45
39 (Reapportionment)	66	20	14	30	54
41 (Welfare limit)	64	22	14	36	48

Needless to say, a tremendous effort was waged on both sides, actively using the state's well-developed "referendum industry" of media consultants. Democratic opponents of these measures appeared to have made particularly skilled use of negative advertising on television. But after all, this is very often the way elections are won in the age of the "permanent campaign."

39. The issues here are both profound and enduring. For a discussion relating to the period 1800–1828, including the War of 1812 and its management, see James Sterling Young, *The Washington Community, 1800–1828* (New York: Columbia University Press, 1966); and for a penetrating comparison of the Union and the Confederacy along this partisan/constitutional dimension, see Eric McKitrick, "Party Politics and the Union and

Confederate War Efforts," *The American Party Systems,* eds. William N. Chambers and Walter Dean Burnham (New York: Oxford University Press, 1967, 1975), pp. 117–151.

40. This term, "interregnum state," was first coined so far as I know by a young MIT scholar, John Coleman, in an as yet unpublished paper "Critical Realignment and the Modern American State."

41. Among some political scientists and publicists, this attack went back as far as the late 1960's. See, for instance, Theodore Lowi, *The End of Liberalism* (New York: Norton, 1969) (the term "interest-group liberalism" is Lowi's). It intensified very substantially across the 1970's. See also, *e.g.,* Kristol and Glazer, *op. cit.*

42. Kevin P. Phillips, *Post-Conservative America* (New York: Random House, 1982).

References and Further Reading

Abramson, Paul R., et al. *Change and Continuity in the 1980 Elections.* Washington, D.C.: CQ Press, 1982.

Blumenthal, Sidney. *The Permanent Campaign.* New York: Simon & Schuster, 1982.

Burnham, Walter Dean. *The Current Crisis in American Politics.* New York: Oxford, 1982.

Ferguson, Thomas, and Joel Rogers, eds. *The Hidden Elections.* New York: Pantheon, 1981.

Fiorina, Morris. *Retrospective Voting in American National Elections.* New Haven: Yale, 1981.

Page, Benjamin I. *Choices and Echoes in Presidential Elections.* Chicago: University of Chicago Press, 1978.

Tufte, Edward R. *Political Control of the Economy.* Princeton, N.J.: Princeton University Press, 1978.

Wattenberg, Martin P. *The Decline of American Political Parties, 1952–1980.* Cambridge: Harvard University Press, 1984.

9

Conclusion:
The Reagan Victory—
Retrospect and Prospect

Ellis Sandoz and Cecil V. Crabb, Jr.

The essays by the contributors to this volume call attention to a number of major implications and problems of the 1984 national election for the nature and development of the American political system.

The Concerns of the Voters

As the essay by Stephen McDonald emphasizes, it seems clear that in 1984, as is customarily true of political behavior in the United States, the American people were motivated primarily by *economic issues* in their decision to give the Reagan-Bush team one of the largest Electoral College majorities in the nation's history. By late 1984, citizens had widely concluded that the Reagan White House had made creditable progress in the campaign against inflation, in raising employment, in tax reduction, in improving the business and investment climate, and generally in restoring an atmosphere of confidence in the economic and financial future of America. If a number of key economic problems remained unsolved— and the ever-mounting federal deficit was a conspicuous example—the people believed that Ronald Reagan and his advisers were at least "on the right track" in their approach to them. At any rate, the electorate discovered little in the solutions offered by the Mondale-Ferraro ticket to convince them that Democratic control of the White House would provide better, and less painful, solutions than those proposed by the Reagan-Bush team.

The 1984 election provided confirmation of a commonplace observation about the political behavior of Americans:

voters are primarily interested in "pocketbook issues" which directly affect their daily lives, and their assessment of the *performance* (or anticipated performance) of presidential candidates in dealing with such issues is likely to be crucial in determining their decisions on Election Day.

This long-standing political behavior trait at least partially explains the American people's evaluation of the Reagan Administration's foreign policy record. Toward diplomatic issues, Americans have traditionally been uninformed and apathetic; in effect, they acknowledge that they "don't know"; and for the most part they are content to leave the resolution of complex foreign policy questions to the president and his advisers. Lacking persuasive evidence to the contrary—and in the election of 1984, the Democratic party was unable to provide it—the people assumed that the Reagan White House was doing as well as could reasonably be expected to protect and promote Americans interests abroad, in an often adverse external environment.

Again, Walter Mondale and his supporters were unable to convince a majority of citizens that their foreign policy proposals offered a better prospect for success than those of the Reagan Administration. A major reason for this perception of course was that many Americans believed that the diplomatic activities of successive Democratic presidents—most recently, Jimmy Carter—were in large part responsible for the fact that Ronald Reagan had been compelled during his first term to *restore* American influence and credibility abroad.

Another tendency highlighted by the 1984 election, and examined in considerable detail by Walter Dean Burnham, is the decline or "decomposition" of political parties as decisive agents in accounting for the political behavior of Americans. The evidence provided by the recent national election indicates that the trend toward "independency" by the American voter continues. Partisan ties and allegiances are perhaps weaker today than in any era of American history. Voters have become highly resistant to appeals for political support merely on the basis of partisan affiliation or loyalty. Despite intensive voter registration drives by Democrats and Republicans alike, citizen participation in the electoral process remains low and did not change significantly in 1984. A substantial number—perhaps even a majority—of voters had made up their minds politically long before the November election; and they had become saturated and enervated by the interminable campaigning which accompanied the primary contests and the election itself. This prolonged partisan contest perhaps was a unique disadvantage for Walter Mondale, who literally exhausted himself, initially in the fight against several Democratic challengers, and then against the skillful GOP campaign effort. With the other obstacles he was required to surmount, this "overexposure" of Mondale unquestionably weakened his appeal to the American people.

As explained more fully in the essay by Charles O. Jones, many of these same tendencies were evident in the congressional campaigns. The 1984 election corroborated the fact that Americans are influenced by different criteria in their decisions about candidates on the national, and on the state-local levels. Moreover, the same considerations which motivated citizens to select a Republican president do not necessarily apply to their selection of legislators. Based on the voters' decisions in 1984, we may anticipate the continued loosening of party ties on Capitol Hill, the exercise of independent judgment by junior members of the House and Senate, and further erosion of the seniority principle which traditionally governed the organization and deliberations of Congress. These tendencies, of course, did not begin in the 1980's; and it remains to be seen whether they will result in enhancing congressional *effectiveness* as a national institution.

Image-Building and the Political Process

Another tendency highlighted by the 1984 election was the crucial role of the media and modern modes of communication in the American political process. All the contributors to our study agree that Ronald Reagan's highly positive "image" with the American people was a key factor accounting for his impressive electoral victory. Better perhaps than any national candidate since Franklin D. Roosevelt, Reagan and his advisers have mastered the art of creating—and what may be even more difficult, *maintaining*—a presidential image which is attractive to the American people. Reagan's political aides also excel in the technique of "news management" to

enhance the President's political appeal and refute the criticisms of his political adversaries.

A remarkable aspect of this phenomenon, however, is that
(in marked contrast with the experience of the Johnson and
Nixon administrations earlier) the Reagan White House has
not been widely accused of "manipulating" the news and has
not suffered politically because of it. In this and other respects, for reasons that are not altogether clear, the American
people have exhibited a more charitable attitude toward Ronald Reagan than was the case with several of his predecessors. They were more disposed to believe the Reagan version
of the facts vis-á-vis the contentions of his critics. Above all
perhaps, Americans were convinced that during the Reagan
administration (in contrast to the 1960's), most of the news
dispensed by the White House was good: at home and abroad,
for the most part conditions were improving, and the Reagan
team was moving in the right direction in its efforts to solve
pressing national problems.

The crucial role played by a candidate's image in determining electoral outcomes in modern American society has several implications identified and discussed by our contributors.
Without a doubt, it *does* confer real advantages upon political
incumbents, especially to congressional incumbents. Their
challengers are often at a serious disadvantage in gaining
comparable public exposure, coverage by the news media,
the funds needed to undertake increasingly expensive political
campaigns, and other requirements of a successful political
race. As the results in 1984 demonstrated, in congressional
and state-local elections today, the odds heavily favor the
return of incumbents to office.

The current preoccupation with the public image of candidates has also been a major factor in the steadily escalating
costs of political campaigns. As the essay by Charles O.
Jones reminds us, on the basis of evidence supplied by the
1984 election, federal and state efforts to "limit" overall
campaign spending have done little to achieve the desired
result. This reality as a rule benefits Republican candidates
more than it does Democrats, although of course there are
often exceptions to this general principle. The effective
regulation of campaign spending remains a problem which
needs to be addressed anew, in frank recognition of the
fact that such attempted regulation to date has done little

to limit the cost of running for public office in the United States.

The American Pragmatic Tradition

The analysis by Thomas E. Cronin underscores the fact that the Reagan presidency has been characterized by paradoxes, anomalies, and contradictions. To the degree that this has been the case, it may be concluded that once again Ronald Reagan has consciously or unconsciously demonstrated a perceptive understanding of the American tradition and ethos. Throughout their political experience, Americans have been a remarkably nonideological people. In nearly all spheres of national life, the American preference has been for evolutionary, piecemeal, and *ad hoc* responses to problems in domestic and foreign affairs. Extremist and ideologically rigid solutions to national problems have customarily had little appeal for the American mind. (This fact does not mean that historically Americans have been indifferent or insensitive to the viewpoints of minorities, protest movements, and other groups which believed their demands and needs were being neglected by the majority. It does mean that, as a general rule, the two major political parties have in time been responsive to such viewpoints and have incorporated minority demands into their own platforms and programs. Third parties and ideologically based movements have thus been influential in the United States mainly because of their impact upon the positions of the two major parties.)

Today, as in the past, Americans expect their leaders to be in the "mainstream" of the society's ideological heritage and traditions. They admire leaders who exhibit flexibility, creativity, moderation, and common sense in adjusting to new conditions inside and outside the United States. Extremist and utopian schemes for restructuring the American society or remaking the world seldom elicit more than the support of a small minority of the American people. In exhibiting this "pragmatic" mentality for some two centuries, Americans have never been unduly troubled by the existence of logical paradoxes and philosophical inconsistences in "the American way of life'' or in their own distinctive conception of democracy.

In this respect, Ronald Reagan can be called a "typical American." The Reagan White House understands better than most of its critics these characteristics of American thought and conduct. In 1984, for example, Republicans were successful in depicting the Mondale-Ferraro ticket as the spokesman for "special interests," fringe groups, and esoteric movements, many of which are viewed by the average citizen as outside the mainstream of the American tradition. In his bid for the White House, Mondale was never able to overcome the damaging accusation that he had been "captured" by a variety of special interests; the implication of course was that, as president, Mondale's approach to public policy questions would largely be dictated by his indebtedness to these minority constituencies. Objectively of course, the accusation was no doubt unfair and largely without foundation. The Reagan-Bush team was not without its own ties to "special interests" which desired a Republican victory. Yet Mondale's efforts to adjust his position during the course of the campaign—and conspicuous examples were his discussions of the problem of national defense and his "tough" stance toward the government of Nicaragua—were politically unavailing and were widely interpreted as mere political "expediency."

By contrast, Ronald Reagan was able to win implicit or explicit public approval for his not infrequent changes of position during his first term. These policy adjustments—amounting in some cases to policy *reversals*—were in the main accepted as evidence of Reagan's flexibility and willingness to adapt to changing circumstances at home and abroad.

A common theme which unifies the essays in our study is that Ronald Reagan remains a political enigma. He is at one and the same time an avowed *political conservative* and also a consummate political *pragmatist*. From time to time (mainly perhaps for the benefit of his conservative political constituents), Reagan fires ideological "broadsides" at his opponents inside and outside the United States. Yet in practice, in both internal and external dimensions of national policy, Reagan has repeatedly modified his position in the light of existing realities; he has "settled for what he can get" in such diverse spheres as tax and welfare reform, achieving consensus with the nation's allies, and negotiations with the Soviet Union.

As well as any occupant of the Oval Office in recent memory, Reagan understands that politics is "the art of the possible," and he has not hesitated to abandon or ignore ideological principles in order to achieve an attainable goal. Yet in contrast to Walter Mondale, Reagan manages to do so without conveying the widespread public impression that his actions are dictated mainly by considerations of mere political expediency.

One key to understanding the phenomenon perhaps can be found in a curious irony of contemporary American political life: Ronald Reagan and his advisers understand better than their Democratic opponents a salient and publicly appealing feature of President Franklin D. Roosevelt's New Deal. After he entered the White House in 1932, FDR informed the nation that he proposed to experiment, to innovate, and to rely upon trial-and-error methods in his administration's efforts to solve the manifold problems accompanying the Great Depression. As all students of the Roosevelt presidency are aware, the New Deal was a patchwork collection of ideas, projects, and programs; it consisted of both carefully "planned" and *ad hoc* responses to existing problems in domestic and foreign affairs. The New Deal had no discernible ideological or philosophical consistency; and many of FDR's actions on one front were at variance with his actions on some other front. Yet as the years passed, this experimental and eclectic quality of the New Deal tended to be forgotten—most of all, perhaps, by Roosevelt's Democratic supporters and admirers!

As the public perception of the Mondale candidacy in 1984 clearly indicated, political leaders and aspirants in the New Deal-Fair Deal-Great Society tradition appeared to have abandoned the spirit of experimentation and improvisation which was the hallmark of the New Deal. In many cases today, the approach of Democratic candidates to urgent national problems has become thoroughly predictable, ritualistic, and ideologically rigid. Millions of voters concluded in 1984 that Democratic candidates for national office offered merely "more of the same," while the Republican party led by Ronald Reagan was endeavoring to experiment, to be flexible, and to adapt existing policies and programs to the exigencies facing the United States at home and overseas.

In a curious reversal of roles, Democratic office-seekers now find themselves in the same position as Herbert Hoover and his followers in 1932. Deliberately or not, Democrats widely convey the impression to the voters that the answer to the problems of the hour is a continuation of the approach that *produced* many of these same problems since the New Deal era. Just as Franklin D. Roosevelt was elected in 1932 to "save" the American capitalistic system, Ronald Reagan received the overwhelming support of the American people in his efforts to "save" the New Deal-Fair Deal-Great Society edifice by correcting its excesses, abuses, and threatened insolvency. In more general terms—and again, the parallel with FDR's election in 1932 is striking—Reagan has succeeded in restoring the *confidence* of the American people that they are able successfully to meet the challenges confronting them in the 1980's. Moreover, Reagan proposed to undertake this assignment in precisely the way Roosevelt attacked the dislocations accompanying the Great Depression: not on the basis of some elaborate and detailed "blueprint" for the salvation of society, but by *accepting* the essentials of existing programs and policies which have evolved over the last half-century and by overhauling, modifying, and otherwise adapting them to current conditions and the needs of the American people. In doing so, Republican policymakers will largely be guided by the old pragmatic principle of *experience*.

A unifying theme of all the essays in this volume is that the meaning of the popular "mandate" which was conferred upon Ronald Reagan in 1984 is ambiguous and unclear—more so perhaps than in most presidential elections in the United States. Despite the ambiguity of the Reagan mandate, however, it would not be amiss to say that by their overwhelming vote of confidence in his leadership, the American people authorized the Reagan White House to respond effectively to the challenges confronting the United States at home and abroad *on a pragmatic basis*. Even more today perhaps than in the past, citizens make their judgments on the merits of candidates on the basis of their actual or expected performance in office, rather than on their ideological appeal or logic of their ideas. The American voters elected Ronald Reagan in 1980, and reelected him again in 1984, primarily because of a two-fold popular conviction: the people believed that Reagan understood correctly the nature and urgency of the problems at the forefront of public concern; and despite his lack of experience and expertise in key policy areas (like economics and diplomacy), Americans believed that Ronald Reagan and his advisers would formulate reasonable and moderate solutions for these problems.

The Presidency in Modern American Life

This leads to another significant implication of the outcome of the 1984 election, which is the major focus of the analysis by Fred I. Greenstein: the high level of public confidence exhibited toward Ronald Reagan testifies to the continuing belief of the American people that the *presidential office* is still the locus of effective decision-making in the national government. Another largely incontrovertible element in Ronald Reagan's popular mandate is the conclusion that Americans do not want "another Jimmy Carter" in the White House.

The outcome of the 1984 presidential race indicates beyond real doubt that relatively few Americans are troubled by Reagan's "detached" style of decision-making—primarily perhaps because they believed that in the end, the Reagan White House will *make a decision* which promotes the interests of the United States in domestic and foreign affairs. Nor are citizens excessively disturbed by continuing evidence of internal policy "dissonance" and bureaucratic infighting among the president's closest advisers. Those Americans who remember the New Deal recall that the Roosevelt Administration was also characterized by frequent quarreling, personal rivalries, and basic policy disagreements among FDR's inner circle—a condition which Roosevelt himself sometimes *encouraged* in order to enhance his own position as chief executive. Both then and today, many citizens viewed such bureaucratic wrangling as in fact a desirable extension of the principle of separation of powers to the executive branch. As in FDR's era, it leaves the president free to serve as the final arbiter among his often ambitious advisers.

In any case, during his first term in the White House Ronald Reagan managed to avoid two extremes in his role as chief executive. For the most part, Reagan escaped the accusation that he and his staff were acting illegally and in defiance of traditional American constitutional principles and ethical values. Except among his more extreme critics, Ronald Reagan has not been accused of operating the kind of "imperial presidency" which was identified with Lyndon Johnson and Richard Nixon.

Conversely, as we have observed, Reagan has also escaped the pitfalls of presidential *immobilism*, which produced the political demise of the Carter Administration. The American people of course expect that the president and all other national officials will respect constitutional norms and requirements, including those which have over the past 200 years become embodied in the "unwritten constitution." (For example, after his reelection in 1984, President Reagan made a concerted effort to consult legislators in the process of initial negotiations with the Soviet Union on arms control, although there is no explicit constitutional requirement that he do so.)

Yet within these parameters, the people unquestionably expect the chief executive *to act*, to exert leadership, to demonstrate the vision required to solve vexatious domestic and international problems, to exude confidence in the future, and to convey the overall impression that the president is "on top of the situation" and not overwhelmed by it. The common sense of the American people tells them that in the final analysis the engine of the ship of state must *run powerfully*, with the president at the helm, if national goals are to be achieved. And if the waters within and outside the United States are sometimes "stormy," that is all the more reason why full power must be available to the captain and his crew to ride out storms successfully.

This in some measure explains why Ronald Reagan has not been held politically liable, in the same degree as some of his predecessors in the Oval Office, for his more conspicuous policy failures, mistakes, and unfulfilled campaign promises. In contrast to Lyndon Johnson during the Vietnam War, for example, in his diplomacy toward Lebanon Ronald Reagan eventually had the eminently good sense to liquidate an unpromising diplomatic venture before it was converted into a national trauma. In effect, Ronald Reagan did what Lyndon Johnson was advised to do when he was urged to declare American military intervention in Southeast Asia "a victory and come home." The Reagan White House knew full well, of course, that the Lebanese venture was not a victory; the

President's critics reminded him of that fact daily; and informed citizens were under no misapprehensions about the fact that the Reagan Administration had failed to achieve its diplomatic objectives in Lebanon. Yet no convincing evidence could be cited to show that this and other misadventures at home and abroad seriously damaged Ronald Reagan's popular appeal.

If the people have been more forgiving of domestic and foreign policy failures by Ronald Reagan than those made by Lyndon Johnson or Jimmy Carter, at least two reasons may be cited to explain the difference. The people did not blame Ronald Reagan for *trying* to bring peace to the turbulent Middle East; that is a goal which most Americans, regardless of their partisan affiliations, broadly share. Nor did citizens find fault with the president for taking a "calculated risk" by engaging in a *limited* military intervention to achieve the goal. In a crisis-ridden world, most responsible citizens realize that the pervasive fear of "another Vietnam" cannot be generalized into a blanket prohibition against reliance upon military force to achieve foreign policy ends. They know also that every crisis facing the United States abroad is not analogous to the situation in Southeast Asia.

On a different front, Ronald Reagan's efforts to reduce the national deficit and to insure the solvency of Medicare, Social Security, and other long-established programs exhibit the same innovative, trial-and-error mentality. It is much too early to predict precisely how the White House and Congress will finally attack the problem of the federal deficit. Even at this stage, however, several assertions about it can be made with confidence. In the end, the campaign to reduce the deficit will consist of a "package" of diverse approaches and steps agreed upon by executive and legislative policymakers. The package will contain several major elements: anticipated increases in federal revenues from at least some segments of the American economy; the elimination or substantial reduction of some existing federal programs; moderate and selective tax increases; reduced spending by most federal agencies (not excluding the Pentagon); more efficient administration of existing programs; and other steps designed to bring the deficit problem under control.

Most reasonably well informed citizens credit the Reagan Administration with two things in its efforts to reverse the nation's half-century tradition of deficit spending. Better than any other chief executive since World War II, President Reagan understands enough economics to know that a steadily escalating national deficit is *an extremely serious problem for the United States,* in both its domestic and foreign affairs. He does not believe that the problem will somehow "go away," solve itself, or otherwise disappear. And most citizens applaud the fact also that the Reagan Administration is at least *trying to solve the problem,* without a wholesale dismantling of programs which have been adopted since the New Deal and without creating widespread social and economic hardships.

The Reagan White House, in other words, is endeavoring to apply the cherished American precepts of moderation and balance, common sense, and flexibility in responding to a difficult and complex condition threatening the well-being of the present and future generations of Americans. That is an approach to problem-solving with which countless millions of Americans are familiar, which they employ in their everyday lives, and which goes far toward accounting for the fact that the United States has recently celebrated its two hundredth anniversary as the world's oldest democracy.

The Parties Face the Future

Two final aspects of the election of 1984 remain to be analyzed briefly: its effect upon the future of the Democratic and Republican parties. The outcome of the election, it hardly needs to be said, was traumatic for the Democratic party, despite its gains in Congress and its victories on the state and local levels. Walter Mondale's spectacular defeat will no doubt produce extended postmortems and soul-searching by party leaders and followers in Washington and throughout the nation at large. What went wrong with the Democratic campaign? Why is it so difficult for Democratic leaders and candidates to elicit the same kind of positive response from the voters which swept the Reagan-Bush ticket into the White House? What must Democratic party strategists do now, in order to avoid another political disaster in the 1988 or 1992 national elections? On the basis of the recent election results, such question are as timely as they are perhaps difficult to answer with assurance.

An easy (and not altogether convincing) answer to such questions is that the principal challenge confronting the Democratic party in the future is to find its own Ronald Reagan—a candidate with comparable charisma, poise, confidence, faith in the future, and other qualities which elicit a favorable response from the voters. Admittedly, based upon the experience of the 1984 presidential campaign, this is an urgent need of the Democratic party. Yet no prominent Democratic figure at the present time seems an obvious choice to become the "Democratic Reagan." The most charismatic Democratic contender in recent months—the Reverend Jesse Jackson—appeals to a constituency which is too small and too ideologically oriented to attract a broad national following in the United States. Several years may be required before the Democratic party is able to offer the nation "fresh" and appealing candidates capable of emulating Ronald Reagan's successful political style.

But this is only part, and quite possibly the least difficult part, of the Democratic party's problem after 1984. As the essay by Walter Dean Burnham emphasizes, the proccupation of the Democratic party in recent years with organizational reforms, rules changes, party procedures, and the like has unquestionably weakened it internally, encouraged conflicts within the party, and diverted its energies into activities only marginally related to the central purpose of political parties in the United States. A not inconsiderable liability has been the fact that intraparty wrangling has provided graphic evidence to the voters that the Democratic party appeared determined to "shoot itself in the foot" when it entered the political arena. Historically of course, the Democratic party has always been a more heterogeneous coalition of interests and groups than its Republican counterpart. The perennial problem of internal factionalism is an inherently more serious problem for the former than for the latter—more so today perhaps than in most other periods of the nation's political experience. Yet if the party's strategists do not somehow manage to overcome or contain its centrifugal tendencies, its prospects for revival will remain limited.

A related disability of the Democratic party on the national level is its pervasive reputation as an organization dominated by, and subservient to, special interests, minority groups, and assorted political causes which sometimes take positions which are not in the mainstream of the American ethos. Early in the eighteenth century, the perceptive Frenchman Alexis de Tocqueville observed that America was a society of loud minorities and quiet majorities—and in recent years, the Democratic party has appeared determined to prove him right. It goes without saying that the American democratic system must remain "open" and responsive to the needs of all its members, that it must be sympathetic to the particular requirements of disadvantaged individuals and groups, and that it must always venerate and respect the principle of minority rights.

At the same time, the opposite side of the coin of democratic government is "majority rule." Ministering to the desires and needs of minorities is not the only legitimate function of government in the twentieth century—and in the last analysis, it may not be the most important. To govern effectively, national leaders must forge a durable majority whose viewpoints are consonant with, and reflect, the consensus existing among the majority of the people. As the experience of the Democratic party in recent years illustrates, this majority is not likely to be created—or if it is created, to prove durable—if it consists of nothing more than a patchwork of minority opinion and fringe group political activity.

In its efforts once more to become the majority party in the United States, the Democratic party must also avoid certain pitfalls—and that will not always prove an easy matter. *First,* as our earlier discussion suggested, it must somehow overcome the pervasive impression that it is ideologically rigid, that its principles have not really changed since the era of the New Deal, and that it has little to offer toward the solution of current and future problems except the remedies proposed long ago by Franklin D. Roosevelt, Harry Truman, and Lyndon Johnson. After the 1984 election, it seems justified to conclude that the American people agree with Ronald Reagan's contention, that many of these old solutions are now passé, unresponsive to contemporary conditions and problems, and incapable of eliciting widespread public support.

Second, the Democratic party must also counteract the idea that it has little to offer the country except obstructionism, harassment of the Reagan White House, an unending barrage of criticisms directed at alleged Republican failures, and a heavy burden of national guilt and self-doubt. Since 1981, President Reagan has had a high level of success in blaming many of his administration's inadequacies on the "Democratic opposition" in Congress, particularly in the House of Representatives. While that may be a technique employed by every chief executive since the era of George Washington, it is also true that substantial numbers of citizens obviously *believe* Ronald Reagan and are convinced that if Congress would just "cooperate with him," problems like the national deficit or the "welfare mess" or even scandalous overspending by the Pentagon could be solved.

Third, in their rebuilding efforts leaders and members of the Democratic party must also avoid the dangers inherent in a position of "me-tooism"—which is likely to be a strong temptation after their defeat in 1984 at the hands of Ronald Reagan. A tendency toward me-tooism is always attractive for an opposition party when it confronts a government in power enjoying broad popular support. It seems undeniable that Ronald Reagan and his political aides correctly understand the temper and mood of the American people in the late twentieth century. They know, for example, that a majority of citizens want to retain many of the programs which have evolved in the United States since the 1930's, while eliminating the more obvious abuses and excesses from them, operating them more efficiently, and reducing their swollen administrative costs. Few responsible Americans really contest the principle that truly deserving individuals should receive welfare. They do not quarrel with the idea that job training programs should be available to rehabilitate the unemployed. In foreign affairs, only a small minority of Americans would reject the idea that the United States ought to provide some form of assistance to needy societies overseas.

In these and other instances, however, responsible citizens also demand that domestic welfare programs be administered honestly and efficiently, that fraud and maladministration be eliminated from them, and that all such programs be reexamined periodically to determine the degree to which their original purposes are being achieved. In foreign relations—and the Reagan Administration's decision to withdraw American representation to UNESCO is a prominent example—the American people may legitimately expect that their aid will be used wisely, for feasible and sensible projects abroad, and that it will encourage a greater degree of self-help and productivity by societies benefiting from it. Conversely, they have every right to insist that the resources of the American society *not* be wasted, used to enrich corrupt officials and "middlemen" abroad, or used in ways to conflict with the overall diplomatic objectives of the United States. These have always been reasonable expectations about federal programs at home and abroad, and it is clear that in recent years they are at the forefront of the American public mind.

Democrats must comprehend this public concern, without in the process adopting a position on internal and external policy questions which is identical to that of the Reagan White House. Democratic contenders can always try to convince the voters, of course, that they are able to administer such programs "better" than Republicans. In some instances, that may indeed be the best course for Democratic office-seekers on the national level to follow. This strategy is, however, admittedly hazardous, since it invites the response from the voter: Why should I vote for Democratic "converts" to this cause when the modern Republican party has already demonstrated its determination to curtail the size of government, eliminate waste, and operate governmental programs less expensively?

In the years after 1984, the Republican party confronts a different set of problems and dilemmas. On the basis of the evidence provided by American political experience since World War II, it seems safe enough to say that Ronald Reagan is sui generis. Only one other chief executive in recent memory (Franklin D. Roosevelt) was Reagan's equal in exhibiting charismatic leadership, communicating with the American people, and when necessary, rallying public support for his administration's position. Republicans may have no easier time than Democrats in finding a successor to Ronald Reagan as an extraordinarily skillful and popular party leader. To the extent that the outcome of the 1984 presidential contest was an intensely "personal" victory for Reagan—which it undoubtedly was—that fact will confront the GOP with the difficult challenge of locating his successor.

The electoral tidal wave which swept the Reagan-Bush team back into office in 1984 was a truly national phenomenon. As much as any other party slate in American history perhaps, the recent Republican ticket drew support broadly from most segments of the population; and it made heavy inroads into several traditionally Democratic sources of strength.

Yet as nearly all our contributors agree, it is too early to conclude that a fundamental "party realignment" has occurred in the United States. Impressive as it was, the massive Republican majority in 1984 *is fragile;* its future durability remains to be demonstrated in the absence of Ronald Reagan's charismatic leadership. It has long been said of the French electorate that its natural political orientation is "to the left, always to the left." In the United States, for over a half-century the Democratic party has been viewed as the "majority party"; more citizens were nominally affiliated with it than with the GOP—even while they were in the process of voting Republican or independently! This kind of popular or nostalgic identification with the Democratic party, we may be quite certain, has not ended because of the Reagan-Bush victory in 1984.

Expressed differently, in the post-Reagan era Republican party strategists need to remember that the standard of "performance" relied upon by Americans to judge elected officials is a double-edged sword. In 1988, the performance of the Reagan White House will doubtless be as carefully scrutinized by the electorate as the records of past Democratic administrations. For reasons that remain elusive even now, in the last election the voters were unquestionably disposed to treat Ronald Reagan's performance during his first four years charitably and to give the President the benefit of the doubt in borderline cases. The voters, however, were inclined to be less charitable in judging the Mondale-Ferraro ticket. Yet there is no reason to expect that Republican candidates after Ronald Reagan will be similarly treated; and there is no convincing reason why they should be.

An old adage of American politics holds that the electorate is not so inclined to vote for a particular candidate as to vote *against* his opponent. It is also a well-known axiom of the American system of government that people who *oppose* a particular program or undertaking are more likely to express their viewpoints strongly and repeatedly than those who favor it. Such precepts cannot be taken too literally, and every informed student of American politics can think of exceptions to them. Nevertheless, they remind us of a challenge confronting the Republican party in the future. Much of Walter Mondale's inability to win the support of the electorate could be explained as a residual public reaction against the Carter Administration. Intentionally or not, Mondale succeeded in convincing millions of Americans that he was Jimmy Carter's "successor" to the position of leadership of the national Democratic party. Once that impression became fixed in the American public mind, Mondale had insuperable obstacles to overcome in his bid for the presidency.

With the passage of time, memories of the inadequacies of the Carter and other Democratic administrations in Washington will begin to fade. In the natural rhythm of the American two-party system, the Democrats will produce candidates who are not associated with past mistakes and unpopular Democratic leaders of an earlier era. When that happens, Republicans will need more than recollections of Ronald Reagan's charisma to convince the voters that they should be returned to office. As the party which has controlled the White House since 1968, except for the Carter presidency (1976–1980), Republicans will be increasingly on the political defensive and will be required to demonstrate that on the basis of their performance they should be returned to power.

Even now GOP strategists, therefore, would be well advised to reflect upon the meaning and lessons of Ronald Reagan's political triumph. If his skill in the art of political communication and image-building has seldom been equaled, it is no less true that *what he communicated* to the American people seemed uniquely suited to the national mood and to the needs of the era. That combination was crucial in returning Ronald Reagan to the White House, and it is likely to be no less decisive in determining the political success of any Republican candidate who follows him.

Landslide Without a Mandate?

Since we readily acknowledge the imprecision of our subject and, hence, of the science of politics, we can agree both with Charles O. Jones that "mandates are inherently implausible" (quoting Raymond Wolfinger) and with Daniel J. Elazar that "the Reagan Administration has pointed the United States in a new direction." Ronald Reagan and his supporters—and probably a majority of his opponents also—believe the endorsement of President Reagan for a second term is not only a personal victory but a policy vindication as well. That adds up to a mandate of sorts. With suitable qualification, then, the editors' answer to the question in our book's subtitle is *no*. The "qualification" is that the mandate is general, not one for a detailed blueprint. The landslide for the Republican national ticket in 1984 *did* signal overwhelming approval of the "new direction" given the country since 1980. One of the editors (Sandoz), rather more strongly than the other (Crabb), *also* believes the long-awaited critical election realigning American politics has occurred and that we now live in the sixth historical period of our politics, one which dates from 1968 and 1972 when Richard Nixon was elected and reelected.

The plausible interpretation given the latter notion by Walter Dean Burnham turns on the observation that *party* realignment in the classic pattern of critical and realigning elections did *not* occur. Rather, realignment took place subtly, in a new mode of American politics. This is dominated by the media and the institutionalization of the "permanent campaign" (following Sidney Blumenthal's analysis) as the major aggregating mechanisms of national politics now eclipsing the declining parties. By that account, 1984 was a "maintaining election"—a preserving of the policy realignment of a decade and a half ago that was reasserted in 1980 and with great power and considerable substance in the recent election. Party decomposition is characteristic of such politics, and such structuring as is present is provided at the elite level by (quoting Burnham) "the mass media, individual candidates, and their staffs of pollsters, media consultants, and image manipulators." Burnham goes on to decide this amounts to a policy realignment *without* an electoral realignment and to designate the present state of things as an *interregnum*, a term which seems preferable to the *dealignment* of other writers. Deadlock and drift would appear to be in prospect after Reagan, if this reading is correct.

The matter should begin to clarify in next year's elections, and by 1988 the Republicans without Ronald Reagan to lead them will be put to the test in a decisive fashion. Deadlock and drift are not what the second Reagan administration has in mind, however, either for itself or for upcoming elections. Rather it is going for the political jugular and appears bent on consolidating the Reagan victories into full-scale electoral realignment by formally capturing the center and assimilating it into the new Republican party—thereby completing a faltering and torturous process begun nearly twenty years ago.

By our reading of recent political history, this process was retarded by the politics of malaise and fragmentation that beset the country in various degrees of severity from the assassination of President John F. Kennedy in 1963 onward: through a period of intense domestic conflict accompanying the civil rights revolution, the frustrations and acrimony of American involvement in Vietnam, the distention of the New Deal and Fair Deal impulse into the excesses of President Lyndon B. Johnson's Great Society, the assassination of Martin Luther King and Robert F. Kennedy and the permanent maiming of Governor George C. Wallace, and the great constitutional crisis and debacle of the imperial presidency that we call the Watergate affair. The *magnification* and frequent distortion of all these (and many other) wrenching events through the power of television is rightly seen as compounding their effects by vaulting them from the basement range of the disconcerting and unsettling through the emotional ceiling of public excitation to reach the shattering and hysterical zones of feeling and reaction.

In short, the decomposition of the parties and disaggregation of American political consensus are no more than aspects of the wider institutional crisis besetting the country in myriad ways in the pressure cooker atmosphere that reached fever pitch at home in 1963 and antedates even that, if the onset of the nation's novel role in the world arena through the start of the Cold War in 1947 be recalled as a benchmark. "Normalcy" in our society has been an elusive quality for a very long time, and the politics of chronic crisis traces back to presidential assassination, and farther back to Cold War and the Truman Doctrine, and yet farther back to Pearl Harbor and World War II, and even back to the beginning of this intelligible Era of Modern America, in the crisis of economic catastrophe called the Great Depression and the rise of the New Deal.

Liberal American politics, in the form familiar through the

New Deal coalition in successive permutations dominant for half a century, was born of despair and catastrophe and retains the birthmark traces of the politics of hysteria down to the present. President Franklin Delano Roosevelt's great line in his first Inaugural Address (1933) is emblematic: "The only thing we have to fear is fear itself." The motif is echoed in the famous Four Freedoms speech he made to Congress in 1941, in which he included "freedom from fear." The Democrats as the assuagers of fear among the impoverished, the down-and-out, minorities discriminated against, unemployed workers at the mercy of avaricious and insensitive big business, and as the friends and patron of the little guy in general, project a central thread of appeal for the party over decades.

As the public outcry grew louder, the rhetoric intensified in shrillness in the last two decades as Vietnam and Watergate took their toll on living color television, and the all too real hazards of terrorism, public corruption, environmental disaster, and nuclear holocaust were vividly added to the list of things the public ought to be terrified about. Scare politics are not a Democratic monopoly, of course, but a bipartisan affair to a considerable degree, as recollection of Joseph McCarthy's Red Scare of the Dwight Eisenhower–Harry Truman period reminds us. But it is fair to say that Republican themes have been more stolid and lackluster ("the business of America is business"), while the Democrats have not without some justification been lampooned as "bleeding heart liberals." As late as 1944 during the last Roosevelt election campaign, the Republicans came on after one of FDR's radio "specials" to "talk facts," and the President's little Scottie dog, Fala, lying at his master's feet promptly fell asleep. Roosevelt quipped: "They've even put my dog to sleep."

Those were the old Republicans. The new Republicans of the Reagan years are another matter. With only two Democratic presidents since FDR elected by a majority of the popular vote (Lyndon Johnson and, with 50.1 percent of the vote, Jimmy Carter), the shrillness of the party's campaign rhetoric tended to intensify. President Carter in 1980 added vocal shrillness to rhetorical shrillness in the scare politics employed against candidate Reagan: he was trigger-happy, likely to start a nuclear war, and would dismantle the welfare programs upon which so many of the poor, Black, Hispanic, unemployed, disabled, sick, and elderly Americans utterly relied. To all of this, Reagan responded with his patented grin: "There you go again!"

While that Reagan response did not succeed in debating Walter Mondale, the politics of hysteria ("Stop the Madness" posters strewn about, with crude pictures of Reagan and a mushroom cloud side by side, for instance) worked even less well for the Democratic ticket in 1984. Reagan had too much credibility with too many of the electorate, including not least of all the little guy who used to identify with FDR, for this strategy to succeed. Scare *cum* candor also did not work for the Democrats. Mondale's promise to raise taxes so as to cope with the astronomic national debt ("Let's tell the truth" . . . Mr. Reagan will raise taxes and so will I. He won't tell you. I just did," uttered at the Democratic national convention in his acceptance speech) was believed true for Mondale and false for Reagan; and 25 percent of those voting against the Democrats said they did so because of the threat of higher taxes. Scare politics gingerly associated with Reagan's advanced age, exploiting in various ways the fears that senility was upon our president and his "handlers" alone knew the country's business and ruled as a committee, crept into the open in the second debate when age overtly was mentioned. Reagan responded in deadpan that he was not going "to exploit my opponent's youth and inexperience" for political advantage. Even Mondale smiled. Substantively, Reagan promised to raise taxes only as a "last resort" and "over my dead body." And he pledged not to reduce Social Security benefits.

The Democrats' appeal to the fringe groups among the electorate created the impression of a montage of special interests being appealed to and the general interest being ignored. "Lemmings left!"—to recall Richard Scammons's and Ben Wattenberg's expression—into the sea. The Democrats' "fairness" appeal cost them votes from the mainstream of the American electorate who are in rebellion against welfarism and attendant policies. For example, it says something that only 30 percent of the potential electorate voted in early 1985 in the Southwest's most cosmopolitan city, Houston, Texas, on a referendum proposition prohibiting discrimination against gays in city government—and then it failed by an 82 to 18 percent margin. As Governor George Wallace of Alabama bluntly told the new Democratic national chairman, Paul Kirk, in declining an invitation to a Southern regional meeting of the party in February 1985: "The party's got to get away from some of the ultraliberal positions that they advocated in the platform during the last election if they ever hope to carry the state of Alabama again." Alabama's state party chairman did attend the meeting, however, and further clarified local thinking: "We in Alabama reserve the right to discriminate against homosexuals," stated Jimmy Knight. No Democratic president in this century has been elected without carrying the South, and the shifting of population in the country to the Sunbelt makes that political real estate more valuable every day.

In sum, the appeal to fear accompanied by the assurance that the Democratic party and its candidates will provide the only safe haven for the mass of the citizenry has not succeeded in national elections of late. Even apocalyptical visions of a dangerous, ill-informed, and unstable ideologue in the Oval Office (sometimes caricatured as "Bonzo" by detractors in the media) threatening to end the world by precipitating nuclear war did not frighten American voters away from Ronald Reagan in sufficient numbers to dent landslide victories. The post-Great Society politics of a paternalistic federal government sheltering a docile and dependent citizenry from the dangerous forces buffeting them socially and economically has grown obnoxious in the public's view and not a little demeaning as well. That working Americans labor on the average until May each year just to pay their taxes is galling enough. That recognition stirs passionate resentment when it also is realized that significant fractions of those taxes go to support able-bodied men and women who refuse to work and to foster a soaring illegitimate birthrate among minority women (55 percent of all births in the Black population, according to Theodore White). The Democrats have been victimized by a revolution in social tolerance as far as welfarism is concerned. Political power is in the center and not on the periphery of the voting population, and the center is revolting against the positive administrative state and demanding its reform. The Republicans are following the *public's* lead.

The New Republicanism

Ronald Reagan's presidential paradigm is supplied by Franklin Roosevelt, as Fred Greenstein suggests. The new Republicanism is not the sort of dead stuff that put little Fala to sleep in 1944 but something quite different. There is a sense of mission and a quite startling fervor about the second administration reminiscent of the urgency of a person who knows his days are numbered and there is work to do. Lou Cannon in also tracing Reagan's idea of the presidency back to the Roosevelt model writes: "Reagan's idea of a president [is] of a leader who [can] rally the country to a cause with the power of his voice and use public opinion as a catalyst for change."

In going for the political jugular, as we have phrased it, the Reagan Republicans appeal to the pantheon of Democratic political heroes and especially to Roosevelt and Kennedy, but also to Truman and even Lyndon Johnson. They conspicuously avoid mention of Nixon and Ford or even Eisenhower in their rhetoric. Democrat-bashing is largely confined to the Carter-Mondale Democrats. There is a clear awareness that, on Election Day 1984, 38 percent of the voters were nominal Democrats and only 32 percent were Republicans. The thread of discourse echoed a quasi-pulpit, born-again rhetorical style and was steadily utilized by Reagan, who lauded the Democratic greats and acknowledged that he was a Democrat himself who never left the party—rather the party left him and the country, too. As Reagan directly said in a speech in Austin, Texas, on the day after conclusion of the Democratic national convention, the Democrats have gone "so far left, they've left the country." Out of pain and soul-searching comes the discovery: the true Democrat is the new Republican! FDR's theme song, "Happy Days Are Here Again," was performed frequently at the Republican convention. A major speech was delivered to the convention by U.N. Ambassador Jeane J. Kirkpatrick, described as an enlightened lifelong Democrat, in praise of Reagan and to welcome other clearheaded Americans who remained members of that party to "our" side. (She formally joined the Republican party in April 1985 as she resigned from her position of Ambassador and returned to private life.)

Not only were Carter-Mondale Democrats untrue to America, they were untrue to the country's religious heritage. In

Reagan's acceptance speech, he remarked: "If our opponents were as vigorous in supporting our voluntary prayer amendment as they are in raising taxes, maybe we could get the Lord back in the schoolrooms and the drugs and violence out." He concluded that speech evoking America as a "shining city on the hill" and proclaiming a "springtime of hope." Geraldine Ferraro was so put out by these tactics that she peevishly called on the Republicans to talk about their own presidents and "leave ours alone," a complaint that fell on deaf ears. Burnham concludes from a preliminary analysis that the appeal to the Democrats was such that Reagan won more *congressional districts* electing Democratic than Republican congressmen (estimated at 185 to 181, or 366 in all); this is even better than Nixon did in 1972, and split-ticket results in congressional races were at 42.8 percent—a rate only exceeded by that in 1972. (See Table 9–1.)

Going for the jugular means raising the Republican party to majority status and electing not only the national ticket but also majorities in the House of Representatives and in the Senate, the litmus paper test of political realignment. The Republicans are very far from this, but this is their project. Ed Rollins states that this is unlikely to occur prior to 1990 or 1992, primarily because of the artful drawing of congressional districts by predominantly Democratic state legislatures after the 1980 reapportionment. The implication is that concentrated attention will be paid to developing the Republican party *as an institution* and to electing Republican state officials in the intervening period—so as to consolidate the realignment of the country's politics.

Still, the wooing of Democrats by Republicans obviously had considerable effect in 1984. It was contributed to by a highly skillful and organized campaign on the Republicans' part no less than by the telegenic prowess of President Reagan. The steady proselytizing of Democrats and appeal to the center of the electorate that we have stressed included such campaign "media events" as awarding a Congressional Gold Medal to Hubert H. Humphrey's widow, Muriel, in the Rose Garden of the White House with Joan Mondale in attendance; and Nancy Reagan's White House luncheon to honor the memory of a great American woman, Eleanor Roosevelt (FDR's wife and widely despised by conservatives and Republicans for her do-goodism), to commemorate the hun-

Table 9–1

Results of the 1984 Election by Congressional District and Incumbency Status*

Category of House Seat	Number of Cases for:		Pres. 1984	Vote Cong. 1984	Cong. 1982	1982–84 Swing	1984 Gap, Cong. - Pres.
	Vote	Swing					
Dem. incumbents, 2 terms & over	147	124	46.7	65.7	69.5	−3.8	+19.0
Dem. incumbents, elected 1982/3	55	53	44.9	60.0	59.1	+0.9	+15.1
All Dem. incumbents, subtotal	202	177	46.2	64.2	66.3	−2.1	+18.0
Open seats, ex-Democrat held	13	10	40.8	53.1	64.6	−11.5	+12.3
All Democratic seats	215	187	45.9	63.5	66.3	−2.8	+17.6
Rep. incumbents, 2 terms & over	125	114	34.8	30.8	36.6	−5.8	−4.0
Rep. incumbents, elected 1982/3	17	16	34.7	32.0	42.1	−10.1	−2.7
All Rep. incumbents, subtotal	142	130	34.7	30.9	37.3	−6.4	−3.8
Open seats, ex-Republican held	13	11	34.9	42.9	37.4	+5.5	+8.0

All Republican seats	155	141	34.8	31.9	37.3	− 5.4	− 2.9
TOTAL USA:	370	328	41.2	50.3	54.1	− 3.8	+ 9.1

*Notes: (1) Percentages and swing based on average (mean) Democratic percentages of the two-party vote in each category. It has been necessary to include a great many estimates of the two-party for president by congressional district, since full data at that level is not yet directly available.

(2) The data throughout are for contested seats only (65 House races in 1984 had no major-party opposition). The number of cases for 1982–84 swing also excludes cases where there was no major-party opposition in 1982, and is hence smaller than the number of cases analyzed for 1984 alone.

(3) Swing represents the net shift by category between 1982 and 1984 percentages Democratic. Where positive, the 1984 Democratic vote was higher than in 1982; where negative, it is lower.

(4) Gap refers to the difference in 1984 between Democratic percentages of the two-party vote for President and U.S. House by category of contested House seats in 1984. Where positive, Democratic congressional vote is larger than presidential vote, and where negative it is smaller.

Prepared by Walter Dean Burnham.

dredth anniversary of her birth. The theme that the Democrats had left America with Carter-Mondale, combined with constant evocation of the greatest and best loved of modern presidents as truly their own by Reagan-Bush, achieved substantive credibility from such strands in Franklin Roosevelt's political career as his saving of the capitalist system from collape in the depression and his vigilantly leading the country against totalitarian dictatorship in World War II. Such Rooseveltian rhetoric, for instance, as one of his campaign speeches in 1936 hovers in the background of the Reagan evocation.

Roosevelt said: "I believe, I have always believed, and I will always believe in private enterprise as the backbone of economic well-being in the United States. . . . It was this Administration that saved the system of free enterprise after it had been dragged to the brink of ruin by these same [Republican] leaders who now try to scare you. . . . I believe in individualism. I believe in it in the arts, the sciences, and professions. I believe in it in business. I believe in individualism in all of these things—up to the point where the individualist starts to operate at the expense of society."

Monopoly and "individualism run wild" were Roosevelt's problems, in part, in succoring the nation in the midst of great misery and economic turmoil. The inundation of the free enterprise system and obliteration of the liberty of the individual by massive federal controls and the positive administrative state are Reagan's chief domestic problems—as he perceives them. Both sets of problems represent extremes that define the resting point of a pendulum swing in American politics. That gravitational point lies in the center of an arc where individual liberty and free enterprise are preserved while the public interest is protected and citizens' well-being served. Both Roosevelt's and Reagan's political strategies seek a rebalance of a traditional norm approached from more or less diametrically opposite circumstances.

The cogency and authenticity of the Reagan-Republican appeal to the distant past of our modern politics no doubt partly contributed to the electoral landslide as a contextual dimension of the Four P's: *prosperity, peace, patriotism, and personality*. It convincingly added a fifth *P*: *populism*, identification with the average American. It brought in the youth vote (18–24 years old) as a potential base for Republican party expansion. It established the notion that Republicans better than present Democrats can lead the country at home and abroad. While the congressional elections showed relatively little for Republicans to cheer about on the surface, they won most of the hotly contested races in the House, ran close in many races they finally lost, and added 4 seats in the Texas delegation and 3 in North Carolina. And although Republicans picked up only one additional governorship, they added over 335 seats in state legislatures across the country with big gains in New Hampshire and Texas and substantial gains in North and South Carolina and in Florida. This adds up to a significant demonstration of grass roots voting strength and a laying of groundwork as the vital infrastructure for the congressional reapportionment effort that is a key to the Republicans' election of a majority in the House in the decade of the 1990's. Such prospective developments would demonstrate realignment of American politics to the most rigorous of political scientists. It also would make the Democratic party in its current configuration as dead as the dodo bird. This is not to forecast but merely to canvass the possibilities, in the humbling awareness of the many strange things that happen in politics and with a healthy regard for the urge to survive that drives the political animal.

Policy Prospects

A substantial manifestation of that urge to survive can be seen in the caution with which the Ninety-ninth Congress began its first session in 1985. To be sure, Speaker O'Neill managed to patronize the president as a "kindly old gentleman." But after playing musical chairs in the White House senior staff and in the Cabinet, the Administration came right at Congress with a series of proposals for major reform legislation. Sensing the power of the Reagan mandate to finish the job begun in the first administration, the President led cheers and then matter-of-factly laid down an agenda of federal retrenchment in domestic programs that promised drastically to thin the herd of sacred cows down on the political farm.

Curtailment of the federal budgetary outlay so as to address the enormous deficit became the chief vehicle for a near freeze proposal that cut into many favorites of the Democrats and of old and new Republicans alike, threatening to reach great segments of the American population. The list includes the phasing out of farm price supports and return of agriculture to free market conditions; reduction of funds for student assistance and guaranteed loans for college students; retrenchment of Medicare and Medicaid; reduction of Veterans Administration support and veterans' benefits and retirement programs; personnel cuts in many federal agencies and possible pay reductions; the ending of the popular revenue-sharing programs whereby federally gathered tax funds flow to states and municipalities and comprise substantial parts of the financial support of both; and the slowing or freezing of Social Security support increases, a program made actuarially sound during the first Reagan administration as one of its major policy achievements. All of this (and much more) was calculated to save around $50 billion from the projected fiscal year 1986 federal budget *deficit* as part of the move to "shrink the system slowly," in the phrase of David A. Stockman (director of the OMB, Office of Management and Budget).

Despite great outcry from the affected constituencies, the Congress itself seems inclined to go along with much of the Reagan economic program. By a kind of squeeze play forced by the budget, even liberals support Reagan. Not only do senators and representatives read the election returns with care and understand that there is one other politician in their states and districts more popular than they are—President Reagan—but they are convinced the budget must come down to preserve economic prosperity. They clearly understand, also, that economic prosperity is fundamental to reelection in 1986 for themselves as incumbents. With nearly half of the senate Republicans up for reelection in 1986, majority leader Senator Robert J. Dole (R-Kan.) observed that the President may be a lame duck, but he and others in the Congress would be dead ducks if a new recession hit in 1986. Other incumbents who are Democrats also prefer survival to principle.

A blending of logic and visceral response to the political future thus may well restore to the Washington vocabulary a word not often heard in recent decades: *bipartisanship*. Self-interest and bowing to the inevitable are major engines of bipartisan politics. The Reagan juggernaut of populist conservatism may well deserve columnist Richard Reeves's olfactory complaint: "The stink of arrogance is heavy in Washington, worst around the White House." But odious as it is, it is the aroma of incumbency success that Congress shared in to an unprecedented degree in 1984 and is eager to continue to enjoy.

Thus, everyone is eager to find ways to reduce the budget deficit and the Administration is generously enlisting the support and ideas of Congress in fashioning the precise texture of the cuts to be enforced—undoubtedly painful though these are, as the chorus of lamentation from all sides proves. Representative Dan Rostenkowski (D-Ill.), chairman of the tax-writing House Ways and Means Committee, surprisingly came out in support of bipartisan tax-simplification plan and pledged to work closely with President Reagan and Treasury Secretary James A. Baker III to that end. Proposal of a "flat tax" or a major revision and simplification of the tax code has been in the air for years and is a popular idea, if it can be executed without further undermining the federal budget. Bipartisanship also emerged in the conciliatory conduct of foreign affairs by Secretary of State George P. Shultz, who moved toward the center in strengthening the reliance of State on career foreign service officers (at the expense of politically appointed conservatives), in supposedly encouraging the exit of hard-liner Jeane Kirkpatrick from the foreign policy-making scene, and in seeking wide consultation and support for the negotiation of a nuclear arms control agreement of some kind with the Soviet Union. (See Appendix for Cabinet and White House officials listing.)

President Reagan, whatever others say, *believes* he received a mandate in 1984 to simplify government further: to return more and more responsibility in the domestic arena to state and local governments; *not* to raise taxes; to restore the free market at home and in international trade to the degree feasible; to continue the military buildup as a means of reestablishing United States' self-respect and preserving parity with Russia as a world power; to oppose communist expansion in the world and especially in this hemisphere; and to effect cost savings and management reform everywhere without damaging the vital "safety net" for the truly needy and unfortunate. The fights with Congress and myriad constituencies will be not so much about principles as about execution of these plans within the horizon of economic health, the restoration of "domestic tranquility," especially through attack on the narcotics and organized crime problems, and continued top-priority attention to national security. Means and parameters will be the focus of the opposition Democrats and others, most often in response to local constituency campaigns and to organized interest-groups pressures.

Foreign and military affairs, and related expenditures, will provoke major disagreements between Congress and the President. Support of the *contras* fighting against the Sandinista rulers of Nicaragua as "freedom fighters" and "our brothers," as the President called them in his first press conference of the new term, aroused intense debate, and initial rejection of a proposed $14 million appropriation by the House of Representatives in April 1985. The Strategic Defense Initiative, ridiculed and discredited as "Star Wars" by the peace movement as part of the politics of hysteria previously discussed, will not be set aside by slogans and "bumper sticker logic," to use the term of the Pentagon's expert, Lieutenant General James A. Abrahamson, director of the SDI Organization for the Air Force. There is evidence, in fact, that the Soviets possess substantial capability of the kind planned for SDI area and have returned to the arms control negotiations in Geneva chiefly to dissuade the United States from going forward with the project.

The success of the Administration in prosecuting its general program of budgetary and legislative reform depends upon skill and luck, of course, but mainly upon the continuation of the record of success that accompanied President Reagan in 1983 and 1984 in the economy. Neither the politicians nor the country will stay with a sinking ship: performance is the acid test.

The kind of governmental success and upbeat politics of hope the country demands is reflected in the testimony given the Senate Foreign Relations Committee by Secretary of State Shultz in mid-January 1985: "Opinions are being revised about which system (ours or the Soviets') is the wave of the future. The free nations, if they maintain their unity and their faith in themselves, have the advantage—economically, technologically, morally. History is on freedom's side."

Final Thoughts

To the three C's of conventional politics—*charisma, campaign,* and *circumstance*—the Reagan Administration has added three others that continue to serve it well: *communication, co-optation,* and *conciliation.* Secretary Shultz's remarks reflect the theme that Ronald Reagan steadily has enunciated that "America is back." It is a theme that the country obviously responds to favorably. It is good politics. Americans generally can see no earthly reason why such a coercive and flawed system as Marxism should succeed as the wave of the future in this hemisphere or elsewhere, whether of the Soviet, Chinese, or Cuban variety. They also see no reason to concede vital interests to covert or overt Soviet or Soviet-surrogate subversion or imperialism. They are willing to gamble with the nation's economic future in order to be prepared militarily, since common sense and recent experience both teach that the lessons of Munich remain valid: strength and resolve are essential in dealing with the bullying of the totalitarian imperialist. Nor can diplomacy be prosecuted effectively from the posture of psychological prostration or military weakness. Power is an ineluctable dimension of politics domestically and internationally. Wisdom and high motivations have never been enough to assure sound political rule, and even Plato in the *Republic* (543B) insisted on the point in summarizing the qualifications for philosopher king: "Kings among them must be those who have shown themselves best both in philosophy and in warfare." Both good arms and good laws are imperative.

The reelection of President Reagan in 1984 served to restore stability to our system of government. No president since Dwight D. Eisenhower (1952–1960) has served two full terms in office. The institutions of the country have been wracked with crisis, corruption, and lack of confidence to the point that the structure of authority itself is alarmingly eroded. Constitutionally, the United States is a government of laws and not of men. This means law and justice must be served if we are to be true to ourselves, and not the narrow purposes of willful and self-serving men. It also means that the government exists for the people and not they for it. The Due Process clauses of the Fifth and Fourteenth Amendments that guarantee no person shall be "deprived of his life, liberty, or property, without due process of law" constitutionally express a fundamental of American political theory, one with roots in the thought of the seminal English thinker John Locke and in constitutional theory back to the Greeks. This tradition, biblical as well as classical, stresses the ultimate dignity and worth of the *individual* human being. We are "Lockean" politically in that sense. And we are said to be "Lockean" economically, also, because this notion of individual dignity attaches to our acquisitive drive and to our material no less than our moral and intellectual personality.

Free enterprise or *laissez faire* economics which rewards the industry and ingenuity of the individual as the great springs of all achievement, and protects the fruits of labor against criminal or arbitrary incursion, is seen as an expression of the natural liberty and rationality of the human being. Society and government exist to provide the conditions for the prosperity and security of the people and of every individual among them. Liberty and justice are inseparable in this view. When the American founders launched the Revolution rather than pay a three-penny tax on tea calling it tyranny, they asserted their indefeasible dignity and the natural right of themselves and posterity to live as free men and women bound only by laws they consented to. When the Constitution was framed in 1787 and enlarged in 1791 to include the Bill of Rights, the same principles obtained; and an extended commercial republic was founded on a federated pattern. In *The Federalist No. 51* James Madison stated the fundamental principle: "Justice is the end of government. It is the end of civil society. It ever has been, and ever will be pursued, until it be obtained, or until liberty be lost in the pursuit."

In saying that this or that administration evokes the unity and pride of the nation, one is really saying that it stirs the spirit of the people and reminds them to be true to themselves and to their own political and economic heritage. The Reagan Administration has succeeded in doing this in a way superior to American experience over the past two decades or more. It has restored self-respect and a sense of purpose to the country. It has given the nation a new direction in keeping with our highest vision of human and national purpose. And it has governed effectively. It has done all of this by evoking our Lockean individualism curbed by national covenant. By such considerations, among others, the "real plurality" of politically involved Americans have expressed their satisfaction and invested their trust in the 1984 reelection. A getting right with ourselves and a restoring of the lost balance in the social and political priorities is sensed, a mood comparable to the one evoked by FDR.

All of this is to the good. But certain cautionary words are in order. A main fear of the Constitution's framers was "tyranny of the majority."

> "O it is excellent
> To have a giant's strength, but it is tyrannous
> To use it like a giant."

So Shakespeare wrote in *Measure for Measure* (Act II, scene 2). The power of the voting majority in a country now struggling to reinstitutionalize its politics can be as dangerous as the framers feared it might become. The politics of the "permanent campaign" conducted by symbol manipulators, media experts, and public-opinion specialists through television and the concentrated power of the other mass media can be abused in a variety of ways (as it has been), including the tyrannizing of the minority. The brute force of an overwhelming silent majority confronting an array of apathetic minorities *can* exacerbate the historical tensions in American society and force a polarization of politics utterly destructive of the national community.

This possibility is the more pronounced to the degree that acculturation to the political and economic history, ethos, and principles of the country is absent because of sloth, ignorance, and the collapse of character-forming and educational institutions. *A Nation At Risk* was only one of nearly 100 studies of American education to appear in the early 1980's to stress the marginal if not outright deplorable condition of education in the country. Brutish Americans are as brutish as anyone anywhere. A rampant majority manipulated by clever demagoguery is a political menace at all times and places. And the ease with which a collapsed political party system can give way to a form of plebiscitary democracy through the power of television constitutes a reasonable ground of concern, and writers as little like George Orwell as Walter Dean Burnham, Kevin Phillips, and Theodore White have expressed that concern. It can happen here, and it can happen through idealism, high moral purpose, and worthy motivation. It begins to happen when the opposition becomes the political enemy, a not unknown phenomenon in our recent past.

The best available therapy is revitalization of the two-party system. The Democrats are, for the moment, cast in the role of the Administration's opposition. This adversarial posture is vital to a healthy country, within certain limits. A conciliating, bipartisan approach to governing by the Reagan Administration implies that not simply the electoral power of a landslide vote given by the determined center of the public controls policy, but that reason and compromise also are at work. Fairness or justice is essential to any sound regime, as Aristotle taught. The capacity of the president to appeal over the heads of Congress to the general public is potent and, doubtless, will be utilized so as to provide *leadership* for the country during the next years. We have had enough of the politics of stalemate since Richard Nixon's resignation from office in 1974. The presidency is, indeed, a bully pulpit and should be used as one. But effective checks and balances need to be at work, too, and this means reliance on the extraconstitutional force of the two-party system's adversarial function to augment the Constitution's division and separation of powers.

The Democrats have governed as a majority party since 1932 on the basis of the New Deal coalition of FDR composed of white Southerners, organized labor, Blacks, other ethnic and minority groups, Jews, Catholics, residents of the big cities, and intellectuals. Since 1952 and the election of the first Republican since Herbert Hoover (Eisenhower), this coalition has been in trouble. In truth, it was in trouble in Harry Truman's presidency, and all the world knows Truman barely squeaked past Republican candidate Thomas E. Dewey in 1948. The coalition now is a shambles. The early unity found in a common desire to foster federal domestic programs economically advantageous to each of the constituent groups has been lost. Economic disparities among these various groups pit the taxpayers against the welfare recipients. The civil rights revolution and such attendant policies as affirmative action intensify racial animosities. The rise of religious-based politics aggravates other tensions. Gay rights and the feminist movement create tensions with white Protestants and anti-abortion Catholics. Hawkish Southerners and dovish intellectuals divided during the long Vietnam period, as the original domestic and economic basis of the coalition had to face foreign involvement by the United States in its role as leader of the free world. And so on. Conflict rather than cooperation has become the rule for the old coalition groupings, and the demographic and economic changes in the country have made the original coalition itself obsolete and barely recognizable.

How this base will be repaired is unclear. The cry for social justice—important as it is—is not adequate to reconstitute the Democratic base, short of another depression. Moreover, the Reagan brand of constitutionalism and conservative populism along with the conciliation and co-optation of the new Republicans promises to defuse much of the appeal to fairness and social justice that a purely ideological, right-wing conservative, or old big-business-dominated Republican party might provoke and be vulnerable to. Still, there is a considerable likelihood that the reforming zeal of the Reagan Administration will leave enough injury and social debris in its wake to restore somewhat, at least, the appeal of the Democrats at the national level.

A substantial number of Americans do, in fact, believe the federal government ought increasingly to provide more services for the people and enlarge, rather than slowly shrink, the material supports of the citizenry. This is essentially the tendency toward socialism that exists in many forms in American society. That considerable segment of the population, combined with the uprooted and bruised sectors of the public that may emerge from Reagan's extremely ambitious reform efforts, *could* make a formidable base for revival of the national party. But the welfare state, quasi-socialist appeal is to antithetical to the current humor of the country, and of its silent majority, that only another economic crisis of great magnitude probably can overcome the tide of free market conservativism and traditional Lockean individualism that is running, not merely in Reagan's American but in Thatcher's Great Britain and even Mitterand's France. In any event, America has no true political left (as Burnham reminds us), and there is no class or ideological foundation for a major party there.

This leaves the Democratic prospects open to the ingenuity of its leadership and to the luck of the draw. The Republicans dominated politics from 1860 until 1932 with little interruption, and the Democrats largely have been dominant from then until 1980, still retain a majority of the House of Representatives, and outnumber formally affiliated Republicans among the voting population. Theodore White concludes, however, that the "election of 1980 marked the end of an era" and calls it "a watershed in American politics." The new Republicans could be in for a long run, for this kind of thing has clear precedent in our political history.

But there is no inevitably in politics. Less than one third of the electorate created the 1984 electoral landslide for President Reagan, and 45 percent of the potential electorate did not bother to vote. Voter registration, recruitment, and mobilization can change the face of American politics. But this requires organization and cooperation, and the Republicans have demonstrated far more of this than the Democrats, who cannot seem to find their constituency and consensus. The struggle for the Republican nomination in 1988, as we have noted, will bring at least some degree of confusion to that party and benefit the Democrats. Nor can landslide elections be counted as proof of invincibility. Herbert Hoover buried Democrat Al Smith in 1928 with 59 percent of the popular vote only to be buried himself by FDR four years later by a slightly larger percentage of the two-party vote. The American economy collapsed in the interim. The great Democratic landslide of 1964 gave way to a Republican victory in 1968, although just what would have happened had George Wallace's American Independent party not garnered nearly 10 million votes then is still unclear. The Republican landslide reelection of Richard Nixon in 1972 dissipated with Watergate into a Democratic victory in 1976 when James Earl Carter eked out a 50.1 percent popular vote to defeat incumbent President Gerald R. Ford, the only man to come to that office through appointment.

All of this reminds us that anything can happen in politics. The great changes in prospect for the structure of the United States through the Reagan Administration's decentralizing reforms called the New Federalism alone are themselves so fraught with uncertainty as to pose a major question mark about the durability of the Republicans' voter support. The pocketbook tends to control in American politics, and the shifting of functions without adequate funding sources back to states and municipalities is a game of political Russian roulette in the short run. How will it all be managed? How will incumbents fare if the transfer of power continues and the shifts in prospect are effected? Never mind the long-term, salutary benefits to the states as polities within a federal system of unprecedented standing and dignity. Politicians think in terms of the next election. There are more questions than answers in this vast arena, and much less money in prospect than is currently being expended. It all sounds grand in theory, but on the ground . . . ?

The same kind of wrenching questions and debates fill the air in the fields of education, farm policy, health and medical protection, and foreign and defense policy. In fact, it is difficult to find in American history a more profound searching of the national soul since the abolition crisis of the 1840's and 1850's than the debate now underway over our institutions and policies. Added to the domestic issues are the great foreign policy and military questions. Not least of all the enormous swelling of the Pentagon, the fearful military-industrial complex so soberly warned against by an expert, President Eisenhower, raises great questions about the ground of political power now and in the future in this country. Even the most determined anticommunist and hard-line critic of the U.S.S.R. can still tremble a little when confronted with the economic and political implications of the huge bite military expenditures represent not merely in dollars and cents but in the shifting of sovereign power from the people to a business-political-military elite, silently and subtly. Our system was designed for a normal operation in peace, yet we steadily have been at war—hot and cold—for nearly half a century. Do we grasp the results of that passage for ourselves and our nation?

Too much that is disruptive is transpiring in the United States not to provide fertile ground for a resuscitated Democratic party and a revitalized two-party system. The very organization and energy of the new Republicans force that issue along with a great many others.

How will it all turn out? What will happen next year, and in 1988? Our crystal ball fills with fog at these questions. We can only lamely answer, time will tell.

Appendices

Appendix I

Official 1984 Presidential Election: Final Tally

Note: Based on official returns from all 50 states and the District of Columbia.

State	RONALD REAGAN (Republican) Votes	%	WALTER F. MONDALE (Democrat) Votes	%	Total Other Candidate Vote	Total Vote	Percentage of 2-Party Vote	Turnout (Percentage of Potential Electorate)
Alabama	872,849	60.5	551,899	38.3	16,965	1,441,713	38.7	50.7
Alaska	138,377	66.7	62,007	29.9	7,221	207,605	30.9	62.0
Arizona	681,416	66.4	333,854	32.5	10,627	1,025,897	32.9	48.6
Arkansas	534,774	60.5	338,646	38.3	10,986	884,406	38.8	52.7
California	5,467,009	57.5	3,922,519	41.3	115,895	9,505,423	41.8	53.3
Colorado	821,817	63.4	454,975	00.0	18,588	1,295,380	35.6	56.6
Connecticut	890,877	60.7	569,597	38.8	6,426	1,466,900	39.0	63.8
Delaware	152,190	59.8	101,656	39.9	726	254,572	40.0	56.8
District of Columbia	29,009	13.7	180,408	85.4	1,871	211,288	86.1	45.2
Florida	2,730,350	65.3	1,488,816	34.7	885	4,180,051	34.7	52.5
Georgia	1,068,722	60.2	706,628	39.8	770	1,776,120	39.8	43.0

State	RONALD REAGAN (Republican) Votes	%	WALTER F. MONDALE (Democrat) Votes	%	Total Other Candidate Vote	Total Vote	Percentage of 2-Party Vote	Turnout (Percentage of Potential Electorate)
Hawaii	185,050	55.1	147,154	43.8	3,642	335,846	44.3	48.1
Idaho	297,523	72.4	108,510	26.4	5,111	411,144	26.7	61.7
Illinois	2,707,103	56.2	2,086,499	43.3	25,486	4,819,088	43.5	59.1
Indiana	1,377,230	61.7	841,481	37.7	14,358	2,233,069	37.9	56.9
Iowa	703,088	53.3	605,620	45.9	11,097	1,319,805	46.3	62.8
Kansas	677,296	66.3	333,149	32.6	11,546	1,021,991	33.0	57.8
Kentucky	821,702	60.0	539,539	39.4	8,104	1,369,345	39.6	51.1
Louisiana	1,037,299	60.8	561,586	38.2	17,937	1,706,822	38.6	55.3
Maine	336,500	60.8	214,515	38.8	2,129	553,144	38.9	67.1
Maryland	879,918	52.5	787,935	47.0	8,020	1,675,873	47.2	52.8
Massachusetts	1,310,936	51.2	1,239,606	48.4	8,911	2,559,543	48.6	60.2
Michigan	2,251,571	59.2	1,529,638	40.2	20,449	3,801,658	40.5	59.5
Minnesota	1,032,603	49.5	1,036,364	49.7	15,482	2,084,449	50.1	69.7
Mississippi	582,377	61.9	352,192	37.4	6,636	941,104	37.7	52.6
Missouri	1,274,188	60.0	848,583	40.0	0	2,122,771	40.0	58.4
Montana	232,450	60.5	146,742	38.2	5,185	384,377	38.7	66.0

302

State								
Nebraska	460,054	70.6	187,866	29.0	4,170	652,090	29.0	56.8
Nevada	188,770	65.9	91,655	32.7	2,292	282,717	32.7	43.1
New Hampshire	267,050	68.7	120,347	31.1	1,620	389,017	31.1	55.5
New Jersey	1,933,630	60.1	1,261,323	39.5	22,909	3,217,862	39.5	59.4
New Mexico	307,101	59.7	201,769	39.7	5,499	514,369	39.7	53.1
New York	3,664,763	53.8	3,119,609	46.0	22,438	6,086,810	46.0	53.7
North Carolina	1,346,481	61.9	824,287	38.0	4,593	2,175,361	38.0	48.4
North Dakota	200,336	64.8	104,429	33.8	4,206	306,871	34.3	63.8
Ohio	2,678,560	58.9	1,825,440	40.1	59,236	4,563,235	40.5	59.0
Oklahoma	861,530	68.6	385,080	30.7	9,066	1,255,676	30.9	52.1
Oregon	685,700	55.9	536,497	43.7	4,438	1,226,527	43.9	64.0
Pennsylvania	2,584,323	53.3	2,228,131	46.0	32,449	4,844,903	46.3	54.8
Rhode Island	212,080	51.8	197,106	47.9	1,306	410,792	48.2	57.8
South Carolina	615,539	63.6	344,459	35.6	8,531	968,529	35.9	41.4
South Dakota	200,267	63.0	116,113	36.5	1,487	317,867	36.7	64.2
Tennessee	990,212	57.8	711,714	41.6	10,068	1,711,994	41.8	49.8
Texas	3,433,428	63.6	1,949,276	36.1	14,867	5,397,571	36.2	48.9
Utah	469,105	74.5	155,369	24.7	5,182	629,656	24.9	62.7
Vermont	135,865	57.9	95,730	40.8	2,966	234,561	41.3	61.8
Virginia	1,337,078	62.3	796,250	37.1	13,307	2,146,635	37.3	52.2
Washington	1,051,670	55.8	807,352	42.9	24,888	1,883,910	43.4	61.2
West Virginia	405,483	55.1	328,125	44.6	2,134	735,742	44.7	51.9

State	RONALD REAGAN (Republican) Votes	%	WALTER F. MONDALE (Democrat) Votes	%	Total Other Candidate Vote	Total Vote	Percentage of 2-Party Vote	Turnout (Percentage of Potential Electorate)
Wisconsin	1,198,584	54.2	995,740	45.0	17,365	2,211,689	45.4	64.5
Wyoming	133,241	70.5	53,370	28.2	2,357	188,968	28.6	53.5
UNITED STATES	54,455,074	58.8	37,577,137	40.6	632,236	92,664,447	40.8	55.0

* Notes: there are some tiny discrepancies between the statewide major-party tallies in some states as between CQ's published data and the returns held by me. With the exception of the 9,000-vote discrepancy in Washington, they are entirely trivial. Arguendo, I accept CQ's statewide and national major-candidate totals. The third-party and total vote, however, differ rather more, and for reasons unknown to me. I count some 10,654 more scattered and "minor" votes than CQ does, hence the discrepancies.

Turnout is based on the estimated 1984 citizen electorate 18 years old and over by state, and not the larger voting-age population base (which includes aliens).

Prepared by Walter Dean Burnham.

Appendix II

Estimated National Presidential and Congressional Vote, 1984, Compared with 1972–1980 Totals

(Votes in Millions)

Year	President Dem.	President Rep.	President Other	President Total	U.S. House Dem.	U.S. House Rep.	U.S. House Other	U.S. House Total
1972	29.2	47.2	1.4	77.7	38.0	33.3	0.9	72.2
1976	40.8	39.1	1.6	81.6	42.6	31.4	1.2	75.3
1980	35.5	43.9	7.1	86.5	39.6	37.5	1.1	78.2
1984est	37.0	53.5	0.4	90.9	43.0	38.5	0.4	81.9

Percentages of the Total and Two-Party Vote

Year	President Total Dem.	President Total Rep.	President 2-Party Dem.	U.S. House Total Dem.	U.S. House Total Rep.	U.S. House 2-Party Dem.	2-Party Gap: P-C
1972	37.5	60.7	38.2	52.6	46.2	53.2	−15.0
1976	50.1	48.0	51.1	56.7	41.7	57.6	−6.5
1980	41.0	50.7	44.7	50.6	47.9	51.4	−6.7
1984est	40.7	58.9	40.9	52.5	47.0	52.8	−11.9

305

Turnout (Percentage Voting of Estimated Citizen Adults) and Partisan Division of House Seats

Year	Est. Potential Electorate (millions)	Turnout: President.	Turnout: U.S. House*	U.S. House Seats Dem.	U.S. House Seats Rep.	U.S. House Seats Total	Majority
1972	136.3	57.0	53.2	243	192	435	51 D
1976	147.7	55.2	51.1	292	143	435	149 D
1980	159.2	54.3	49.2	243	192	435	51 D
1984	168.3	53.0	48.8	252	182	434**	70 D

* U.S. House turnout excludes the District of Columbia from the population base (i.e., the 1984 House base is 167.9 million).
** One seat undecided (8th Indiana), and pending lengthy recount proceedings. Final margin will either be 71 D or 69 D, depending on the outcome.

Prepared by Walter Dean Burnham

Appendix III

Turnout Rates by State, 1960 and 1980–1984*

State	% Voting of Estimated Potential Electorate			Turnout Shift, 1960– 1980	Turnout Shift, 1980– 1984
	1960	1980	1984		
Alabama	31.2	49.3	49.2	+18.1	-0.1
Alaska	48.0	59.2	50.3	+10.2	-8.9
Arizona	56.7	46.4	47.7	-10.3	+1.3
Arkansas	41.2	52.0	51.9	+10.8	-0.1
California	71.0	52.4	51.8	-18.6	-0.6
Colorado	72.6	57.7	53.3	-14.9	-4.4
Connecticut	80.8	63.8	63.1	-17.0	-0.7
Delaware	74.7	55.8	56.2	-18.9	+0.4
Dist. Columbia	...	36.6	42.6	...	+6.0
Florida	51.6	52.2	50.0	+0.6	-2.2
Georgia	30.5	42.0	42.8	+11.5	+0.8
Hawaii	58.1	47.6	48.0	-10.5	+0.4

307

State	% Voting of Estimated Potential Electorate			Turnout Shift, 1960–1980	Turnout Shift, 1980–1984
	1960	1980	1984		
Idaho	81.7	69.3	60.8	−12.4	−8.5
Illinois	77.7	59.5	58.3	−18.2	−1.2
Indiana	77.5	58.3	54.8	−19.2	−3.5
Iowa	77.1	63.4	62.1	−13.7	−1.3
Kansas	70.8	57.5	57.0	−13.3	−0.5
Kentucky	59.4	50.3	50.6	−9.1	+0.3
Louisiana	45.1	54.2	54.4	+9.1	+0.2
Maine	75.0	66.4	66.5	−8.6	+0.1
Maryland	58.2	51.4	50.3	−6.8	−1.1
Massachusetts	79.5	61.4	59.4	−18.1	−2.0
Michigan	74.5	61.2	59.1	−13.3	−2.1
Minnesota	78.1	71.2	69.0	−6.9	−2.2
Mississippi	25.5	52.4	52.3	+26.9	−0.1
Missouri	72.3	59.4	57.9	−14.4	−1.5
Montana	72.4	66.0	60.1	−6.4	−5.9
Nebraska	72.3	57.4	55.0	−14.9	−2.4
Nevada	62.9	43.3	42.8	−19.6	−0.5

State					
New Hampshire	82.0	59.2	54.6	−22.8	−4.6
New Jersey	74.7	57.4	58.5	−17.3	+1.1
New Mexico	63.2	52.4	52.3	−10.8	−0.1
New York	70.6	50.4	51.9	−20.2	+1.5
North Carolina	53.7	44.1	48.1	−9.6	+4.0
North Dakota	79.5	65.6	62.7	−13.9	−2.9
Ohio	72.4	56.2	57.7	−16.2	+1.5
Oklahoma	64.1	53.2	51.8	−10.9	−1.4
Oregon	73.6	62.7	60.3	−10.9	−2.4
Pennsylvania	71.8	52.8	54.1	−19.0	+1.3
Rhode Island	77.9	60.6	55.8	−17.3	−4.8
South Carolina	30.6	41.2	37.3	+10.6	−3.9
South Dakota	78.8	67.7	63.9	−11.1	−3.8
Tennessee	50.4	49.3	49.7	−1.1	+0.4
Texas	42.9	46.7	48.8	+3.8	+2.1
Utah	81.8	66.7	61.9	−15.1	−4.8
Vermont	74.6	59.4	60.3	−15.2	+0.9
Virginia	33.6	48.6	52.0	+15.0	+3.4
Washington	74.3	59.7	54.6	−14.6	−5.1
West Virginia	77.9	53.3	51.1	−24.6	−2.2
Wisconsin	74.4	68.5	63.9	−5.9	−4.7

State	% Voting of Estimated Potential Electorate			Turnout Shift 1960–1980	Turnout Shift 1980–1984
	1960	1980	1984		
Wyoming	75.4	55.0	52.5	–20.4	–2.5
NON-SOUTH	72.8	56.6	55.6	–16.2	–1.0
SOUTH	41.4	48.1	48.8	+6.7	+0.7
UNITED STATES	65.4	54.3	54.1	–11.1	–0.2

*Notes 1. The turnouts for 1960 and 1980 are based on complete official returns for president. The denominators (potential electorate estimates) are based on voting-age citizen population at the time of the election (as citizenship is not given in the 1960 census, though it is at the state level for 1950, 1970, and 1980; interpolations for 1960 from the 1950 and 1970 census data are used to make the estimate for that year). It is assumed that the fraction of total voting-age population who had citizenship status was identical in 1984 to its 1980 census figure, and voting-age population estimates for 1984 are adjusted downwards accordingly.

2. Except for Texas and Colorado, where apparently complete returns for president including minor-party votes are available at the time of compilation, turnouts are based on the totals for Reagan and Mondale only, based on the most complete figures currently available (USA Today, November 8, 1984). Obviously, the actual turnouts will be higher in the end, both because of possible additions to the major-party totals and because of the addition of minor-party votes. There is, however, excellent reason to believe that they will not go up very substantially for either reason—possibly by about 0.3–0.8 percent.

Prepared by Walter Dean Burnham

Appendix IV

Inaugural Address
President Ronald W. Reagan

(January 21, 1985, Washington, D.C.)

Senator Mathias, Chief Justice Burger, Vice President Bush, Speaker O'Neill, Senator Dole, Reverend Clergy, members of my family, and my fellow citizens:

There are no words adequate to express my thanks for the great honor you have bestowed on me. I will do my utmost to be deserving of your trust.

This is the fiftieth time we the people have celebrated this historic occasion. When the first president, George Washington, placed his hand upon the Bible, he stood less than a single day's journey by horseback from raw, untamed wilderness.

There were four million Americans in a union of 13 states. Today, we are 60 times as many in a union of 50 states. We have lighted the world with our inventions, gone to the aid of our fellow citizens of the world wherever they cried out for help, journeyed to the Moon and safely returned.

So much has changed. And yet, here again we stand, together as centuries ago. And, once again, an American president freely chosen by a sovereign people has taken the oath prescribed by the Constitution that guides us still. This alone is cause for rejoicing, but there is more.

When I took this oath four years ago, I did so in a time of economic stress. Voices were raised saying we had to look to our past for the greatness and glory that had marked our two centuries as a nation. But we, the present-day Americans, are not given to looking backward. In this blessed land, there is always a better tomorrow.

Four years ago, I spoke to you of a new beginning, and we

have accomplished that. But in another sense, our new beginning is a continuation of that beginning created two centuries ago; that break with the past when, for the first time in history, a people said, government is not our master but our servant; and government's only power will be that which we the people allow it to have.

Our bedrock principles have never failed us. But, for a time, we failed those principles. Over recent years we asked things of the federal government that it was not equipped to give. We yielded authority to government that properly belonged at local or state levels or in the hands of the citizenry. We allowed taxes and inflation to rob us of our earnings and savings. We watched the great industrial machine that had made us the most productive people on Earth slow and the number of unemployed mount.

By 1980, we knew it was time to embrace again the great promise of our American Revolution; time to renew our faith; to dream heroic dreams; to strive with all our strength toward the ultimate in individual freedom, consistent with an orderly society.

We believed then and repeat today: There are no limits to growth and human progress when men and women are free to follow their dreams. And we were right to believe. Tax rates have been reduced, inflation cut dramatically, and more people are employed today than ever in our history.

We are creating a new America, a rising nation once again vibrant, robust, and alive. But the promise of our revolution was meant for all people for all future time. There are many mountains yet to climb. We will not rest until every American, from countryside to inner city, enjoys the fullness of freedom dignity, and opportunity which is our birthright as citizens of this great republican.

If we meet this challenge, these will be years of American renewal:

> When Americans restored their confidence and tradition of progress;
> When our values of faith, family, work, and neighborhood were revived and restated for a modern age;
> When our economy was finally freed from government's grip, and the American eagle soared to new heights;

When we made sincere efforts at meaningful arms reduction, and also, by rebuilding our defenses, our economy, and developing new technologies, strengthened our position and helped preserve peace in a troubled world;

And, yes, the years when America courageously supported the struggle for individual liberty, self-government, and free enterprise throughout the world, and turned the tide of history away from totalitarian darkness and into the warm sunlight of human freedom.

My fellow citizens, our nation is poised for greatness. We must do what we know is right, and do it with all our might. Let history say of us, these were golden years—when the American Revolution was reborn, when freedom gained new life, when America reached for her best.

Our two-party system has served us well over the years, but never better than in times of great challenge, when we come together not as Democrats or Republicans, but as Americans united in this common cause.

Two of our founding fathers, a Boston lawyer named Adams and a Virginia planter named Jefferson, both members of that remarkable group who met in Independence Hall and dared to think they could start the world over again, left us an important lesson. They had become political rivals in the government they helped create.

In the presidential election of 1800, they were bitterly estranged. Only years later when both were retired, and age had softened their anger, did they begin to speak to each other through letters.

In 1826, the fiftieth anniversary of the Declaration of Independence, they both died, died on the same day, within a few hours of each other. The day was the Fourth of July.

In one of those letters exchanged in the sunset of their lives, Jefferson wrote, "It carries me back to the times when, beset with difficulties and dangers, we were fellow laborers in the same cause, struggling for what is most valuable to man, his right of self-government. Laboring always at the same oar, with some wave ever ahead threatening to overwhelm us, and yet passing harmless . . . we rode through the storm with heart and hand."

With heart and hand, let us stand as one today: One people

under God determined that our future shall be worthy of our past. As we do, we must not repeat the well-intentioned errors of our past. We must never again abuse the trust of working men and women, by sending their earnings on a futile chase after the spiraling demands of a bloated federal establishment. You elected us in 1980 to end this prescription for disaster. I do not believe you reelected us in 1984 to reverse course.

At the heart of our efforts is one idea vindicated by 25 straight months of economic growth: Freedom and incentives unleash the drive and entrepreneurial genius that are the core of human progress. We have begun to increase rewards for work, savings, and investment, reduce the increase in the cost and size of government and its interference in people's lives.

Rather than limit our challenge to growth, let us challenge the limits of growth. We must simplify our tax system, make it more fair and bring tax rates down for all who work and earn. We must think anew and move with new boldness, so every American who seeks work can find work; so the least among us have an equal chance to achieve the greatest things—to be heroes who heal our sick, feed the hungry, protect peace among nations, and leave this world a better place.

The time has come for a new American Emancipation—a great national drive to tear down economic barriers and liberate the spirit of enterprise in the most distressed areas of our country. My friends, together we can do this, and do it we must, so help me God.

From new freedom will spring new opportunities for growth, a more productive, fulfilled, and united people, and a stronger America—an America that will lead the technological revolution, and also open its mind, heart, and soul to the treasures of literature, music, and poetry, and the values of faith, courage, and love.

A dynamic economy, with more citizens working and paying taxes, will be our strongest tool to bring down budget deficits. But an almost unbroken 50 years of deficit spending has finally brought us to a time of reckoning.

We have come to a turning point, a moment for hard decisions. I have asked the Cabinet and Staff a question, and now I put that same question to you. If not us, who? If not now, when? We know the answer. It must be done now, by all of us going forward with a program aimed at reaching a balanced budget. We can then begin reducing the national debt.

I will shortly submit a budget to the Congress aimed at freezing government program spending for the next year. Beyond that we must take further steps to permanently control government's power to tax and spend.

We must act now to protect future generations from government's desire to spend its citizens' money and tax them into servitude when the bills come due. Let us make it unconstitutional for the federal government to spend more than it takes in.

We have already started returning to the people and to state and local governments responsibilities better handled by them. There is a place for the federal government in matters of social compassion. But our fundamental goals must be to reduce dependency and upgrade the dignity of those who are infirm or disadvantaged. And here, a growing economy and support from family and community offer our best chance for a society where compassion is the way of life, where the old and infirm are cared for, the young and, yes, the unborn protected, and the unfortunate looked after and made self-sufficient.

There is another area where the federal government can play a part. As an older American, I remember a time when people of different race, creed, or ethnic origin in our land found hatred and prejudice installed in social custom and law. There is no story more heartening in our history than the progress we've made toward the ''brotherhood of man'' that God intended for us. Let us resolve there will be no turning back or hesitation on the road to an America rich in dignity and abundant with opportunity for all our citizens.

Let us resolve that we the people will build an American opportunity society, in which all of us—white and black, rich and poor, young and old—will go forward together, arm in arm. Again, let us remember that, though our heritage is one of blood lines from every corner of the Earth, we are all Americans pledged to carry on this last, best hope of man on Earth.

I have spoken of our domestic goals and the limitations we should put on our national government. Let me turn now to a task that is, above all, the primary responsibility of national government—the safety and security of our people.

Today, we utter no prayer more fervently than the ancient prayer for peace on Earth. Yet history has shown that peace does not come, nor will our freedom be preserved, by goodwill alone. There are those in the world who scorn our vision of human dignity and freedom. One nation, the Soviet Union, has conducted the greatest military buildup in the history of man, building arsenals of awesome, offensive weapons.

We have made progress in restoring our defense capability. But much remains to be done. There must be no wavering by us, nor any doubts by others, that America will meet her responsibilities to remain free, secure, and at peace.

There is only one way safely and legitimately to reduce the cost of national security, and that is to reduce the need for it. This we are trying to do in negotiations with the Soviet Union. We are not just discussing limits on any further increase of nuclear weapons. We seek, instead, to reduce them. For the sake of each child in every corner of the globe, we seek, one day, the total elimination of nuclear weapons from the face of the Earth.

For decades, we and the Soviets have lived under the threat of mutual assured destruction; if either resorted to the use of nuclear weapons, the other could retaliate and destroy the other. Is there either logic or morality in believing that, if one side threatens to kill tens of millions of our people, our only recourse is to threaten tens of millions of theirs?

We seek another way—a far better way. I have approved a research program to see if a security shield can be developed that will destroy nuclear missiles before they reach their target. Such a shield would not kill people, but destroy weapons; it would not militarize space, but help demilitarize the arsenals of Earth. Such a shield could render nuclear weapons obsolete. So, we will meet with the Soviets hoping that we can agree on a formula for ridding the world of the threat of nuclear destruction.

And as we strive for peace and security, we are heartened by the changes all around us. Since the turn of the century, the number of democracies in the world has grown fourfold. Today, human freedom is on the march, and nowhere more so than in our own hemisphere. Freedom is one of the deepest and noblest aspirations of the human spirit. People worldwide hunger for the right of self-determination, for those inalienable rights that make for human dignity and progress.

America must remain freedom's staunchest friend, for freedom is our best ally, and the world's only hope to conquer poverty and preserve peace. Every blow we inflict against poverty will be a blow against its dark allies of oppression and war. Every victory for human freedom will be a victory for world peace.

So we go forward today, a nation still mighty in its youth and powerful in its purpose. With our alliances strengthened, with our economy leading the world to a new age of economic expansion, we look to a future rich in possibilities. All this because we worked and acted together, not as members of political parties, but as Americans.

My friends, we live in a world lit by lightning. So much is changing and will change, but so much endures and transcends time.

History is a ribbon, always unfurling; history is a journey. And as we continue our journey, we think of those who traveled it before us. We stand again at the steps of this symbol of our democracy, and we see and hear again the echoes of our past.

A general falls to his knees in the hard snow of Valley Forge; a lonely president paces the darkened halls and ponders his struggle to preserve the Union; the men of the Alamo call out encouragement to each other; a settler pushes west and sings a song, and the song echoes out forever and fills the unknowing air.

It is the American sound: hopeful, big-hearted, idealistic—daring, decent, and fair. That is our heritage, that is our song. We sing it still. For all our problems, our differences, we are together as of old, as we raise our voices to the God who is the Author of this most tender music. And may He continue to hold us close as we fill the world with our sound—in unity, affection, and love. One people under God, dedicated to the dream of freedom He has placed in the human heart, called upon now to pass that dream on to a waiting and hopeful world.

God bless you and may God bless America.

Appendix V

President Ronald W. Reagan's State of The Union Address, February 6, 1985

(Text of Address as transcribed when delivered by the President.)

The President: Mr. Speaker, Mr. President, distinguished members of the Congress, honored guests, and fellow citizens, I come before you to report on the state of our Union, and I'm pleased to report that after four years of united effort, the American people have brought forth a nation renewed, stronger, freer, and more secure than before.

Four years ago, we began to change, forever I hope, our assumptions about government and its place in our lives. Out of that change has come great and robust growth—in our confidence, our economy, and our role in the world.

Tonight, America is stronger because of the values that we hold dear. We believe faith and freedom must be our guiding stars for they show us truth, they make us brave, give us hope, and leave us wiser than we were. Our progress began not in Washington, D.C., but in the hearts of our families, communities, workplaces, and voluntary groups which, together, are unleashing the invincible spirit of one great nation under God.

Four years ago, we said we would invigorate our economy by giving people greater freedom and incentives to take risks and letting them keep more of what they earned. We did what we promised. And a great industrial giant is reborn.

Tonight, we can take pride in 25 straight months of economic growth, the strongest in 34 years; a 3-year inflation average of 3.9 percent, the lowest in 17 years; and 7.3 million new jobs in two years, with more of our citizens working than ever before.

New freedom in our lives has planted the rich seeds for future success:

For an America of wisdom that honors the family, knowing that as the family goes, so goes our civilization;

For an America of vision that sees tomorrow's dreams in the learning and hard work we do today;

For an America of courage whose servicemen and women, even as we meet, proudly stand watch on the frontiers of freedom;

For an America of compassion that opens its heart to those who cry out for help.

We have begun well. But it's only a beginning. We're not here to congratulate ourselves on what we have done, but to challenge ourselves to finish what has not yet been done.

We're here to speak for millions in our inner cities who long for real jobs, safe neighborhoods, and schools that truly teach. We're here to speak for the American farmer, the entrepreneur, and every worker in industries fighting to modernize and compete. And, yes, we're here to stand, and proudly so, for all who struggle to break free from totalitarianism; for all who know in their hearts that freedom is the one true path to peace and human happiness.

Proverbs tells us, without a vision the people perish. When asked what great principle holds our Union together, Abraham Lincoln said, "Something in (the) Declaration giving liberty, not alone to the people of this country, but hope to the world for all future time."

We honor the giants of our history not by going back, but forward to the dreams their vision foresaw. My fellow citizens, this nation is poised for greatness. The time has come to proceed toward a great new challenge, a Second American Revolution of hope and opportunity; a revolution carrying us to new heights of progress by pushing back frontiers of knowledge and space; a revolution of spirit that taps the soul of America, enabling us to summon greater strength than we've ever known; and a revolution that carries beyond our shores the golden promise of human freedom in a world of peace.

Let us begin by challenging our conventional wisdom. There are no constraints on the human mind, no walls around the human spirit, no barriers to our progress except those we ourselves erect. Already, pushing down tax rates has freed our economy to vault forward to record growth.

In Europe, they're calling it "the American Miracle." Day

by day, we are shattering accepted notions of what is possible. When I was growing up, we failed to see how a new thing called radio would transform our marketplace. Well, today, many have not yet seen how advances in technology are transforming our lives.

In the late 1950's, workers at the AT&T semiconductor plant in Pennsylvania produced five transistors a day for $7.50 apiece. They now produce over a million for less than a penny apiece.

New laser techniques could revolutionize heart bypass surgery, cut diagnosis time for viruses linked to cancer from weeks to minutes, reduce hospital costs dramatically, and hold out new promise for saving human lives.

Our automobile industry has overhauled assembly lines, increased worker productivity, and is competitive once again.

We stand on the threshold of a great ability to produce more, do more, be more. Our economy is not getting older and weaker, it's getting younger and stronger. It doesn't need rest and supervision, it needs new challenge, greater freedom. And that word freedom is the key to the second American revolution that we need to bring about.

Let us move together with an historic reform of tax simplification for fairness and growth. Last year, I asked Treasury Secretary then Regan to develop a plan to simplify the tax code, so all taxpayers would be treated more fairly and personal tax rates could come further down.

We have cut tax rates by almost 25 percent, yet the tax system remains unfair and limits our potential for growth. Exclusions and exemptions caused similar incomes to be taxed at different levels. Low-income families face steep tax barriers that make hard lives even harder. The Treasury Department has produced an excellent reform plan whose principles will guide the final proposal that we will ask you to enact.

One thing that tax reform will not be is a tax increase in disguise. We will not jeopardize the mortgage interest deduction that families need. We will reduce personal tax rates as low as possible by removing many tax preferences. We will propose a top rate of no more than 35 percent, and possibly lower. And we will propose reducing corporate rates while maintaining incentives for capital formation.

To encourage opportunity and jobs rather than dependency

and welfare, we will propose that individuals living at or near the poverty line be totally exempt from federal income tax. To restore fairness to families, we will propose increasing significantly the personal exemption.

And tonight, I am instructing Treasury Secretary James Baker—I have to get used to saying that—to begin working with congressional authors and committees for bipartisan legislation conforming to these principles. We will call upon the American people for support, and upon every man and woman in this chamber. Together, we can pass, this year, a tax bill for fairness, simplicity, and growth, making this economy the engine of our dreams and America the investment capital of the world—so let us begin.

Tax simplification will be a giant step toward unleashing the tremendous pent-up power of our economy. But a second American revolution must carry the promise of opportunity for all. It is time to liberate the spirit of enterprise in the most distressed areas of our country.

This government will meet its responsibility to help those in need. But policies that increase dependency, break up families, and destroy self-respect are not progressive, they're reactionary. Despite our strides in civil rights, Blacks, Hispanics and all minorities will not have full and equal power until they have full economic power.

We have repeatedly sought passage of enterprise zones to help those in the abandoned corners of our land find jobs, learn skills, and build better lives. This legislation is supported by a majority of you.

Mr. Speaker, I know we agree that there must be no forgotten Americans. Let us place new dreams in a million hearts and create a new generation of entrepreneurs by passing enterprise zones this year. Tip, you could make that a birthday present.

Nor must we lose the chance to pass our Youth Employment Opportunity wage proposal. We can help teenagers who have the highest unemployment rate find summer jobs, so they can know the pride of work and have confidence in their futures.

We'll continue to support the Job Training Partnership Act which has a nearly two-thirds job placement rate. Credits in education and health care vouchers will help working families shop for services that they need.

Our administration is already encouraging certain low-income public housing residents to own and manage their own dwellings. It's time that all public housing residents have that opportunity of ownership.

The federal government can help create a new atmosphere of freedom. But states and localities, many of which enjoy surpluses from the recovery, must not permit their tax and regulatory policies to stand as barriers to growth.

Let us resolve that we will stop spreading dependency and start spreading opportunity; that we will stop spreading bondage and start spreading freedom.

There are some who say that growth initiatives must await final action on deficit reductions. Well, the best way to reduce deficits is through economic growth. More businesses will be started, more investments made, more jobs created, and more people will be on payrolls paying taxes. The best way to reduce government spending is to reduce the need for spending by increasing prosperity. Each added percentage point per year of real GNP growth will lead to cumulative reduction in deficits of nearly $200 billion over five years.

To move steadily toward a balanced budget, we must also lighten government's claim on our total economy. We will not do this by raising taxes. We must make sure that our economy grows faster than the growth in spending by the federal government. In our fiscal year 1986 budget, overall government spending will be frozen at the current level. It must not be one dime higher than fiscal year 1985, and three points are key.

First, a social safety net for the elderly, the needy, the disabled, and unemployed will be left intact. Growth of our major health care programs, Medicare and Medicade, will be slowed, but protections for the elderly and needy will be preserved.

Second, we must not relax our efforts to restore military strength just as we near our goal of a fully equipped, trained, and ready professional corps. National security is government's first responsibility, so in past years defense spending took about half the federal budget. Today it takes less than a third. We've already reduced our planned defense expenditures by nearly $100 million over the past four years and reduced projected spending again this year.

You know, we only have a military-industrial complex

until a time of danger, and then it becomes the arsenal of democracy. Spending for defense is investing in things that are priceless: peace and freedom.

Third, we must reduce or eliminate costly government subsidies. For example, deregulation of the airline industry has led to cheaper airfares, but on Amtrak taxpayers pay about $35.00 per passenger every time an Amtrak train leaves the station. It's time we ended this huge federal subsidy.

Our farm program costs have quadrupled in recent years. Yet I know from visiting farmers, many in great financial distress, that we need an orderly transition to a market-oriented farm economy. We can help farmers best not by expanding federal payments, but by making fundamental reforms, keeping interest rates heading down, and knocking down foreign trade barriers to American farm exports.

We—we're moving ahead with Grace Commission reforms to eliminate waste and improve government's management practices. In the long run, we must protect the taxpayers from government. And I ask again that you pass, as 32 states have now called for, an amendment mandating the federal government spend no more than it takes in. And I ask for the authority used responsibly by 43 governors to veto individual items in appropriation bills. Senator Mattingly has introduced a bill permitting a two-year trial run of the line-item veto. I hope you'll pass and send that legislation to my desk.

Nearly 50 years of government living beyond its means has brought us to a time of reckoning. Ours is but a moment in history. But one moment of courage, idealism, and bipartisan unity can change American history forever.

Sound monetary policy is key to long-running economic strength and stability. We will continue to cooperate with the Federal Reserve Board, seeking a steady policy that ensures price stability without keeping interest rates artificially high or needlessly holding down growth.

Reducing unneeded red tape and regulations, and deregulating the energy, transportation, and financial industries have unleashed new competition, giving consumers more choices, better services, and lower prices. In just one set of grant programs we have reduced 905 pages of regulations to 31.

We seek to fully deregulate natural gas to bring on new supplies and bring us closer to energy independence. Consistent with safety standards, we will continue removing restraints on the bus and railroad industries; we will soon end up legislation—or send up legislation, I should say—to return Conrail to the private sector where it belongs, and we will support further deregulation of the trucking industry.

Every dollar the federal government does not take from us, every decision it does not make for us, will make our economy stronger, our lives more abundant, our future more free.

Our second American revolution will push on to new possibilities not only on earth, but in the next frontier of space. Despite budget restraints, we will seek record funding for research and development.

We've seen the success of the space shuttle. Now we're going to develop a permanently manned space station and new opportunities for free enterprise, because in the next decade, Americans and our friends around the world will be living and working together in space.

In the zero gravity of space, we could manufacture in 30 days lifesaving medicines it would take 30 years to make on earth. We can make crystals of exceptional purity to produce supercomputers, creating jobs, technologies, and medical breakthroughs beyond anything we ever dreamed possible.

As we do all this, we'll continue to protect our natural resources. We will seek reauthorization and expanded funding for the Superfund program to continue cleaning up hazardous waste sites which threaten human health and the environment.

There's another great heritage to speak of this evening. Of all the changes that have swept America the past four years, none brings greater promise than our rediscovery of the values of faith, freedom, family, work, and neighborhood.

We see signs of renewal in increased attendance in places of worship; renewed optimism and faith in our future; love of country rediscovered by our young, who are leading the way. We've rediscovered that work is good in and of itself, that it ennobles us to create and contribute no matter how seemingly humble our jobs. We've seen a powerful new current from an old and honorable tradition, American generosity.

From thousands answering Peace Corps appeals to help boost food production in Africa, to millions volunteering time, corporations adopting schools, and communities pulling together to help the neediest among us at home, we have refound our values. Private sector initiatives are crucial to our future.

I thank the Congress for passing equal access legislation giving religious groups the same right to use classrooms after school that other groups enjoy. But no citizen need tremble, nor the world shudder, if a child stands in a classroom and breathes a prayer. We ask you again, give children back a right they had for a century-and-a-half in this country.

The question of abortion grips our nation. Abortion is either the taking of a human life or it isn't. And if it is—and medical technology is increasingly showing it is—it must be stopped.

It is a terrible irony that while some turn to abortion, so many others who cannot become parents cry out for children to adopt. We have room for these children. We can fill the cradles of those who want a child to love. Tonight I ask you in the Congress to move this year on legislation to protect the unborn.

In the area of education we're returning to excellence, and again, the heroes are our people, not government. We're stressing basics of discipline, rigorous testing, and homework while helping children become computer-smart as well. For 20 years, Scholastic Aptitude Test scores of our high school students went down. But now they have gone up two of the last three years.

We must go forward in our commitment to the new basics, giving parents greater authority and making sure good teachers are rewarded for hard work and achievement through merit pay.

Of all the changes in the past 20 years, none has more threatened our sense of national well-being than the explosion of violent crime. One does not have to be attacked to be a victim. The woman who must run to her car after shopping at night is a victim. The couple draping their door with locks and chains are victims; as is the tired, decent cleaning woman who can't ride a subway home without being afraid.

We do not seek to violate the rights of dependents—defendants. But shouldn't we feel more compassion for the victims of crime than for those who commit crimes? For the first time in 20 years, the crime index has fallen 2 years in a row. We've convicted over 7,400 drug offenders and put them, as well as leaders of organized crime, behind bars in record numbers.

But we must do more. I urge the House to follow the Senate and enact proposals permitting use of all reliable evidence that police officers acquire in good faith. These proposals would also reform the habeas corpus laws and allow, in keeping with the will of the overwhelming majority of Americans, the use of the death penalty where necessary.

There can be no economic revival in ghettos when the most violent among us are allowed to roam free. It's time we restored domestic tranquillity. And we mean to do just that.

Just as we're positioned as never before to secure justice in our economy, we're poised as never before to create a safer, freer, more peaceful world.

Our alliances are stronger than ever. Our economy is stronger than ever. We have resumed our historic role as a leader of the free world. And all of these together are a great force for peace.

Since 1981, we've been committed to seeking fair and verifiable arms agreements that would lower the risk of war and reduce the size of nuclear arsenals. Now our determination to maintain a strong defense has influenced the Soviet Union to return to the bargaining table. Our negotiators must be able to go to that table with the united support of the American people. All of us have no greater dream than to see the day when nuclear weapons are banned from this Earth forever.

Each member of the Congress has a role to play in modernizing our defenses, thus supporting our chances for a meaningful arms agreement. Your vote this spring on the Peacekeeper missile will be a crucial test of our resolve to maintain the strength we need and move toward mutual and verifiable arms reductions.

For the past 20 years we've believed that no war will be launched as long as each side knows it can retaliate with a deadly counterstrike. Well, I believe there's a better way of eliminating the threat of nuclear war.

It is a Strategic Defense Initiative aimed ultimately at finding a nonnuclear defense against ballistic missiles. It's the most hopeful possibility of the nuclear age. But it's not very well understood.

Some say it will bring war to the heavens—but its purpose

is to deter war in the heavens and on earth. Now some say the research would be expensive. Perhaps, but it could save millions of lives, indeed humanity itself. And some say if we build such a system, the Soviets will build a defense system of their own. Well they already have strategic defenses that surpass ours; a civil defense system where we have almost none; and a research program covering roughly the same areas of technology that we're now exploring. And finally some say the research will take a long time. Well, the answer to that is: "Let's get started."

Harry Truman once said that, ultimately, our security, and the world's hopes for peace and human progress, "lie not in measures of defense or in the control of weapons, but in the growth and expansion of freedom and self-government."

And tonight, we declare anew to our fellow citizens of the world: freedom is not the sole prerogative of a chosen few; it is the universal right of all God's children. Look to where peace and prosperity flourish today. It is in homes that freedom built. Victories against poverty are greatest and peace most secure where people live by laws that ensure free press, free speech, and freedom to worship, vote, and create wealth.

Our mission is to nourish and defend freedom and democracy, and to communicate these ideals everywhere we can. America's economic success is freedom's success; it can be repeated a hundred times in a hundred different nations. Many countries in East Asia and the Pacific have few resources other than the enterprise of their own people. But through low tax rates and free markets they've soared ahead of centralized economies. And now China is opening up its economy to meet its needs.

We need a stronger and simpler approach to the process of making and implementing trade policy, and we'll be studying potential changes in that process in the next few weeks. We've seen the benefits of free trade and lived through the disasters of protectionism. Tonight, I ask all our trading partners, developed and developing alike, to join us in a new round of trade negotiations to expand trade and competition, and strengthen the global economy—and to begin it in this next year.

There are more than three billion human beings living in third world countries with an average per capita income of $650 a year. Many are victims of dictatorships that impoverished them with taxation and corruption. Let us ask our allies to join us in a practical program of trade and assistance that fosters economic development through personal incentives to help these people climb from poverty on their own.

We cannot play innocents abroad in a world that's not innocent. Nor can we be passive when freedom is under siege. Without resources, diplomacy cannot succeed. Our security assistance programs help friendly governments defend themselves and give them confidence to work for peace. And I hope that you in the Congress will understand that dollar for dollar, security assistance contributes as much to global security as our own defense budget.

We must stand by all our democratic allies. And we must not break faith with those who are risking their lives on every continent, from Afghanistan to Nicaragua, to defy Soviet-supported aggression and secure rights which have been ours from birth.

The Sandinista dictatorship of Nicaragua, with full Cuban-Soviet-bloc support, not only persecutes its people, the church, and denies a free press, but arms and provides bases for communist terrorists attacking neighboring states. Support for freedom fighters is self-defense and totally consistent with the O.A.S. and U.N. charters. It is essential that the Congress continue all facets of our assistance to Central America. I want to work with you to support the democratic forces whose struggle is tied to our own security.

Tonight, I've spoken of great plans and great dreams. They're dreams we can make come true. Two hundred years of American history should have taught us that nothing is impossible.

Ten years ago, a young girl left Vietnam with her family, part of the exodus that followed the fall of Saigon. They came to the United States with no possessions and not knowing a word of English. Ten years ago. The young girl studied hard, learned English, and finished high school in the top of her class. And this May, May 22nd to be exact, is a big date on her calendar. Just ten years from the time she left Vietnam she will graduate from the United States Military Academy at West Point.

I thought you like—I thought you might like to meet an American hero named Jean Nguyen.

Now there's someone else here tonight, born 79 years ago.

She lives in the inner city where she cares for infants born of mothers who are heroin addicts. The children, born in withdrawal, are sometimes even dropped on her doorstep. She helps them with love. Go to her house some night and maybe you'll see her silhouette against the window as she walks the floor talking softly, soothing a child in her arms—Mother Hale of Harlem, and she, too, is an American hero.

Jean, Mother Hale, your lives tell us that the oldest American saying is new again: Anything is possible in America if we have the faith, the will, and the heart. History is asking us once again to be a force for good in the world. Let us begin in unity, with justice, and love. Thank you and God bless you.

Appendix VI

President Ronald W. Reagan's 1985 Budget Message to the U.S. Congress, February 4, 1985

To the Congress of the United States:

In the past 2 years we have experienced one of the strongest economic recoveries of the postwar period. The prospect of a substantially brighter future for America lies before us. As 1985 begins, the economy is growing robustly and shows considerable upward momentum. Favorable financial conditions presage a continuation of the expansion. Production, productivity, and employment gains have been impressive, and inflation remains well under control. I am proud of the state of our economy. Let me highlight a few points:

- The economy expanded at a 6.8 percent rate in 1984 and at a 6 percent annual rate over the 2 years since the recession trough at the end of 1982—faster than any other upturn since 1951.
- Confidence in the economy has prompted business firms to expand their capital facilities. Real investment in new plant and equipment has grown 15.4 percent annually since the end of 1982—faster than in any other postwar recovery.
- The ratio of real investment to real GNP has reached its highest level in the post-war period.
- Industrial production is 23 percent above its level at the recession trough in November 1982—a greater advance than in any other recovery since 1958.
- Corporate profits have risen nearly 90 percent since the recession trough in 1982—the fastest 8-quarter increase in 37 years.

The Budget Dollar
Fiscal Year 1986 Estimate

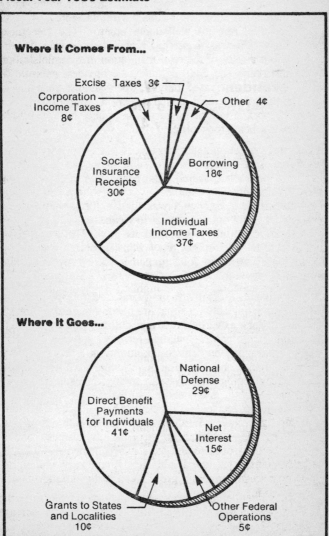

Where It Comes From...

- Excise Taxes 3¢
- Corporation Income Taxes 8¢
- Other 4¢
- Social Insurance Receipts 30¢
- Borrowing 18¢
- Individual Income Taxes 37¢

Where It Goes...

- National Defense 29¢
- Direct Benefit Payments for Individuals 41¢
- Net Interest 15¢
- Grants to States and Localities 10¢
- Other Federal Operations 5¢

- Civilian employment has grown 7.2 million over the past 25 months, and the number of unemployed has fallen by 3.7 million. In the last 4 months alone, more than 1.1 million Americans have found jobs.
- Inflation remains well under control. The December 1984 CPI was 4 percent higher than a year earlier, about a third of the rate of inflation this administration inherited. The GNP deflator, the broadest measure of inflation, increased only 3.5 percent last year and at only a 2.4 percent annual rate in the fourth quarter.
- The prime rate of interest is now only half of what it was when I took office.

Contrast our current circumstances with the situation we faced just 4 years ago. Inflation was raging at double-digit rates. Oil prices had soared. The prime rate of interest was over 20 percent. The economy was stagnating. Unemployment had risen sharply and was to rise further. America's standing in world opinion was at low ebb.

All that, mercifully, is behind us now. The tremendous turn-around in our fortunes did not just happen. In February 1981, I presented the four fundamentals of my economic program. They were:

- Reducing the growth of overall federal spending by eliminating activities that are beyond the proper sphere of federal government responsibilities and by restraining the growth of spending for other activites.
- Limiting tax burdens to the minimum levels necessary to finance only essential government services, thereby strengthening incentives for saving, investment, work, productivity, and economic growth.
- Reducing the federal regulatory burden where the federal government intrudes unnecessarily into our private lives, the efficient conduct of private business, or the operations of state and local governments.
- Supporting a sound and steady monetary policy, to encourage economic growth and bring inflation under control.

Four Years of Accomplishment

These policies were designed to restore economic growth and stability. They succeeded.

The past four years have also seen the beginning of a quiet but profound revolution in the conduct of our federal government. We have halted what seemed at the time an inexorable set of trends toward greater and greater government intrusiveness, more and more regulation, higher and higher taxes, more and more spending, higher and higher inflation, and weaker and weaker defense. We have halted these trends in our first four years.

- The rate of federal spending growth was out of control at 17.4 percent a year in 1980. Under my budget proposals the growth of programmatic spending—that is, total federal spending except for debt service—will be zero next year—frozen at this year's levels.
- Further, spending will grow only 30 percent over the four years from 1982 to 1986, compared to its record pace of 66 percent between 1977 and 1981, and this despite legislated additions to my program and the needed rebuilding of our defense capabilities.
- The federal tax system was changed for the better— marginal tax rates were reduced and depreciation reform introduced. These reforms were designed to increase incentives for work, training and education, saving, business growth, and capital expansion. Tax loopholes have been closed, improving the equity of the system.
- Domestic spending, which previously grew faster than any other major part of the budget (nearly fourfold in real terms between 1960 and 1980), will have been virtually frozen from 1981 to 1985.
- Our defense capabilities are now getting back to a level where we can protect our citizens, honor our commitments to our allies, and participate in the long-awaited arms control talks from a position of respected strength.
- Federal credit programs, which had also grown out of control, have been cut back, and their management has been vastly improved.

- The rapid growth of regulations and red tape has also been halted. The number of federal rules published by agencies has fallen by over 35 percent during the past four years, and many unnecessary old rules have been eliminated. For the first time, the Federal Register of new regulatory actions has grown shorter for four consecutive years; it is now 41 percent shorter than it was in 1980.
- Major management improvement initiatives are underway that will fundamentally change the way the federal government operates. The President's Private Sector Survey on Cost Control has completed its report, and many of its recommendations are included in this budget. The President's Council on Integrity and Efficiency has reported $46 billion in improved use of funds through reduction of waste and fraud.
- The federal nondefense work force has been reduced by over 78,000.

The proposals contained in this budget will build on the accomplishments of the last four years and put into action a philosophy of government that is working and that has received the overwhelming endorsement of the American people.

The 1986 Budget Program

If we took no action to curb the growth of spending, federal outlays would rise to over a trillion dollars in 1986. This would result in deficits exceeding $200 billion in each of the next five years. This is unacceptable. The budget I propose, therefore, will reduce spending by $51 billion in 1986, $83 billion in 1987, and $105 billion in 1988. Enactment of these measures would reduce the deficit projected for 1988 to $144 billion—still a far cry from our goal of a balanced budget, but a significant step in the right direction and a 42 percent reduction from the current services level projected for that year.

Last year my administration worked with Congress to come

up with a downpayment on reducing the deficit. This budget commits the government to a second installment. With comparable commitments to further reduction in the next two budgets, and, I hope, other spending reduction ideas advanced by the Congress, we can achieve our goal in an orderly fashion.

The budget proposes a one-year freeze in total spending other than debt service. This will be achieved through a combination of freezes, reforms, terminations, cutbacks, and management improvements in individual programs. For a number of reasons, a line-by-line budget freeze is not possible or desirable. Further, such an approach would assume that all programs are of equal importance. Taken together, the specific proposals in this budget hold total federal spending excluding debt service constant in 1986 at its 1985 level.

The budget proposals provide for substantial cost savings in the Medicare program, in federal payroll costs, in agricultural and other subsidies to business and upper-income groups, in numerous programs providing grants to state and local governments, and in credit programs. A freeze is proposed in the level of some entitlement program benefits, other than Social Security, means-tested programs, and programs for the disabled, that have hitherto received automatic "cost-of-living adjustments" every year. The budget proposes further reductions in defense spending below previously reduced mid-year levels.

Despite the reforms of the past four years, our federal tax system remains complex and inequitable. Tax rates are still so high that they distort economic decisions, and this reduces economic growth from what it otherwise could be. I will propose, after further consultation with the Congress, further tax simplification and reform. The proposals will not be a scheme to raise taxes—only to distribute their burden more fairly and to simplify the entire system. By broadening the base, we can lower rates.

There will be substantial political resistance to every deficit reduction measure proposed in this budget. Every dollar of current federal spending benefits someone, and that person has a vested self-interest in seeing these benefits perpetuated and expanded. Prior to my administration, such interests had been dominant and their expectations and demands had been met, time and time again.

The Budget Totals
(in billions of dollars)

	1984 actual	1985 estimate	1986 estimate	1987 estimate	1988 estimate
Receipts	666.5	736.9	793.7	862.7	950.4
Outlays	851.8	959.1	973.7	1,026.6	1,094.8
Deficit (–)	–185.3	–222.2	–180.0	–164.9	–144.4

Note: Totals include outlays that are off-budget under current law, proposed to be included on-budget.

Freeze on Programmatic Outlays

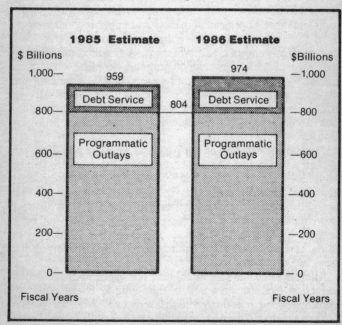

At some point, however, the question must be raised: "Where is the political logrolling going to stop?" At some point, the collective demands upon the public Treasury of all the special interests combined exceed the public's ability and willingness to pay. The single most difficult word for a politician to utter is a simple, flat "No." The patience of the American people has been stretched as far as it will go. They want action; they have demanded it.

We said "no" frequently in 1981, and real spending for discretionary domestic programs dropped sharply. But we did not accomplish enough. We now have no choice but to renew our efforts with redoubled vigor. The profusion of federal domestic spending programs must be reduced to an acceptable, appropriate, and supportable size.

It will require political courage of a high order to carry this program forward in the halls of Congress, but I believe that with good faith and goodwill on all sides, we can succeed. If we fail to reduce excessive federal benefits to special interest groups, we will be saddled either with larger budget deficits or with higher taxes—either of which would be of greater harm to the American economy and people.

1986 Management and Regulatory Program

Not only must both the scope and scale of federal spending be drastically cut back to reduce the deficit: we must also institute comprehensive management improvements and administrative reforms to make sure that we use available funds as efficiently as possible.

Tough but necessary steps are being taken throughout the federal government to reduce the costs of management and administrtation. Substantial savings in overhead costs have been achieved under provisions of the Deficit Reduction Act of 1984. A 5 percent federal civilian employee salary cut has been proposed; a 10 percent reduction in administrative overhead has been ordered; termination of programs that have outlived their usefulness is proposed; outmoded, inefficient agency field structures that have evolved over the past half-century are being consolidated and streamlined to take advantage of efficiencies made possible by modern transporation, communication, and information technology.

Administration of federal agencies is being made more efficient through the adoption of staffing standards, automation of manual processes, consolidation of similar functions, and reduction of administrative overhead costs. A program to increase productivity by 20 percent by 1992 in all appropriate government functions is being instituted, as are improved cash and credit management systems and error rate reduction programs.

This management improvement program will result in a leaner and more efficient federal structure and will be described in a management report that I am submitting to the Congress for the first time shortly after my annual budget submission.

We have also made a great deal of progress in reducing the costs imposed on businesses and state and local governments by federal regulations. These savings are estimated to total $150 billion over a 10-year period. We have reduced the number of new regulations in every year of my first term and have eliminated or reduced paperwork requirements by over 300 million hours each year. In addition, the regulations are more carefully crafted to achieve the greatest protection for the least cost, and wherever possible to use market forces instead of working against them.

A recent executive order will strengthen the executive branch coordination that has made these accomplishments possible. For the first time, we will publish an annual program of the most significant regulatory activities, including those that precede the publication of a proposed rule. This will give Congress and the public an earlier opportunity to understand the administration's regulatory policies and priorities.

Conclusion

The key elements of the program I set out four years ago are in place and working well. Our national security is being restored; so, I am happy to report, is our economy. Growth and investment are healthy; and inflation, interest rates, tax rates, and unemployment are down and can be reduced further. This proliferation of unnecessary regulations that stifled both economic growth and our individual freedoms has been halted. Progress has been made toward the reduction of unwarranted and excessive growth in domestic spending programs.

But we cannot rest on these accomplishments. If we are to attain a new era of sustained peace, prosperity, growth, and freedom, federal domestic spending must be brought firmly under control. This budget presents the steps that I believe must be taken. I do not exclude other economies that Congress may devise, so long as they do not imperil my fundamental constitutional responsibilities to look after the national defense and the general welfare of the American people.

Let us get on with the job. The time for action is now.

Appendix VII

Presidents of the United States
(1789–Present)

1	George Washington *(1732–1799)*	Federalist	1789–1797
2	John Adams *(1735–1826)*	Federalist	1797–1801
3	Thomas Jefferson *(1743–1826)*	Dem.-Rep.	1801–1809
4	James Madison *(1751–1836)*	Dem.-Rep.	1809–1817
5	James Monroe *(1758–1831)*	Dem.-Rep.	1817–1825
6	John Quincy Adams *(1767–1848)*	Dem.-Rep.	1825–1829
7	Andrew Jackson *(1767–1845)*	Democrat	1829–1837
8	Martin Van Buren *(1782–1862)*	Democrat	1837–1841
9	William Henry Harrison *(1773–1841)*	Whig	1841
10	John Tyler *(1790–1862)*	Whig	1841–1845
11	James Knox Polk *(1795–1849)*	Democrat	1845–1849
12	Zachary Taylor *(1784–1850)*	Whig	1849–1850
13	Millard Fillmore *(1800–1874)*	Whig	1850–1853
14	Franklin Pierce *(1804–1869)*	Democrat	1853–1857
15	James Buchanan *(1791–1868)*	Democrat	1857–1861
16	Abraham Lincoln *(1809–1865)*	Republican	1861–1865
17	Andrew Johnson *(1808–1875)*	Democrat	1865–1869
18	Ulysses Simpson Grant *(1822–1885)*	Republican	1869–1877
19	Rutherford Birchard Hayes *(1822–1893)*	Republican	1877–1881
20	James Abram Garfield *(1831–1881)*	Republican	1881
21	Chester Alan Arthur *(1830–1886)*	Republican	1881–1885
22	Grover Cleveland *(1837–1908)*	Democrat	1885–1889
23	Benjamin Harrison *(1833–1901)*	Republican	1889–1893
24	Grover Cleveland *(1837–1908)*	Democrat	1893–1897
25	William McKinley *(1843–1901)*	Republican	1897–1901

26	Theodore Roosevelt *(1858–1919)*	Republican	1901–1909
27	William Howard Taft *(1857–1930)*	Republican	1909–1913
28	Woodrow Wilson *(1856–1924)*	Democrat	1913–1921
29	Warren Gamaliel Harding *(1865–1923)*	Republican	1921–1923
30	Calvin Coolidge *(1872–1933)*	Republican	1923–1929
31	Herbert Hoover *(1874–1964)*	Republican	1929–1933
32	Franklin Delano Roosevelt *(1882–1945)*	Democrat	1933–1945
33	Harry S Truman *(1884–1972)*	Democrat	1945–1953
34	Dwight David Eisenhower *(1890–1969)*	Republican	1953–1961
35	John Fitzgerald Kennedy *(1917–1963)*	Democrat	1961–1963
36	Lyndon Baines Johnson *(1908–1973)*	Democrat	1963–1969
37	Richard M. Nixon *(1913–)*	Republican	1969–1974
38	Gerald R. Ford *(1913–)*	Republican	1974–1977
39	Jimmy Carter *(1924–)*	Democrat	1977–1981
40	Ronald R. Reagan *(1911–)*	Republican	1981–

Appendix VIII

Principal Officials in the Second Reagan Administration

The Cabinet

Vice President	George Bush
Secretary of State	George P. Shultz
Secretary of the Treasury	James A. Baker III
Secretary of Defense	Caspar W. Weinberger
Attorney General	Edwin Meese III
Secretary of the Interior	Donald Paul Hodel
Secretary of Agriculture	John R. Block
Secretary of Commerce	Malcolm Baldrige
Secretary of Labor	William E. Brock
Secretary of Health and Human Services	Margaret M. Heckler
Secretary of Housing and Urban Development	Samuel R. Pierce, Jr.
Secretary of Transportation	Elizabeth Hanford Dole
Secretary of Energy	John S. Herrington
Secretary of Education	William J. Bennett
Director, Office of Management and Budget	David A. Stockman
Director, Central Intelligence Agency	William J. Casey
United States Trade Representative	Clayton Yuetter
Chief of Staff to the President	Donald T. Regan

Assistants to the President (Selected)

Press Secretary	James S. Brady
Counsel to the President	Fred F. Fielding
National Security Affairs	Robert C. McFarlane
Director of Communications	Patrick J. Buchanan
Legislative Strategy Coordinator	Max Friedersdorf

342

Political and Governmental Affairs Edward J. Rollins
Director of Special Support Services Edward V. Hickey, Jr.
Principal Deputy Press Secretary Larry M. Speakes
Legislative Affairs M. B. Oglesby
Management and Administration &
 Director of the Office of
 Administration J. F. W. Rogers
Policy Development John A. Svahna
Intergovernmental Affairs Lee Verstandig
Public Liaison Faith Ryan Whittlesey
Executive Assistant to the Chief of Staff
 and Deputy Assistant to the President Thomas C. Dawson
Cabinet Secretary
 and Deputy Assistant to the President Alfred H. Kingon

Contributors

WALTER DEAN BURNHAM is professor of political science at Massachusetts Institute of Technology and the author of a number of articles and books on American politics and electoral behavior, including: *Presidential Ballots, 1836–1892; Critical Elections and the Mainsprings of American Politics;* with William N. Chambers, eds., *The American Party Systems;* with Martha W. Weinberg, eds., *American Politics and Public Policy;* and *The Current Crisis in American Politics.*

CECIL V. CRABB, JR., is professor of political science at Louisiana State University and author of numerous books and articles on international relations and American foreign policy, including: *Bipartisan Foreign Policy: Myth or Reality; Nations in a Multipolar World; American Foreign Policy in the Nuclear Age,* 4th ed.; with Ellis Sandoz, eds., *A Tide of Discontent: The 1980 Elections and Their Meaning; The American Approach to Foreign Policy: A Pragmatic Perspective;* and *The Doctrines of American Foreign Policy: Their Meaning and Role.*

THOMAS F. CRONIN teaches political science at Colorado College. A former White House aide and White House Fellow, Cronin serves as associate editor of *Presidential Studies Quarterly* and is a past president of the Presidency Research Group. He is author, coauthor, or editor of several books, including: *The State of the Presidency; Government by the People; Rethinking the Presidency; The Presidential Advisory System; U.S. v. Crime in the Streets;* and *State and Local Politics.*

DANIEL J. ELAZAR is professor of political science and director of the Center for the Study of Federalism at Temple University, and head of the Institute of Local Government at

Bar Ilan University (Israel). He is editor of *Publius: The Journal of Federalism* and author of numerous articles and books on American government and Jewish politics, including: *The American Partnership: Federal-State Relations in the Nineteenth Century; American Federalism: A View from the States; The American System: A New View of Government in the United States; Community and Polity: The Organizational Dynamics of American Jewry; Cities of the Prairie;* and *Governing Peoples and Territories*.

FRED I. GREENSTEIN teaches political science at Princeton University as the Henry Luce Professor of Politics, Law, and Society and has published widely in the fields of political psychology and American politics, including the following books: *The American Party System and the American People; Children and Politics; Personality and Politics: Theoretical and Methodological Issues; The Dynamics of American Politics; The Hidden-Hand Presidency: Eisenhower as Leader;* and *The Reagan Presidency: An Early Appraisal*.

CHARLES O. JONES is Robert Kent Gooch Professor of Government and Foreign Affairs at the University of Virginia, former editor of the *American Political Science Review*, and author of numerous articles and books on American politics and the Congress, including: *Party and Policy-Making: The House Republican Policy Committee; The Republican Party in Politics; The Minority Party in Congress; An Introduction to the Study of Public Policy; Limiting Presidential and Congressional Terms; The United States Congress: People, Place and Policy:* and coauthor, *American Democracy: Institutions, Policies, and Politics*.

STEPHEN L. McDONALD is professor of economics and Jack S. Josey Professor of Energy Studies at the University of Texas at Austin, a former economist for Humble Oil and Refining Company (now Exxon USA), and staff associate of the Brookings Institution; his books include: *Federal Tax Treatment of Income from Oil and Gas; Petroleum Conservation in the United States; The Leasing of Federal Lands for Fossil Fuels Production*, and numerous articles in professional journals.

ELLIS SANDOZ is professor of political science at Louisiana State University and member of the National Council on the

Humanities. He has published in the fields of political theory, American government, and constitutional law, and his books include: *Political Apocalypse: A Study of Dostoevsky's Grand Inquisitor; Conceived In Liberty: American Individual Rights Today;* with Cecil V. Crabb, Jr., eds., *A Tide of Discontent: The 1980 Elections and Their Meaning; The Voegelinian Revolution: A Biographical Introduction;* and ed., *Eric Voegelin's Thought: A Critical Appraisal. A Government of Laws: The Political Theory of the American Founders* is forthcoming.

Index

MENTOR Books of Special Interest

(0451)

☐ **A DOCUMENTARY HISTORY OF THE UNITED STATES by Richard D. Heffner.** A unique collection—35 important documents that have shaped America's history, with a commentary showing their significance.
(622510—$3.95)

☐ **THE FEDERALIST PAPERS with an Introduction by Clinton Rossiter.** Political essays by Alexander Hamilton, James Madison, and others, which influenced the acceptance of our Constitution and remain prime examples of political theory. (619072—$2.95)

☐ **THE LIVING U.S. CONSTITUTION by Saul K. Padover.** A comprehensive, expanded, and completely updated guide to understanding the Constitution and the men who framed it. Includes the complete text of the Constitution with an informative Index; historic Supreme Court decisions; and new precedent-setting cases concerning civil liberties. Second Revised Edition.
(621743—$4.95)

☐ **TWO TREATISES OF GOVERNMENT by John Locke.** Critical edition based on the recently discovered manuscript believed to be Locke's final version of his most famous work. Offers evidence that Locke's attack on the divine right of kings was a call for what became the Glorious Revolution rather than a plea in its defense. Introduction and Notes by Peter Laslett. Footnotes. Bibliography. Index. (622020—$4.95)

Buy them at your local bookstore or use coupon on next page for ordering.

Recommended MENTOR Books

(0451)

☐ **THE AFFLUENT SOCIETY by John Kenneth Galbraith.** Fourth Revised Edition with a new Introduction. The book that added a new phrase to our language, a new classic to literature, and changed the basic economic attitudes of our age. In this new revision, Galbraith has extensively updated the information and widened the perspectives of his basic argument "... Daring ... a compelling challenge to conventional thought." —*The New York Times* (623940—$4.95)*

☐ **THE NEW INDUSTRIAL STATE by John Kenneth Galbraith.** Third Revised Edition. One of our most distinguished economists and author of such bestsellers as *The Affluent Society* offers a comprehensive look at modern economic life and the changes that are shaping its future. (620291—$3.95)

☐ **UNDERSTANDING THE ECONOMY: For People Who Can't Stand Economics by Alfred L. Malabre, Jr.** The U.S. economic scene made easily comprehensible and intensely interesting ... "Millions of readers can learn from this lively book."—Paul Samuelson, Nobel Prize-winning economist. (621409—$3.50)

☐ **BAD MONEY by L.J. Davis.** "The author has managed to integrate such seemingly disparate events of the 1970s as the collapse of the railroads in the Northeast; the bankruptcy of a major mass retailer; the overextension of some of our largest banks; the OPEC connection; the Eurodollar economy; and the attempt to corner the silver markets. All of these point to the dangers which should be of enormous concern ..."—Senator Frank Church (622456—$3.50)*

*Price is higher in Canada.

Buy them at your local bookstore or use this convenient coupon for ordering.

NEW AMERICAN LIBRARY,
P.O. Box 999, Bergenfield, New Jersey 07621

Please send me the books I have checked above. I am enclosing $_____ (please add $1.00 to this order to cover postage and handling). Send check or money order—no cash or C.O.D.'s. Prices and numbers are subject to change without notice.

Name_____

Address_____

City_____State_____Zip Code_____
Allow 4-6 weeks for delivery.
This offer is subject to withdrawal without notice.